Faith-Based Education That Constructs

Faith-Based Education That Constructs

A Creative Dialogue between Constructivism and Faith-Based Education

EDITED BY
HEEKAP LEE

WIPF & STOCK · Eugene, Oregon

FAITH-BASED EDUCATION THAT CONSTRUCTS
A Creative Dialogue between Constructivism and Faith-Based Education

Biblical quotations are from the New Revised Standard Version

Wipf & Stock
An imprint of Wipf and Stock Publishers
199 W. 8th Ave., Suite 3
Eugene, OR 97401

ISBN: 978-1-60608-674-2

www.wipfandstock.com

Contents

Foreword

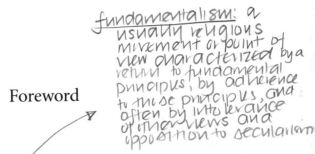

fundamentalism: a usually religious movement or point of view characterized by a return to fundamental principles, by adherence to those principles, and often by intolerance of other views and opposition to secularism

WHILE IT MAY BE SO obvious as to be obtuse and so often repeated as to be clichéd, I must observe that our society, the American society within which this book was principally constructed, is a divided society. Indeed, the world that we live in is a divided community of nations, faiths, and cultures. The most obvious divisions are between the left and the right (politically), the sacred and the secular (spiritually), and even between fundamentalist and modernist (now postmodernist, religiously). These observations are a necessity in the face of the above potential criticisms simply because this book is all about unity and division. It is about what can be taken from diverse and even opposing philosophical positions and be used in harmony with each perspective within the context of public education and private Christian education in America.

At this writing, the situation in our world appears to be becoming more and more divided, with the extreme ends of the opposing sides becoming more and more the strident voice of each philosophy (or theology). Politically in America this is perhaps most obvious in the nearly unanimous agreement that to win an election the goal must be to gain the middle ground. Whichever side can more persuasively argue that they really represent the centrist position, whether or not the argument represents sound principle or integrity with the proponent's actual position, is more likely to win the election. Whether the "promises" made to the middle during the campaigns are ever kept is a matter of argument after-the-fact, and the public has become increasingly and rightfully cynical in that regard. Truly we live in a postmodern age where at least political opposites avoid "all pretensions to depth and substance in favor of surface style and fashion, dethroning truth and making image the dominant source of meaning and identity" (chapter 2, Fennema paraphrasing Jenkins, 1996).

And thus, we have a society, and a world, that is being driven to extremes, both politically and socially. There is no better place to bridge those extremes and bridge our diversity of thought about our world than in the teaching and learning relationship. That is where this book excels.

CONSTRUCTIVISM AND EDUCATION

HeeKap Lee (chapter 4) suggests that there are three facets (or "faces") of constructivism as it is applied in education. They are philosophical, theoretical, and pedagogical. As with political and religious divisions, the most extreme divisions occur at the philosophical and theoretical levels. That is, it is the ideologue that tends to make the most extreme statements in order to make his or her position clear. However in the teaching and learning environment, the needs of children or adult learners cause many of the extreme positions to fade into the background as real people attempt to solve real, everyday instructional and learning problems.

Calvin G. Roso (chapter 5) and Lee (chapter 4) and others discuss Jesus' teaching style positively in comparison to constructivist principles. But Roso goes beyond that and identifies characteristics that borrow from philosophical and theoretical approaches that are not purely constructivist (e.g., "teaching with authority"). I would also add that listing "teaching through discipline and correction" as a constructivist strategy is questionable. But then his point is that one must draw on multiple teaching strategies in the classroom in order to meet the needs of all learners, just as Jesus did.

Likewise, Rhoda Sommers-Johnson (chapter 8) examines Jesus' techniques of instruction as a class research project (or series of projects), and she too concludes that Jesus used multiple methods. While she admits a bias toward identifying constructivism as Jesus' main approach, earlier in the chapter she cites Beswick (2005) as saying, in essence, that any teaching technique can be constructivist. That works well in terms of drawing together diverse practices as advocated above. However, it becomes somewhat problematic for a philosophical or theoretical position. That is, the perspectives of Lee, Roso, and Sommers-Johnson work well for the classroom teacher, but they might find difficulty confronting one of the ideologues in constructivist philosophy.

CONCLUSION

The chapters in *Faith-Based Education That Constructs* present a rich array of thoughtful prose on the topic of constructivism in education, particularly as it relates to Christian education. The divide between constructivism and Christian educational philosophy exists in terms of ontological, epistemological, and axiological perspectives. These differences are not unimportant. However, as one moves from the philosophical to the practical aspects of education, the differences diminish and the ability to move methods of instruction from one philosophical position to another, or to view one method from varying philosophical perspectives, increases. Stephen P. Metcalfe (chapter 17) seems to agree with this position in the following quotation:

> Similarity of perspectives regarding learning and understanding between constructivist thought and Christian faith-based education may outnumber differences, if an agreed upon understanding for both positions is presumed to be centrist-held rather than that of beliefs held by the more peripheral radical elements of either group.

Thus, while having a philosophical perspective is critical as a professional, it is equally critical that master teachers see across boundaries and use methods that meet the unique needs of their students as individuals. With adherence to one and only one set of methods comes the risk implied in the old adage, "when the only tool you have is a hammer, every problem is a nail." The professional educators writing in this book do not have to worry about that.

Stephen W. Ragan
Vice President for Academic Affairs
April 3, 2010
MidAmerica Nazarene University
Olathe, Kansas

Preface

Why This Book at This Time?

CONSTRUCTIVISM IS EVERYWHERE, INCLUDING philosophy, education, technology, and even in religion. Especially in the newly published educational psychology and technology textbooks, constructivism has emerged as a viable topic. As a subset of philosophy, constructivism can be identified by answering three essential questions: what is real? (metaphysics), what is true? (epistemology), and what is good? (axiology). Constructivists reply that reality is always subjective. Firstly, there is no inherent, predefined reality, and each person's reality is different. Secondly, truth is internal and is identified through each person's experiences and environments. So, how do we build up truth in a society? The answer to this is by negotiating and collaborating among people. Hence, the key learning procedure is sharing each person's truth among learners. Jean Piaget, Jerome Bruner, John Dewey, and Lev Vygotsky are important figures whose theories have developed constructivism, a highly effective and qualitative educational approach.

However, can constructivism be applied to faith-based education? Is constructivism compatible with Christian education? The answer to all of these questions is yes, for many reasons. First of all, the theories and practices of constructivism have strengthened faith-based education by emphasizing self-directed students, the teacher as a facilitator, and well-organized learning experiences. In fact, Jesus knew that learning was an active knowledge-creating process through learners' full participation. He always encouraged his disciples to think deeply, knowing that learning was not simply memorizing facts or reciting the law of Moses. This kind of learning contrasts with the passive learning paradigm of exact memorization established by the Jewish leaders of Jesus' day.

However, many arguments have been raised against the constructivist approach when it is applied to faith-based education. For example, constructivists claim that meaning is imposed on the world by us rather than existing in the world independently from us. Therefore, they proclaim that truth is relative to particular times, places, and people. However, is truth changeable and constructible based on personal backgrounds or particular contexts? As Christians, we know that there is an ultimate, shared reality of truth. We know that God created all things perfect without defect, but, since the fall, we are fallen creatures, for now we see *through a glass* (1 Cor 13:12). We may construct differently not because reality has no inherent structure, but because we each have an incomplete and distorted perspective. However, we do know that the truth always leads us perfect knowledge. So, if constructivism is a useful and effective approach in education, can we use this approach to improve effectiveness in faith-based education? If we can, what methods or approaches may we use? Is there any educational or learning model of a constructivism-oriented faith-based education? In this book, readers will find a unique approach that may appropriately apply constructivism to a faith-based education setting.

This book is a result of thorough and systematic communications for the last two years on constructivism among sixteen Christian professors who teach in Christian education institutes. When I was serving as an editor-in-chief of a Christian teacher education research journal, *Teaching with Compassion, Competence, Commitment*, the special theme of the May 2008 issue was constructivism and faith-based education. Since then, I have stayed in communication with the contributors and other colleagues concerning their contributions to articles on constructivism.

This book consists of three parts. In part 1, the book describes trends and issues of constructivism in the field of faith-based education, with four chapters identifying historical and theoretical backgrounds of constructivism along with key characteristics and features of that theory. Part 2 deals with practical applications of constructivism in faith-based educational settings. The chapters contained in this section offer many opportunities for applying constructivism to faith-based education. Part 3 provides final reflections and raises further concerns regarding constructivism when used in faith-based education. One author (chapter 17) concludes that constructivism actually allows the image of God to be revealed through the learning process. In the final chapter, the authors claim that constructivism provides a meaningful tool for school innovation.

I am proud to have edited this book. However, I know that I am indebted to all chapter contributors and Dr. Stephen Ragan, whose energy and efforts have been reflected in this book. In addition, the encouragement of Wipf and Stock Publishers helped bring this effort to fruition. I am also thankful for my immediate family (Yoon, Isaac, and Sharon), who have constantly encouraged this project. Finally, most of all, I thank God who inspired me daily during this extensive editing process.

HeeKap Lee
May, 2010
Azusa Pacific University

List of Contributors

Christina Belcher, Ph.D. candidate, Monash University, Australia, is currently an associate professor of education at Redeemer University College, Ancaster, Ontario, Canada. She finds students inspiring and enjoys engaging dialogue on the topics of literacy, worldview, and cultural/educational issues. Her research interests include literacy, worldview, higher education, and interdisciplinary collaboration. She may be reached at cbelcher@redeemer.ca.

Michael D. Dixon, Head of School of Parkside Christian Academy (PS–6) and Cross Factor Academy (7–12), Jamaica Plain, Massachusetts, grew up on the south side of Chicago, went to public schools, and then went to MIT for undergraduate work as a physics major. He graduated from MIT in 1988 and received his master of divinity with a concentration on Christian education and a doctorate in curriculum and instruction at Boston College. He taught at Gordon College in Wenham for two years preparing students for middle and secondary education, with a focus on math and science. Now he and his wife Crystal have taken a leadership position at Parkside Christian Academy (www.parksideca.org), initiating many educational projects. He may be reached at dixonmi@alum.mit.edu.

Gloria Edwards, Associate Professor of Education, Georgian Court University, Lakewood, New Jersey, teaches graduate and undergraduate courses in technology integration and instructional design. Her research interests focus on digital and web-based tools and how the ability or inability to use such tools impacts the attitudes and productivity of diverse groups of learners in classrooms (traditional and nontraditional) and in the workplace. She can be reached at gedwards@georgian.edu.

Debra Espinor, Assistant Professor of Educational Psychology and Education Foundations and Director of Partnerships and Placement in the School of Education, Seattle Pacific University, has developed partnerships in Beijing, China; Guatemala City, Guatemala; and many local school districts and schools. She teaches courses on assessment, classroom management, educational foundations, and educational psychology in both the undergraduate and graduate programs. She has had a long career as a music teacher, principal, and educator at the university level. Her interests have expanded to include new teacher induction, coteaching, and cluster placement, as well work with the Lilly Foundation in area of vocation and calling. She can be reached at espinor@spu.edu.

Jack Fennema, Professor of Education Emeritus, Covenant College, Lookout Mountain, Georgia, is the author of *The Religious Nature and Biblical Nurture of God's Children*. He presently lives in Columbus, Ohio. In his retirement he commutes to Beijing, China, several times a year to teach in the Chinese Teacher Training Center, a part of Leadership Development International. His interests continue to lie in the theological, philosophical, and psychological foundations of education.

Harry Hall, Associate Dean for Institutional Effectiveness, Indiana Wesleyan University, Marion, Indiana. As a gifted student who failed the twelfth grade, he has always had an interest in learning and motivation. This interest was nurtured during a twenty-eight-year career in the U.S. Army and during his enrollment at Augusta University, where he earned a bachelor's degree in psychology in 1975. Upon retiring from the U.S. Army in 1991, he entered public education as a teacher in an inner-city high school in Charlotte, where he was struck by the lack of student engagement and motivation. During the next ten years, he earned a masters degree in school administration and a doctorate in education leadership from the University of North Carolina–Charlotte. During that same period he also served in several positions, such as high school assistant principal and elementary principal. In 2001, he was hired to begin an online master's degree in education at Indiana Wesleyan University, where he continued to study learning and motivation. Other areas of interest are electronic portfolios, accreditation, international education, educational leadership, and institutional effectiveness. His most constant references are the Bible, *Zen and the Art of Motorcycle Maintenance*, and *The Prince*.

Cindy Harvel, Ph.D., Guidance Counselor, Tianjin International School, China, is enjoying the challenge of incorporating online strategies in assisting high school juniors and seniors in an international setting prepare and apply for college. She can be reached at charvel@ tiseagles.com.

Jillian N. Lederhouse, Professor and Chair of the Department of Education, Wheaton College, Illinois, teaches and coordinates an urban elementary partnership with a Chicago public school. She is the current president of the Association of Independent Liberal Arts College in Teacher Education. Her research interests include urban education, teacher voice, and the experience of Christian teachers in public schools. She can be reached at Jill.N.Lederhouse@wheaton.edu.

HeeKap Lee, Associate Professor in Teacher Education, Azusa Pacific University. Before he joined Azusa Pacific University, he has had many years of experience teaching higher education in various states, such as Indiana, Kentucky, and Ohio. His writing and research is mainly focused on developing effective teaching and learning methods in a faith-based education setting. He has been invited to speak at national and international seminars on many occasions (located in China, Korea, and Thailand), lecturing on such topics as teachers' disposition, multicultural education, educational technology, curriculum development, training evaluation and assessment, Christian education, and school change. In addition, he has served as editor for *Teaching with Compassion, Competence, Commitment*, a Christian teacher education journal. He can be reached at hlee@apu.edu.

Martha E. MacCullough, Dean of the School of Education, Philadelphia Biblical University, specializes in learning theory, philosophy of education, and methodology. She earned her doctorate in education from Temple University, a master of arts in Christian education from Wheaton College, and the bachelor of science in Bible from Philadelphia Biblical University (formerly Philadelphia College of Bible). She taught in the city of Philadelphia for four years and held teaching and administrative posts for six years at a Christian school in Pennsylvania. For six years she was a member of the faculty at Lancaster Bible College where she initiated a program in teacher education. She began teaching at Philadelphia Biblical University in 1980 and developed the teacher education program and served as chair until 2001 when she was appointed dean of the School of Education. During her tenure at Philadelphia Biblical University, twelve programs granting both public-school and Christian-school certification and double degrees have been developed and accredited by state, regional, and national accrediting bodies. She teaches in the undergraduate, graduate, and international divisions of the Philadelphia Biblical University School of Education. In addition to her teaching and administrative responsibilities, she conducts workshops at Christian education and teacher education conventions and conferences at regional, national, and international venues. She also conducts seminars for women on a variety of subjects. She can be reached at mmaccullough@pbu.edu.

Stephen P. Metcalfe, Professor of Education, Mount Vernon Nazarene University. He received a bachelor of arts in psychology from Eastern Nazarene College, an Ed.M. in community counseling from Boston University, an M.Ed. in moderate special needs from Eastern Nazarene College, and a Ph.D. in curriculum and instruction from Boston College. His research interests include at-risk student population success, historical social influences on public education, and personal influences on professional practice. He is a lover of eclectic modern electric and acoustic musical styles. He can be contacted at smetcalf@mvnu.edu.

C. Damon Osborne, Associate Professor of Education, Mount Vernon Nazarene University, Ohio, teaches coursework on educational technology. Additionally, he serves as the institution's instructional technologist, spearheading the university's online learning initiative. He holds a master's degree in integrating technology into the curriculum, and a Ph.D. in instructional design for online learning. His research interests include the study of community development among online learners, as well as identifying best practices for the integration of emerging technologies into the classroom. He can be contacted at dosborne@mvnu.edu.

Pamela M. Owen, Professor of Education, Mount Vernon Nazarene University, Ohio, teaches courses about curriculum, play, democratic education, content reading, and research design. She enjoys designing and teaching online instruction as well as teaching in the traditional face-to-face venue. Her research interests include the role of male teachers in the field of early childhood education. She can be reached at powen@mvnu.edu.

Calvin G. Roso, Associate Professor, Oral Roberts University Graduate School of Education, has been a professional educator, serving in several capacities at Christian schools and universities, since 1990. He has published several teachers' guides through Progeny Press in Eau Claire, Wisconsin and has published various articles regarding curriculum and instruction. He has traveled to Christian schools in Colombia, England, Honduras, Mexico, Nigeria, Spain, and Sweden, as well as throughout the United States, speaking at conferences and assisting in school improvement and accreditation. He earned a doctorate degree in educational leadership and a masters degree in curriculum development from Oral Roberts University, and a bachelors degree in English education from the University of Wisconsin–Madison. He can be contacted at croso@oru.edu.

Rhoda Sommers-Johnson, Dean of the School of Education and Associate Professor of Education, Malone University, Canton, Ohio, taught in elementary and middle schools in Ohio and Pennsylvania for thirteen years and has been involved in teacher education since 1996. Her research interests are focused on effective instructional practices. She can be reached at rsommers-johnson@malone.edu.

Bruce Young, Associate Professor of Education, Covenant College, teaches Educational Psychology, a curriculum course in the Master of Education program, and early childhood content and method courses in science and math. His research interest is in effective instructional practices for science and math education. He can be contacted at bryoung@covenant.edu.

Part 1

Trends and Issues of Constructivism

Introduction

HAVE YOU UNDERSTOOD ALL things (Matt 13:51[1])? Do you still not understand (Mark 8:21)? This is the way Jesus teaches. The purpose of Jesus' teaching for the disciples is to be understood. What does "understand" mean? It is more than memorizing or reciting something, which were the main teaching activities of Jewish leaders. Jesus' teaching can be identified through four stages of active inquiry process, which began with identifying teachable moments. Then he guided inquiry with intriguing questions. He never gave the answer directly to his disciples; rather, he allowed his disciples to explore a hypothesis to find the answer to the question. Learners constructed and organized his teaching based on their own experiences and personal contexts. Once his disciples understood the lesson, Jesus applied the lesson to their lives, usually saying, "go and do it likewise" (Luke 10:37).

Part 1 of this book addresses the theoretical issues of constructivism, especially its congruence to the faith-based educational setting. Identifying the key characteristics of constructivism as a learning theory and connecting it with faith-based education, chapter 1 introduces three of the most prevalent learning theories in the last century: behaviorism, cognitivism, and constructivism. After presenting each theory individually, the author seeks to establish a basis for constructivism in the faith-based school or faith-based classroom. Because people learn through their own experiences and subsequent reflection on those experiences, the author suggests that constructivism teaches students how to ask the "big" questions and learn through exploration by reflecting on past experiences.

Chapter 2 analyzes and evaluates the educational theory of constructivism from a biblical worldview. The postmodern foundations

1. Unless otherwise indicated, all Scriptures quoted are from the New International Version (NIV) of the Holy Bible.

of constructivism are examined first. This is followed by a definition and then a critique of constructivism itself in the areas of philosophy, anthropology, learning theory, curriculum development, instructional strategies, assessment, and research. The conclusions that are drawn indicate both compatibility with biblical norms in certain areas and a lack of compatibility in others.

Since constructivism is deeply embedded in a philosophy that denies absolute truth and that encourages students to construct their own truth while acknowledging that multiple truths exist, many Christians might ask if any good can come out of such an approach. Chapter 3 evaluates constructivist philosophy and methods in light of a biblical worldview by comparing constructivism to the Bible's approaches to instruction and the teaching methods of Jesus. The author summarizes negative aspects of constructivist philosophy and presents the positive outcomes of constructivist learning theory and classroom methodology. Finally, the author examines how constructivist ideas relate to a biblical perspective and Jesus' teaching, demonstrating how Christian educators can use constructivism in the classroom.

Despite constructivism's positive influence on education, confusion with the term has restricted its proper implementation into the classroom. Chapter 4 clarifies the term "constructivism" with the analogy of three faces and establishes possible connections between constructivism and faith-based education: a postmodern educational philosophy, a post-positivist research paradigm, and a set of pedagogical practices and instructional methods that emphasize active participation of learners. The author also suggests some implications for constructivism in faith-based education for each "face."

1

Overview of Learning Theories

Debra Espinor

Excellence, then, being of two kinds, intellectual and moral, intellectual
excellence in the main owes both its birth and its growth to teaching
(for which reason it requires experience and time) . . .

—Aristotle, *Nichomachean Ethics*

INTRODUCTION

VIRTUALLY EVERYONE WOULD AGREE that the role of the school is
to help students learn. The school, as an institution of education,
must incorporate a sense of morality or values. This said, the methods
of incorporating morality and values into education vary. This chapter
explores three of the most common learning theories of the last fifty
years: behaviorism, cognitivism, and constructivism. Each section will
take a brief glance at the history, background, and definition of each of
the theories. Then, the chapter will turn to the strengths and weaknesses
of each of the theories, illuminating their role in supporting students'
learning. In addition, we will examine how these specific learning theories can be combined with faith in the classroom, in the home-school
environment, and in other educational settings. Table 1.1 offers a summary of the three learning theories discussed in this chapter.

Table 1.1 Summary of learning theories

Theory	Behaviorism	Cognitivism	Constructivism
Definition	Behavior should be explained by all things observed, not by mental processes.	Mental function can be understood and explained, and psychology is the medium for the explanation.	The learner is at the center of the educational stage. Knowledge cannot be handed down from one person to another but must be constructed by learners themselves.
Strengths	A new behavioral pattern is repeated until it becomes automatic.	The focus is on the mental structures that cause our physical actions.	Learning is the constant effort to assimilate new information.
Weaknesses	Classical conditioning can create fear in learners. The method is unable to deal with complex human behavior.	The idea that mental functions can be described through an information processing model is a weakness.	The method does not fit with the current standards-based testing that has developed in the United States.
Applications to the classroom	Teachers can use this model to develop classroom rules and procedures.	The use of multiple and emotional intelligences could influence the development of lessons and curriculum.	Scaffolding the questions, clues, or suggestions that help students link prior knowledge to new information can improve the classroom environment.
Key people	John Watson B. F. Skinner Albert Bandura	Noam Chomsky Donald E. Broadbent Jerome Bruner	John Dewey Jean Piaget Lev Vygotsky

BEHAVIORISM

Education is what survives when what has been learned
has been forgotten.

—B. F. Skinner

History and Background

American psychologist John Watson was the original thinker behind behaviorism. He suggested that behavior was the only thing that psychology should be concerned with and discounted the mind and the feelings of human consciousness (Alonso, Lopez, Manrique, & Vines, 2008). He went on to propose that rats, apes, and humans should all be studied objectively and in the same way.

Behaviorism strongly emphasizes experience, specifically reinforcement and punishment, as these determine human learning and behavior. Ivan Pavlov (1928) studied animal responses to conditioning. His is best known for his experimentation with dogs. Pavlov would ring a bell when feeding a group of dogs. Eventually, the dogs began to salivate at the ringing of a bell and equated the sound with the coming of another meal. The behavior was later reversed: Pavlov would ring a bell but offer no food, yet the dogs still salivated. Pavlov and Watson believed that humans could be conditioned in the same manner.

B. F. Skinner tested Watson's theories in the laboratory. He rejected Watson's stress on conditioning. Skinner believed that people respond to their environment and that they are aware that their environment affects their behavior. Skinner (1985) believed that people act in response to their environment yet also operate under the conviction that the environment produces consequences. Skinner's theory of "operant conditioning"— the idea that humans behave the way they do because their behavior had consequences in the past—considers each person as an individual (Cohen, 1987). Consequences—rewards and punishments—are contingent on the behavior of the person studied. Reinforcement (reward) is a consequence that increases the probability that a behavior will occur, while punishment is a consequence that decreases the probability a behavior will occur. Reinforcement of behavior strengthens behavior. Using positive reinforcement, the frequency of a response increases because it is followed by a rewarding stimulus. Negative reinforcement elicits a similar response because the frequency of a desired response increases as a negative stimulus is removed. In summary, positive reinforcement occurs when a pleasant stimulus is added and negative reinforcement occurs when an unpleasant stimulus is removed.

Albert Bandura (1974) has also provided a modified approach to these theories, suggesting that people learn from one another via observation, imitation, and modeling. His theory has become a bridge between behaviorist and cognitive learning theories because it includes attention, memory, and motivation. Bandura's "reciprocal determinism" looks at the reciprocation of the person's behavior in direct connection to their world. Behaviorists essentially believe that one's environment causes one's behavior. Bandura also suggested that our behavior shapes our environment as well. Lastly, Bandura (1997) considered personality as an interaction between the three components of environment, behavior, and one's psychological processes (the ability to entertain images in minds and language).

From Watson to Bandura, the history of behaviorism has grown to include more than behavior modification. The development of the original theories of behaviorism has led to a clearer understanding of how people exist in their environment and interact with one another. The roots of behaviorism offer a foundation for working with the students in the classroom and assist teachers in creating procedures and consequences that will facilitate learning.

Strengths

One of the greatest strengths of the behaviorist theory is its relevance to classroom management. Positive teaching and applied behavior approaches receive continual research attention with regard to managing students in the classroom setting. Skinner advocated and popularized the use of positive reinforcement to promote desired learning in the classroom. Connecting learning to rewards and feelings of pleasure is part of a system of reinforcement designed by behaviorists to support desired behaviors. In the classroom, extrinsic rewards are gradually used less and less as students acquire the targeted behavior. Self-satisfaction then becomes its own reward. The teachers' goal is to move the learner from extrinsic to intrinsic reward systems.

One of behaviorism's greatest strengths has come recently with the use of technology. In particular, technology has allowed for many of the principles of behavioral teaching to be reexamined with state-of-the-art computer equipment and programs, including the recent technology of online browsers and phones (McInerney, 2005, 2006). Sophisticated computer programs not only allow realistic simulation of learning situations but provide immediate correction and feedback. There are many alternative learning paths and "intelligent" reactions to the choices that learners make. By measuring students' responses to intelligent computer programs, scientists and teachers have a better chance at understanding how to modify behavior for optimal learning.

Weaknesses

independent/
self governing

Critics of behaviorism speak to the disbelief in the autonomy of the individual. They wonder if people are little more than selfish "reward machines." Can people be manipulated through clever social engineering? Do teachers desire complete control over their students and their students' learning? Behaviorism is also seen as unable to deal with complex human behavior (Ingvarsson, 2004). Some argue that Skinner's theory is not about learning; instead, it is about manipulating human behavior. In that setting, the student is passive, waiting for orders and not capable of critical thinking (Faryadi, 2007). Although not always considered a weakness, behaviorists measure learning in small discrete skills such as how well students apply mathematical operations and remember facts specific to individual subjects (Rivera, 2005). These different methods contribute to a view of a person as the sum of behaviors and ignore the mind that both unites and critiques such behaviors.

Use in Faith-Based Settings

While there is application in all classroom settings, behaviorist theory is particularly applicable to faith-based classrooms. When studying classroom management, behaviorism takes precedence over making rules or enforcing consequences. There are three ways to view the use of behaviorist theory in the classroom: as positive reinforcement, negative reinforcement, or punishment as a consequence.

The first viewpoint—positive reinforcement—offers students the opportunity to identify and learn by constructive support. For example, a student asks a question that is applicable to a lesson, and the teacher commends that student for asking a "good" question. The result is praise from the teacher. Praise can take place in any form depending on the age group and interest of the students. In some cases, praise can be both verbal and physical (the offering of a sticker or star, etc.). The student would then be inclined to ask more good questions in the future.

The same concept holds for negative reinforcement; however, the praise is reversed. A teacher may criticize a student for not turning in their homework on time by communicating with the student disappointment or concern for the student's academic well-being. So, the student then begins to turn in the homework because he or she desires to please the teacher or not be subjected to the disappointment or oral concern of the teacher. As a result, the teacher stops disparaging the student, and the student is more inclined to turn in their homework in the future.

The last considers the teacher's use of punishment as a consequence for breaking rules in a classroom setting. For example, a student interrupts the teacher, and the teacher verbally reprimands the student. This direct communication of the teacher's sentiment toward the interruption would likely direct the student in not interrupting the teacher again.

Given these fundamental examples, one may conclude that behaviorism is already deeply imbedded in our educational systems, in both non- and faith-based environments. My experience of over twenty years in a faith-based school gives me reason to state that faith-based institutions actually are more behavior based.

Behaviorism is embedded in sociology and in the belief that moral values are rooted in biology. However, there are some presuppositions within behaviorism that run counter to faith-based education. For behaviorists there is the belief that a person is someone without a soul or mind and that it is the workings of the brain that reacts to outside stimuli that is the reality. Therefore, behaviorists argue that the material world is the ultimate reality. This idea does not align with the belief of those who have a deep faith structure.

Do you believe that humans are nothing more than machines? That humans only respond to conditions? David Cohen states that "the central tenet of behaviorism is that thoughts, feelings, and intentions, mental processes all, do not determine what we do. Our behavior is the product of our conditioning. We are biological machines and do not consciously act; rather we react to stimuli" (Cohen, 1987, p. 71). The biblical view is dissimilar to the idea of humans being machines. Christians believe that our minds have influence on our actions and that we are made in an image of an inspired, creative God. The Bible teaches that we are basically covenantal creatures, not just biological creatures.

Some view behaviorism as a manipulative theory. Skinner's (1985) work makes the suggestion that behaviorism can be the root for influencing all of society. This is contrary to the biblical view that we should love our neighbors and not manipulate our neighbors. In the biblical view, humans are not reduced to pure biological creatures, stripped of responsibility, freedom, and dignity. To the contrary, we are God's creatures, able to make decisions (whether right or wrong) for ourselves. Behaviorism has its place in the role of classroom teacher, especially in the area of classroom management. However, Christian teachers must consent to love their neighbors, which includes loving their students in a manner that does not control their behavior, but teaches them ways to control their own lives.

COGNITIVISM AND SOCIAL COGNITIVISM

The shred guess, the fertile hypothesis, the courageous leap to a tentative conclusion—these are the most valuable coins of the thinker at work. But in most schools guessing is heavily penalized and is associated somehow with laziness.

—Jerome Bruner

History and Background

Cognitivism became the dominant force in psychology in the late twentieth century. It replaced behaviorism as the most popular way to view the mind. Cognitivism adopts a positivist approach. (Knowledge is only authentic knowledge when it is based on actual sense experience or has been arrived at through the scientific method). Cognitive psychologists challenge the limitations of behaviorism in its focus on observable behavior.

Cognitive psychologists are really interested in the inner workings of human thought and the process of knowing. Mental processes such as memory, thinking, knowing, and problem solving are what they explore. Knowledge can be seen as schema (symbolic) mental constructions. Symbolic reasoning, then, is a "uniquely human talent. It may have arisen from our need to understand one another's intentions and motivations, allowing us to coordinate within a group" (Medina, 2009).

The emphasis on mental structures and content was popularized in the 1950s when Miller (1956) and others showed how ideas from information theory could be modified to characterize the flow of information within the organism (Broadbent, 1963). Abstract ideas such as attention, set, immediate memory, rehearsal, and response bias were made more tangible as these models served to suggest ways in which perception, attention, memory, and action might be related to each other and contribute to overall functioning.

Noam Chomsky (2000) suggested that, although man is a biological organism, there are mystical properties having to do with the theory of mind. Cohen (1977) justifies Chomsky's theory of mystical properties by arguing that "we as biological organisms will not have within our range the theory which would, in fact, explain it."

Later in his career, Jerome Bruner (1966) was influential in the 1950s and 60s as he began to develop the "New Look" in psychology. This idea dealt with how people viewed the world around them and how they responded to different visual stimuli. Bruner had a profound interest in the cognitive development of children and in outlining a form of education that best suited children. He suggested that any subject could be taught to any child at any age of development, if presented in the proper manner. Bruner remains one of the most influential cognitive theorists of our time.

Strengths

Bruner (1983) suggests that being human involves being part of a culture that empowers us to "look outside the human skin for the sources of human competence." Human beings interact with others verbally and are able to make connections while constructing materials necessary for their survival. Once they have made a new connection, humans can examine their perception of each other to expand their understanding.

Cognitivists assert that experts do not simply have more knowledge than novices; rather, the structure of the knowledge differs. Experts understand the patterns of interaction and the underlying principles; therefore, they are more able to plan ahead. Novices will rely on superficial features such as appearance with consideration of underlying principles. Cognitive scientists assert that collaboration and problem solving increase the potential for knowledge construction when both experts and novices work together, sharing ideas and interpretations (McInerney, 2006).

Cognitivist research has shown that meaningful information is easier to learn and remember; it is also easier to remember items from the beginning or the end of a list rather than from the middle of a list. Other strengths include the recognition that much of learning involves associations established through contiguity and repetition. There is also value in reinforcment; indeed, cognitivists stress that providing feedback about whether a response is correct is more important than acting as a motivator (Brophy, 1987).

Weaknesses

Cognitive psychologists have been criticized for not seeing the need to consider our human environment in conducting and evaluating experiments (Overskeid, 2008). From a behaviorist viewpoint, all cognition is behavior. Most human behavior is assumed to respond favorably to conditioning and reinforcement. When cognitivists moved away from behaviorism, they disregarded the behaviorist's knowledge of the relationships of behavior—the way the activity of humans is shaped by the consequences of their own behavior. Why do certain behaviors occur? We communicate to influence the behavior of others, and successful communication depends on our ability to predict the response of the other.

Use in Faith-Based Settings

"Cognitivism exerts great influence over most of psychology" and other related disciplines. "Unlike behaviourism, cognitivism does not reject consciousness"; thus, it acknowledges aspects of mental life, including intentionality, emotional responses, and subjectivity (Pickering, 1995). This knowledge opens the door for a discussion into how cognitivism could influence a faith-based classroom.

The development of faith calls upon some of the Aristotelian ideals of moral education, in particular the education of human virtue. Virtue for Aristotle is about both actions and emotions. Virtue, as with other character traits, arises through repeated practice; we become kind by performing kind actions (Kristjansson, 2000). People can acquire many virtuous dispositions through habit. Gradually, external conditioning plays a less significant role in character formation; more and more, disposition becomes established as a result of an individual's own deliberation and choice.

When educators read Howard Gardner (1983) or Daniel Goleman (1995), there is an understanding that there are more factors than IQ tests that determine how well people fare in school, or even in life. Goleman argues that noncognitive skills can matter as much as IQ in success in education while Gardner suggests that humans have more than mathematical or literacy intelligence. Even so, Gardner's theory does not give us accurate ways to measure the way people experience right and wrong emotions in the right circumstances.

Our very presence as educators puts us at the forefront of how faith, morality, and acceptable emotional responses are taught to our students. Children and young adults "catch" our moral attributes, attitudes, beliefs, and habits from their teachers, both good and bad. Rather than indoctrinating them, we should adhere to the code of ethics that asserts all teachers are required to be responsible for good behavior in their classrooms.

CONSTRUCTIVISM

The belief that all genuine education comes about through experience does not mean that all experiences are genuinely or equally educative.

—John Dewey

History and Background

The premise of constructivism is that learners construct knowledge based upon their own experiences and prior beliefs. Therefore, what is learned cannot be separated from the context of where that learning took place (Roehl & Snider, 2007). Teachers facilitate the construction of knowledge by including opportunities for meaningful and authentic exploration, by designing engaging activities, and by utilizing interactive group work.

Constructivism asserts that knowledge cannot be just handed from one person to another, to be put on like an article of clothing. Knowledge must be constructed (or "sewed," using the clothing metaphor) and tried on and "fitted" to the new learner. Constructivists believe that people continually try to order and make sense of their world. Constructivism, built on the work of Jean Piaget and Lev Vygotsky, reflects cognitive psychologists' view that learning is the constant effort to assimilate new information.

John Dewey (1938) intended his pragmatist approach as a way to know what changes the environment and then reflect on that change. He viewed genuine knowledge as coming neither by thinking about it abstractly or by acting uncritically, but rather by integrating thinking as well as doing.

Therefore, constructivism is built upon the foundation that students are not just "empty heads" that can be filled with knowledge by teachers and great curriculum. Because learning is active and the student must be actively involved in the creation of that knowledge, it is not a product for behaviorists to quantitatively measure but a process of negotiation between one's personal understanding and public knowledge (Marcum-Dietrich, 2008).

Jean Piaget was the originator of the cognitive constructivist viewpoint. He put emphasis on the importance of the cognitive processes that are individual to each person. As individuals try to make sense of the world through experiences, they rely on physical, mental, and social processes (Palmer, 2005). In Piaget's classroom, the child is the subject, with that child's cognitive development as the primary goal.

Lev Vygotsky (1978) took this concept to a different level with the idea of "social consturctivism." He put emphasis on the importance of society, culture, and language. The cognitive constructivist and social constructivist perspectives emphasize different paths towards knowledge construction, but there are commonalities. One source of common ground is the characteristics of students' conceptions or ways of seeing reality.

The cognitive constructivist and social constructivist perspectives emphasize different paths towards knowledge construction, but there are commonalities. One source of common ground is the characteristics of students' conceptions or ways of seeing reality. Both views suggest that learning is an active process as each individual reconstructs knowledge in response to the environment (the classroom).

In summary, constructivism is learner centered; it suggests that class-rooms should support many perspectives and interpretations of reality by the use of context-rich, experienced-based activities. Constructivism focuses on knowledge construction, not knowledge reproduction. The human mind is crucial to the interpretation of events. We each have a different "worldview" based upon our learning environment and our experiences in the world.

Strengths

In thinking of the strengths of constructivism, Brooks (1993) expands on how constructivism fits within a classroom environment or educational setting. Traditionally, students in classrooms primarily work alone with the curriculum presented from part to whole, with the emphasis on basic skills. The constructivist classroom would present curriculum from whole to part, with the emphasis on the big concept. Students would be allowed the opportunity to see the "big picture" before they start putting the puzzle together.

Students in a constructivist classroom work in groups where there is freedom to ask questions outside of the existing curriculum. The curriculum itself relies heavily on primary sources whereas in a traditional classroom the curricular activities rely on textbooks. As a result, students are viewed as thinkers with emerging viewpoints on the world and their role in that world.

As a teacher, the role of a guide is quite appealing to me. It offers a visual of climbing a mountain and pointing out all the interesting details along the way to those who walk with me. I may have more knowledge and understanding of the environment we travel, but each day that same mountain looks different, eliciting new and different questions. The constructivist teacher seeks the students' point of view in order to understand how they learn, which in turn influences how new lessons and concepts are presented.

One final strength is present in the area of assessment. In traditional classrooms, assessment of student learning is viewed as separate from teaching and is directly linked to formal and informal testing. In the constructivist classroom, the assessment of student learning is interwoven with the teaching and learning that occurs through teacher observation of students at work and through their portfolios and reflections.

Weaknesses

Some researchers suggest that learning is active and transforms the learner. Research into teaching, though, demonstrates the importance of direct instruction, which is largely based on behavioral principles (McInerney, 2005). Maybe this paradox exists because there has not been a strong enough definition of exactly what "learning" looks like? Do we think it looks like a "traditional" classroom with a teacher up in front talking? Or do we see learning in the context of a classroom formed around table groups, with conversations and the teacher mingling among the groups like a guide? One thing is clear: more research needs to be done to understand what our outcomes should be.

The use of computers in classrooms is a fine example of constructivist methodology. With the onset of online high schools and continuation of many collegiate classes that are held online, there is the assumption that the students want to learn the material taught and that they want to explore and stay focused on the tasks at hand (Weigel & Gardner, 2009). When students begin to own their own learning, teachers must learn to relinquish control of the classroom, the curriculum, and the assessment. This can be a strength for students in the classrooms of America as they have choice in their construction of knowledge.

Lastly, there is a view that constructivism leaves open the possibility of pluralism since unshared interests would be permissible so long as they don't conflict with the vital interests of the classroom (Wright, 2006). Thus teachers may view students' interests in the area of morality as viable so as not to interrupt their learning. Individual teachers may want to identify common themes and goals for the classroom setting so as to avoid conflict in other subjects.

numerous distinct ethnic, religious, or cultural groups coexist within one nation

Use in Faith-Based Settings

Brooks and Brooks (1993) identify five tenets of constructivism for application in the classroom. The first of these tenets begs the question, how do we find out where students have entry? Student's points of view hold strong value in a constructivist classroom. When formulating lessons and beginning to differentiate instruction, teachers must have a grasp of the students' interests and needs.

Once there is a starting point, the next tenet asks, what can instruction do to build the bridge from a learned concept to a new concept

2. or understanding of a lesson? Bridging offers teachers the opportunity to structure lessons that challenge their students' existing suppositions. Every student, young and old, comes to the classroom with unique life experiences that shape their view of how the world works. When educators permit students to construct knowledge that is challenging, then true learning begins to take shape. Therefore, teachers must question and know their students before this authentic learning can take place.

3. Practicing concepts and building projects around the students' real life experiences outside the classroom, leading the student to ask questions, is the third of these five tenets. Teachers can recognize that students must attach relevance to any curriculum. Students will be more interested in learning when lessons in school reflect on their daily activities and interests.

4. The fourth tenet asks the question, what are the major concepts that students should understand? Exposing students to a whole concept before detailed information can assure a stronger understanding. Teachers who instruct in this manner structure their lessons around the big ideas first.

5. The last of the five principles focuses on the teacher, asking, how might teachers move from right-or-wrong judgments to monitoring students' understanding? This is a question of assessment. Teachers who use constructivist methods assess student learning in a different manner. Assessment is done as part of daily routines, not as "end of the unit" or "end of the chapter" events. Creative assessment strategies can help the students demonstrate their knowledge every day in a variety of ways that go beyond paper-and-pencil assessments. Of course, this may mean more work for the teacher to design and implement a more individualized assessment to students, but there will be the opportunity to truly quantify what a student has learned, rather than what they have memorized.

Now, let's distinguish these five tenets under the lens of faith-based teaching. What might it look like in the classroom? If every human is made in the image of God, then the first tenet (how do we find out where students have entry?) would fit nicely into the faith-based worldview. If we view our students as having the attributes of God, then each one has been made individually, with different life experiences, gifts, and talents. Our curriculum may be standardized but our methodology does not need to be.

Proverbs 2:10 states, "For wisdom will enter your heart, and knowledge will be pleasant to your soul." Our goal for our students is that they use the knowledge they receive from their teachers to live in and improve the world around them. The second tenet speaks of building bridges from learned knowledge to new knowledge. Teachers in the faith-based classroom must be open to helping all students build new knowledge by using and bridging previous knowledge.

The third tenet speaks to the idea of service learning, taking the classroom into the community and exploring all facets of society from inside and outside of the classroom setting.

The issue of relevance taken from the fourth tenet changes the focus of control. For a student to attach relevance to a lesson, that student first must have interest in the subject matter. The teachers' responsibility is to know the students, their interests and their backgrounds, so as to formulate lessons that will "stick." The question of what knowledge is of most worth has been around for centuries. Curriculum that is faith-driven has answered that question whether the faith is derived from the Bible or any other holy book. If you home-school or work in a school with faith-based standards, then your students should also be aware of those expectations.

Assessment needs from the fifth tenet are constant in any educational setting. Teachers must have a way to evaluate student learning. They may not necessarily be the judgment of the beliefs of students, but there is the necessity of making sure they are learning the content that is required by the school or institution or state.

In summary, constructivism allows the role of the student and the role of the teacher to interchange based upon mutual interests and curriculum requirements. Let me leave you with three classroom-based suggestions for a strong faith-based constructivist model.

1. Design your classroom environment (climate) to be characterized as nonjudgmental and non-self-conscious for your students and yourself.

2. Encourage spiritual discourse. In a nonjudgmental classroom, this will open doors to rich discussions about "important" issues that are on the minds of your students and yourself.

3. When designing curriculum and individual lessons, look for opportunities to make those lessons meaningful in a spiritual manner.

Tie lessons back to those spiritual discussions, and plan field trips, events, and book readings to invest in deeper moral meanings for your students.

CONCLUSION

If we go back to the quote from Aristotle at the beginning of the chapter, he is talking about excellence in two areas: intellectual excellence and moral excellence. Those of us that work and teach in faith-based environments are fortunate to have the ability to present new knowledge from a viewpoint of a particular belief structure. The role of the teacher is to be a facilitator and an example, both in intellectual knowledge and moral knowledge. Learning must be well organized, with the goal of having self-directed students. Highly qualified educators have the ability to provide learning experiences that grow students as intellectuals and as strong moral citizens. The questions below are designed to help readers understand learning theories as they apply to faith-based education.

1. How can you present new material to your students in a manner that challenges their current conceptions and encourages them to construct their own personal meaning?

2. In a faith-based classroom, there may not be an emphasis on multiple perspectives, especially in the area of religion. How will you present differing viewpoints in a manner that allows students to restructure their own faith story?

REFERENCES

Alonso, F., Lopez, G., Manrique, D., & Vines, J. (2008). Learning objects, learning objectives and learning design. *Innovations in Education and Teaching International,* 389–400.

Bandura, A. (1974). Behavior theory and the models of man. *American Psychologist, 29,* 859–869.

Bandura, A. (1997). *Self-efficacy: The exercise of control.* New York: W. H. Freeman.

Broadbent, D. E. (1963). Flow of information within the organism. *Journal of Verbal Learning and Verbal Behavior, 50,* 34–39.

Brooks, J. G. (1993). *In Search of understanding: The case for constructivist classrooms.* Alexandria, VA: Association for Supervision and Curriculum Development.

Brophy, T. G. (1987). *Looking in classrooms.* New York: Harper & Row.

Bruner, J. (1966). *Toward a theory of instruction.* Cambridge, MA: Harvard University Press.

Bruner, J. (1983). *In search of mind: Essays in autobiography.* New York: Harper & Row.

Chomsky, N. (2000). *The architecture of language.* New York: Oxford University Press.

Cohen, D. (1977). *Psychologists on psychology: Modern innovators talk about their work.* New York: Taplinger.

Cohen, D. (1987). Behaviorism. In R. Gregory (Ed.), *The Oxford companion to the mind* (pp. 231–264). New York: Oxford University Press.

Dewey, J. (1938). *Experience and education.* New York: Macmillan.

Faryadi, Q. (2007). *Behaviorism and the construction of knowledge.* Malaysia: Self-published.

Gardner, H. (1983). *Frames of mind: The theory of multiple intelligence.* New York: Basic Books.

Goleman, D. (1995). *Emotional intelligence.* New York: Bantam Books.

Ingvarsson, E. T. (2004). Post-Skinnerism, post-Skinner or neo-Skinnerism? *Psychological Record, 54*(4), 497.

Kristjansson, K. (2000). Teaching emotional virtue: A post-Kohlbergian aproach. *Scandinavian Journal of Educational Research, 44,* 405–422.

Marcum-Dietrich, N. (2008). Using constructivist theories to educate the "outsiders." *Journal of Latinos and Education, 7*(1), 79–87.

McInerney, D. (2005). Educational psychology: Theory, research, and teaching; A 25-year retrospective. *Educational Psychology, 25*(6), 585–599.

McInerney, D. (2006). *Educational Psychology: Constructing learning.* Sydney: Prentice Hall Australia. (3rd ed.)

Medina, J. (2009). *Brain rules.* Seattle, WA: Pear Press.

Miller, G. A. (1956). The magical number seven, plus or minus two: Some limits on our capactiy for processing information. *Psychological Review,* 81–96.

Overskeid, G. (2008). They should have thought about the consequences: The crisis of cognitivism and a second chance for behavior analysis. *Psychological Record,* 131–151.

Palmer, D. (2005). A motivational view of constructivist-based teaching. *International Journal of Science Education, 27*(15), 1853–1881.

Pavlov, I. (1928). *Lectures on conditioned reflexes.* New York: Liveright.

Pickering, J. (1995). Buddhism and cognitivism: A postmodern appraisal. *Asian Philosophy, 5,* 23–39.

Rivera, J. (2005). Finding Aristotle's golden mean: Social justice and academic excellence. *Journal of Education, 186*(1), 79–85.

Roehl, R., & Snider, V. (2007). Teachers' beliefs about pedagogy and related issues. *Psychology in the Schools, 44*(8), 873–886.

Skinner, B. F. (1985). Cognitive science and behaviorism. *British Journal of Psychology, 76*(3), 291.

Vygotsky, L. S. (1978). *Mind in society: The development of higher psychological processes.* Cambridge, MA: Harvard University Press.

Weigel, M., & Gardner, H. (2009). The best of both literacies. *Educational Leadership, 66*(6), 38–42.

Wright, J. (2006). Moral discouse, pluralism, and moral cognitivism. *Metaphilosophy, 37*(1), 3–12.

2

Constructivism: A Critique from a Biblical Worldview

Jack Fennema

INTRODUCTION

THREE FORCES APPEAR TO be operative within the realm of education today, each of which is germane to the topic of this article. They are the "transcendent" way of viewing things, represented by the metanarrative of a religious worldview; the "objective" way of viewing things, represented by the standards movement; and the "subjective" way of viewing things, represented by constructivism. Each of these forces within education is informed by the "spirit of their times," the transcendent by the tenets of the premodern era, the objective by the tenets of the modern era, and the subjective by the tenets of the postmodern era (Fennema, 1997).

Until the 1960s, public education in the United States embraced tenets from each of these three forces or movements. A Judeo-Christian ethic colored much that took place within classrooms, while at the same time the back-to-the-basics movements of traditional education continually vied for dominance with Dewey's progressive approach. With the advent of Supreme Court decisions that enforced a separation of church and state within tax-funded institutions, however, the transcendent gave way to an official policy of secularism within public education. This left only the traditional and the progressive approaches as direction-giving authorities, with the transcendent or religious worldview relegated to the private sector.

Wiles and Bondi (2007) cite this struggle within public education today as being between the standards movement that came into full bloom through the No Child Left Behind Act of 1992 and the advent of the internet in the 1990s and its obvious compatibility with a constructivist approach to learning and curriculum development. They appear to believe that the tensions between these two forces are somewhat irreconcilable and that a decision needs to be made on which approach is to guide education's future. They tend to side with the problem-solving discovery approach of constructivism, which aligns itself so naturally to the internet. For them, education should teach *how* to think rather than *what* to think. Standing in the wings, however, are Christian educators who say that any approach to education that does not begin from a biblical perspective is not true and complete education. They opine that education must operate from an "open" system that receives transcendent direction from outside of itself (Fennema, 2008). Even with the many changes that have taken place within society and education over the last fifty years, the original three forces cited above continue to jockey for position within education today.

The question is whether this is an *either-or* proposition or one that is *both-and*. Are these three positions competitively exclusive or can they be cooperatively inclusive? Are they three separate options, or can they find common ground? The position of this article is that merit can, indeed, be found in each position, as well as a degree of mutual compatibility.

This article deals primarily with two of these three forces—the religious, if you will, and constructivist. The standards movement *is* dealt with, albeit tangentially. A clearer understanding of what each of these three forces brings to the educational table cannot but help benefit all educators. At the same time, the practical application of a biblical worldview to the dominant educational theory of the day should prove particularly helpful to Christian educators.

APPLYING A BIBLICAL WORLDVIEW

The very nature of the title of this article illustrates the tensions that exist between these varied approaches to education. From a constructivist view, using a biblical worldview to analyze or critique it as a valid approach to education is not epistemologically possible. Whereas Christian educators claim a biblical worldview to be the metanarrative by which all other narratives are judged, a true constructivist would deny the existence of such transcendent standards. In fact, in this "age of tolerance," the constructivist educator would take offense at such an attempt, declaring it to be unprofessional and divisive. So, from a constructivist perspective, this may be, at best, a nonarticle.

Sadly but really, this may leave Christian educators as the primary audience for whom this article is written. Only they agree that the Bible serves as the basic standard for life, education, and faith. Only they are willing to accept the truth of the written word of God as the criteria by which education is to be evaluated.

Two truths about using a biblical worldview should be noted, however, before proceeding. First, due to the noetic effects of the fall, everyone "sees through a glass darkly." Perfect insight into the mind of God is impossible. Both diminished eyesight and a foggy environment tend to produce limited understanding. Consequently, one should not "stake the whole farm" on any particular position. Secondly, it is my belief that every person, institution, and artifact comports well with biblical truth in some ways and fails to do so in other ways. This will be evidenced as we seek to critique constructivism from a biblical perspective. In certain ways it aligns itself well and could be considered "faithful to Holy Writ"—quite useable by the Christian educator. In other ways, it will no doubt fall short.

POSTMODERNISM DRIVES CONSTRUCTIVISM

The Nature of Postmodernism

The worldview that provides the theoretical foundation for constructivism is postmodernism. Postmodernism rejects the positivism of the modern era—that knowledge must be based on sense perceptions and the investigations of objective science. In other words, positivists believe that the scientific method—which produces empirically verifiable data—is the means for arriving at truth. This view is rejected by postmodernists.

In contrast, three philosophical movements have been especially influential in giving birth to postmodernism: pragmatism, existentialism, and Marxism (Knight, 1998). The first philosophical movement cited, pragmatism, in turn, led to progressivism, exemplified by John

Dewey. Progressivism, too, has influenced postmodernism. Its tenets include: Students are innately good. They are self-directing, autonomous individuals, themselves the source of their own truth. Students learn through active involvement in personally meaningful learning experiences. In this way they develop their abilities and assign personal meaning to what they learn. Teachers facilitate learning by providing positive learning environments that stimulate active, self-directed learning (Van Brummelen, 2002).

Postmodernism has been shaped by a number of characteristics: First, it aims to totally discredit the belief that some sort of universal order, objective meaning, and social harmony can be constructed by human beings. Second, it focuses instead on the individual, the subjective, the fragmentary. Third, it denies the possibility of there being a metanarrative, a universal story that binds humankind. Fourth, it deconstructs all human attempts to build systems of belief; and, finally, it avoids all pretensions to depth and substance in favor of surface style and fashion, dethroning truth and making image the dominant source of meaning and identity (Jenkins, 1996). Postmodernism has divorced itself from the objectivity of modernity. Truth, if indeed there is such a thing, resides and is constructed internally—within the individual—and is, thus, subjective; external, objective truth, according to the postmodernist, does not exist. The postmodern answer to the epistemological question of how one knows, then, is that one knows subjectively through the internal construction of knowledge.

A Biblically Based Critique of Postmodernism

From a biblical viewpoint, postmodernism, on first examination, can appear to be an improvement over modernism. In his *Primer on Postmodernism*, Stanley Grenz (1996, pp. 8–9) states that postmodernism is "post individual, post rationalistic, and post dualistic." This is good news for Christians who have had to deal with the individualism, rationalism, and dualism of the modern age.

Modernism tended to be individualistic, with the rich getting richer and the marginalized and disenfranchised being neglected. In contrast, postmodernists' social concerns comport well with Scripture. Modernism was rationalistic, placing too much optimism on the unaided abilities of the human mind. The Bible states that not only is the human mind finite, it is also fallen. Sin limits the cognitive abilities of all humankind. Modernism was dualistic; it promoted a sacred-secular dichotomy. The immanent and the transcendent did not meet. Faith was viewed as a private matter, at best, that had nothing to do with reality. In contrast, postmodernism provides room at the table for faith-based perspectives. Modernism was also exclusive, whereas postmodernism is inclusive.

Seemingly, the Christian now has equal voice with the other "conversations" that are taking place in the world today. There is, allegedly, tolerance for all stories, even the one the Bible tells. Postmodernism, then, has certain features that are more in harmony with scriptural principles than was true for modernism. But the reverse is true, as well. A number of postmodern tenets fail to align with biblical truth. One is the absence of a metanarrative, in particular, the metanarrative of the Bible. With postmodernism, all stories must be equal; one cannot trump another. Thus no room exists for a story that encompasses all other stories, a claim made by biblical Christianity. The diversity of many narratives trumps the unity found in one metanarrative. In scriptural contrast to this position, while diversity is acknowledged and celebrated, unity, ultimately, always trumps diversity as the "greater good."

A second failure of postmodernism to comport with biblical norms is its denial of absolutes. Truth is viewed as being subjective and relative—found "in the eye of the beholder." In contrast, the Bible emphasizes the immutability of God and God's Word; they are unchangeable. A third variance of postmodernism with Scripture is found in the realm of epistemology. Postmodernism claims that all knowledge is constructed; the Bible states that all knowledge and wisdom is revealed—by God, through God's Word. This, perhaps, is the most serious of conflicts. Finally, the postmodern view of students differs from that offered by the Bible. Postmodernism claims that students are born either morally good or morally neutral, whereas the Bible teaches that all children have been conceived and born with sin-directing natures. Related to this is the postmodern belief that students are autonomous and self-directing; the Bible, in contrast, views children as being dependent creatures of the Almighty who are to be directed by parents and teachers in God's ways. Because postmodernism is the worldview that drives constructivism, many of its positives and negatives can also be applied to constructivism. These are dealt with more fully in the remainder of this article.

CONSTRUCTIVISM

What Is It?

Constructivism is by far the dominant educational theory of the early twenty-first century. Other options do exist, however—two in particular. One includes the traditional approaches to education based on essentialist and perennialist positions. A second involves the process-mastery orientation based on the empirical positivist position mentioned above. The standards movement fits well here, as does behaviorism.

Constructivism *per se* actually exists in three forms (Archer, 1998): social constructivism, individual constructivism, and sociocultural constructivism. Social constructivism states that knowledge is socially constructed; it is a product of the collective (O'Conner, 1998). Knowledge does not exist independently, nor does it preexist for the knowers. It exists only when the facts of a story and how they are connected and construed are agreed upon by the parties involved.

Individual constructivism has been influenced primarily by Jean Piaget. The individual learner is presented as an active participant in the learning process, constructing and organizing new knowledge by building upon previous knowledge. The learner, in seeking cognitive equilibrium, either assimilates or accommodates new information into an existent but constantly developing set of "schemes" or knowledge structures. These schemes are idiosyncratic, built upon the learner's unique life experiences. This may create communication problems at times, for what the teacher thinks is being communicated cannot be identical to that which is actually received by the learner's schema or unique "scheme of things." This is especially true if the worlds of the teacher and learner do not overlap sufficiently.

Sociocultural constructivism has been primarily influenced by Lev Vygotsky, a Soviet psychologist of the 1930s. He believed that learning is embedded not in the collective (the social constructivist view) or in the individual (as in the Piagetian view) but in the interaction between the individual and the collective. Vygotsky (1978) described a zone of *proximal development* that indicates the range of potential thinking and reasoning an individual may accomplish with peer or expert assistance as a complement to the traditional recognition of the zone of *actual development* describing independent accomplishments and achievement. In summary, Vygotsky stated that "individual knowledge always has its origin in the imitation of more accomplished members of society or from apprenticeship activities" (Barrett & Klanderman).

Assumptions of Constructivism

According to Duffy and Jonassen (1992), all three approaches to constructivism share a common set of assumptions: (1) the world is real; but (2) structure is not a part of this reality; rather, meaning is imposed on the world by our experience; (3) there are many ways to "structure" the world; thus, many meanings or perspectives may be generated on the same data; (4) none of the meanings is inherently correct; and (5) meaning is rooted in experience. This view is summarized by Bednar, Cunningham, Duffy, and Perry (1992, p. 91): "Learning is a constructive process in which the learner is building an internal representation of knowledge, a personal interpretation of experience."

A scriptural critique of these five assumptions finds some agreement, but mostly disagreement. First, indeed, the world is real. Second, however, structure is a fundamental—metaphysical—part of this reality (Wolters, 2005). Through the creation process, God posited lawful structure into the cosmos. In Scripture we read that "in (Christ) all things hold together" (Col 1:17b) and that the Son sustains "all things by his powerful word" (Heb 1:3b). Third, indeed, many perspectives can be generated on the same data, but the truthfulness of the perspective is determined by the standards of Scripture. Fourth, God's posited meaning is "correct," yes, but because of the fall, humankind often has difficulty viewing that meaning correctly. Finally, meaning is rooted in God and God's revelatory Word.

Constructivism states that "process or experience is everything"—the source of all personal meaning. In contrast, a biblical view states that reality consists of *both* structure (i.e., product) *and* process. The world can be known because it is structured in a lawful and unified way, and our minds have been created in a like manner. Constants and absolutes do exist.

It is important to note, however, that this, too, is a *both-and* issue rather than one that is *either-or*. Constructivists rightly decry teachers who mindlessly carry out prescribed curriculum directives. Such teachers place all of their pedagogical eggs in the "content" or "product" basket with an absence of the "higher level thinking" of process. Constants and absolutes taken to this extreme create ossification (or indoctrination). I call this "party line" teaching; the *status quo* is the norm. The result is that students become committed to the dominant cultural values without ever questioning them or considering alternatives. In response, constructivists identify with critical theorists who first critique formal curricula and then alter them to become tools for social change. This "liberated" curricula "highlight race and gender rights, community life that resists individualism, and the social problems resulting from societal conflict and hierarchical authority" (Van Brummelen, 2002, p. 7).

Indeed, Christ's Sermon on the Mount (Matt 5–7) contains many radical imperatives. All Christians are mandated to be transformers of society and culture as they live out the new order of the kingdom that Christ inaugurated during his earthly ministry. Seeking justice and righteousness for the marginalized and disenfranchised is part of being Christ's disciple. In this area of concern, there is harmony between constructivism and Scripture.

A BIBLICAL CRITIQUE OF CONSTRUCTIVISM

How, then, does constructivism hold up next to the light of Scripture? Given the thesis that every theory is both faithful and unfaithful to biblical norms, constructivism should be a "mixed bag," with some components being faithful or in harmony with Scripture and some not. The following critique will systematically examine several key educational areas to which constructivism speaks: philosophy, anthropology, learning theory, curriculum development, instructional strategies, assessment, and research.

Philosophy

Three subareas comprise the essence of philosophy: metaphysics, which deals with the "What is real?" question; epistemology, which deals with the "How do we know?" question; and axiology, which deals with the "What do we value?" question. The brief response of the constructivist to these questions is: "We create our own reality, we create our own answers, and we create our own values." Constructivism rejects metaphysical schemes—any universal order; for it, knowledge does not copy or reflect an external reality. Objective, external truth does not exist; truth is viewed as being constructed subjectively.

In contrast, Scripture promotes the metaphysical scheme (i.e., creation order) designed by God in God's creative act that since has been "held together" by Christ. God and God's Word represent external, unchanging, objective truth. But this truth—represented ultimately by Christ himself—is also organic, dynamic, and living. According to the Bible, truth is represented both through form and function, product and process. Scripture also states epistemologically that we know reality solely through the revelation of God's Word—Christ the *logos*. The three manifestations of this *logos* are (1) Jesus Christ—the Word incarnate, (2) the Bible—the Word inscripturated, and (3) created reality—the Word in creation. One cannot know reality and truth apart from divine revelation. Regarding values, they are God-ordained and are to be God-reflecting. The criteria for the axiological categories of beauty and goodness originate in the nature and character of God.

In conclusion, commonalities, then, may be found in two areas. Indeed, truth has a living or "process" aspect. And, knowledge does contain a subjective dimension. But, it appears that in all other areas constructivism and Scripture are philosophically at opposite poles.

Anthropology

Anthropology is a subset of metaphysics, an area not dealt with, for the most part, by contemporary educators. (When did you last take a course in educational anthropology?) But the "nature of the learner" is a valid area of study for educators, for different views of children spawn different views of learning and behavior. There is some agreement, however, on the natures of children. Both the constructivist and scriptural positions believe that children are interactive. They can both initiate and respond. That fact obviously has an impact on the teaching-learning process. The concept of self-esteem is very important to constructivists, at times trumping productivity. The Bible teaches that children are image-bearers of God. For that reason, they, indeed, should have a "high" view of themselves, but only in the light of what God has endowed them to be.

Learning Theory

Learning theory is, perhaps, the area of greatest commonality between Scripture and constructivism. Except for Piaget's evolutionary basis for his schema theory, the theory itself seems to align well with a biblical view of reality (e.g., structured, knowable) and the knowing process (e.g., interactive engagement). Indeed, we do learn by synthesizing new experiences into what we already know. Yes, learning is all about making connections and seeing relationships. The Bible would credit this phenomenon, however, to the unity and relationality of God and God's created reality.

The two positions differ on the source of knowledge. The Bible states that the fear of the Lord is the beginning of wisdom (Prov 1:7) and that God is the source of all wisdom and knowledge (Rom 11:33–36). Constructivists, as previously stated, believe that knowledge is constructed internally by the learner. For them, learning begins with children's own ideas, hypotheses, and explorations. That difference could be bridged, perhaps, if the word "knowledge" were replaced by "understanding." Semantics may be at play here.

Curriculum Development

If the commonalities of positions on learning theory can be represented by overlapping circles in a Venn diagram, those same circles would have to separate entirely when dealing with curriculum development. Because a constructivist curriculum, at least in theory, is a student-generated curriculum, there can be no all-encompassing curricular model. This is a direct offshoot of constructivist rejection of metaphysical schemes, for curriculum directly reflects one's view of reality and its source. If knowledge is internally generated by students, either individually or collectively, then preplanned, objective (even standards-based) curriculum appears to be superfluous. This disconnect with reality (pun not intended) exposes a serious flaw in constructivist reasoning if taken to its logical (or illogical) end (Van Brummelen, 2002).

Constructivism, if taken at its word, is essentially content-free; or, at least the content is not the point of it all. It rejects a common knowledge base. Knowledge is relative and constantly changing. Process is everything; thus, the constructivist curriculum is comprised primarily of process objectives. Meaningful activities are valued more than right answers. Meaning for the learner is rooted in experience; in fact, meaning is imposed on the world by the learning experience. The student addresses the world rather than the other way around. That process does not bode well for traditional or standards-based approaches to curriculum development.

A biblical curricular model is based on a covenant-kingdom metanarrative—the story that trumps all of the smaller stories. This provides the context or field for learning. The curriculum *comes from* somewhere. That viewpoint, obviously, has to be rejected by the constructivist. A Bible-based curriculum also *goes* somewhere; it is teleo-logical in nature. This world is being guided by God toward God's own divine end, that of the consummation of the kingdom of the Son at the end of time. This, too, has a goal-oriented and purposeful bearing on curriculum that the constructivist must reject.

Instructional Strategies

A biblical view of the authority of the teacher differs greatly from the constructivist's view of the position and role of the teacher. With con-structivism, the teacher is not seen as a "sage on the stage" or tour guide; rather, the teacher is viewed as a facilitator. Within this construct, stu-dents are responsible for and negotiate their own learning. Ideally, they set the agenda; the teacher is relegated to the position of "guide on the side." In response, teachers seek and value learners' constructions, view-points, and solutions. If one accepts the constructivist view of learning and curriculum, this all makes perfect sense. The constructivist position, indeed, has internal consistency.

Process-oriented instructional strategies, for the most part, align themselves well with biblically based approaches. But scriptural instruc-tion also "instructs"; content (i.e., the truth of God posited in created real-ity) is presented authoritatively by the teacher. In brief, then, other than in differences over the pedagogical role and authority of the teacher, the two positions do have a number of teaching-learning strategies in common.

Assessment

Regarding assessment, in a nutshell, constructivism uses subjective rather than objective instruments for assessment. That simply follows its metaphysical position that reality and truth are relative, subjective, and constantly changing. There are no "wrong" answers or "misconcep-tions." But what, then, can be assessed?

One measure of assessment is whether students' work is coherent and useful and helps them to open their perceptual windows further. Another is the degree to which process goals are achieved. These relate to student constructions and solutions to problems. Again, having "right" answers (i.e., content answers) is not sought; rather, the teacher looks for a demon-stration of processes that help students grow in their knowledge building. "As long as a student's solution to a problem achieves a viable goal, it has to be credited" (McCarty & Schwandt in Phillips, 2000, p. 49).

Three approaches to assessment appear to be in harmony with the constructivist philosophical and pedagogical position. One, preference is given to anecdotal reporting over letter grades. A descriptive report of progress replaces anything that would smack of objective standards or class standing. Two, authentic (i.e., real life) assessments are favored over any form of standardized assessment. In this case, authentic learning experiences and assessments simply reflect the constructivist the subjective nature of the learning process. The boiler-plate approach, where one size fits all, gives way to the tailor-made approach. Three, portfolios, projects, and performances replace the paper-and-pencil approach. Again, since learning is considered to be a very personal and individualized experience, assessment must be as well.

In critique of constructivist assessment, there probably is not much that doesn't comport with biblical standards. Again, the difference comes with what is left unsaid. Biblically speaking, assessing understanding of content concepts must be an additional part of the mix. Measuring how well predetermined outcome objectives have been met is in line with the Bible's position on the existence of objective and unchanging truth. So, in summary, a biblical worldview on education might say that objective assessment of how well content standards have been achieved needs to be added to such things as portfolios, projects, and performances if a balanced approach to the learning process is to be achieved.

Research

Constructivism promotes action research and actually denigrates traditional research—particularly that which is quantitative in nature. That stance is entirely consistent with a personal and subjective approach to education in general. Traditional research seeks to be objective, valid, and reliable so that replication studies can be done in an orderly and faithful manner by others. Results are intended to be broadly applicable. In contrast, action research is "one and done," and seldom has relevance to others beyond the original researcher.

Mills (2007, p. 6) describes critical action research as "emancipatory action research because of its liberation through knowledge gathering." From what must one be liberated through research? He responds: "from the dictates of tradition, habit, and bureaucracy." We must seek "enlightenment." There is, no doubt, some merit in this. But to take on tradition in carte blanche fashion as an evil that needs to be faced squarely ignores content lessons that history alone can provide. Again, constructivism steps outside the purview of Scripture on this.

CONCLUSION

As is true of all people, institutions, and theories, the line of demarcation for the application of the standard of biblical faithfulness runs *through* constructivism rather than *around* it. Stated in other words, it is neither all good nor all bad; it is neither fully in harmony with scriptural norms nor totally in disharmony. Indeed, it is a mixed bag.

Beginning with the positive, much about the constructivist's view that "process" is crucial for learning fits well with a biblical position. Again, the creation mandate is very much oriented toward a discovery approach to unearthing the creation potential posited by God in the beginning. Questions need answers, problems need solving. In keeping with that, Piaget's schema theory and his emphasis on "seeking equilibration" have much to offer.

But for this one positive, there are two negatives. To begin, the presuppositions or assumptions of constructivism about virtually everything stand in stark contrast to biblical positions. That should be evident as the philosophical basis for constructivism was examined throughout the paper. Secondly, the omission of unchanging content by constructivists simply doesn't comport with the Bible's position on reality and truth. Education that follows biblical standards includes both process and content, and education is seen as a three-fold subjective, objective, and transcendent activity (Fennema, 1997).

Finally, this paper sought to apply a biblical worldview or set of standards to the theory of constructivism. On some matters the theory is faithful to biblical standards; on other matters the theory is unfaithful. Christian educators who seek to be biblically faithful in their teaching need, then, to be discerning. The answer is not found in any one theory. Beginning with the framework of a biblical worldview, they are called to analyze all theories, evaluate each of their components against biblical criteria or standards, and then synthesize an approach that is comprised of the parts that have been found faithful. That would be following the Apostle Paul's admonition to, first, "demolish arguments and every pretension that sets itself up against the knowledge of God," and, secondly, to "take captive every thought to make it obedient to Christ" (1 Cor 10:5).

REFERENCES

Airasian, P., & Walsh, M. (1997). Constructivist cautions. *Phi Delta Kappan, 78*(6), 444–449.

Archer, A. (1998). *Constructivism and Christian teaching*. Presented at the 23rd International Faith and Learning Seminar, University of Eastern Africa, Baraton, Kenya.

Barrett, J., & Klanderman, D. A. Christian constructivist? The impact of worldview on learning theories and the mathematics education research community. *Journal of the Association of Christians in the Mathematical Sciences*. Retrieved from http://www.acmsonline.org/journal/2006/KlandermanBarrett.pdf

Bednar, A., Cunningham, D., Duffy, T, & Perry, J. (1992). Theory into practice: How do we link? In T. M. Duffy & D. H. Jonassen (Eds.), *Constructivism and the technology of teaching: A conversation* (pp. 17–34). Hillsdale, NJ: Erlbaum.

Duffy, T., & Jonassen, D. (1992). Constructivism: New implications for instructional technology. In T. M. Duffy & D. H. Jonassen (Eds.), *Constructivism and the technology of teaching: A conversation* (pp. 1–16). Hillsdale, NJ: Erlbaum.

Fennema, J. (1997). *Knowing in a postmodern age: The Christian's answer begins with a Word—the Logos*. Presented at the With Heart & Mind Conference, Toronto.

Fennema, J. (2008). The three marks of *truly* Christian education (and how to achieve them). Unpublished paper.

Grenz, S. (1996). *A primer on postmodernism*. Grand Rapids, MI: Eerdmans.

Jenkins, J. (1996). *Shaping the Christian mind! Our modernist presuppositions may be showing!* Presented at the Scholarly Conference on Shaping the Christian Mind, Sydney, Australia.

Karpol, B. (1998). *Teachers talking back and breaking bread*. Cresskill, NJ: Hampton.

Knight, G. (1998). *Philosophy and education: An introduction in Christian perspective*. Berrien Springs, MI: Andrews University Press.

Mills, G. (2007). *Action research: A guide for the teacher researcher*. Upper Saddle River, NJ: Pearson.

O'Conner, J. (1998). Can we trace the "efficacy of social constructivism"? In P. D. Pearson & A. Iran-Nejad (Eds.), *Review of Research in Education* (Vol. 23, pp. 25–71). Washington, DC: American Educational Research Association.

Phillips, D. (2000). *Constructivism in education: Opinions and second opinions on controversial issues*. Ninety-ninth yearbook of the National Society for the Study of Education. Chicago: National Society for the Study of Education.

Van Brummelen, H. (2002). *Steppingstones to curriculum: A biblical path*. Colorado Springs, CO: Purposeful Design. (2nd ed.)

Wiles, J., & Bondi, J. (2007). *Curriculum development: A guide to practice*. Upper Saddle River, NJ: Pearson Education. (7th ed.)

Wolters, A. M. (2005). *Creation regained: Biblical basics for a Reformational worldview*. Grand Rapids, MI: Eerdmans.

Vygotsky, L. (1978). *Mind in society: The development of higher psychological processes*. Cambridge, MA: Harvard University Press.

3

Constructivism in the Classroom: Is It Biblical?

Calvin G. Roso   my professor.

INTRODUCTION

CONSTRUCTIVIST LEARNING THEORY IS believed by many to be based on a postmodern educational philosophy that states that learning happens when students are given the opportunity to construct their own knowledge and meaning (Baines & Stanley, 2000; Chrenka, 2001; Olsen, 1999; Windschitl, 1999). At an extreme, this philosophy denies absolute truth and asserts that students can, and should, construct their own knowledge and truth (Chrenka, 2001; von Glaserfeld, 1995). Nevertheless, constructivism encourages student participation in the learning process, moving students away from a teacher-centered classroom and offering learning that connects to students' interests and learning styles and, ultimately, improves student learning. Because of its controversial philosophy, some conservative Christian educators argue against using constructivist methodologies (Baines & Stanley, 2000; Smerdon, Burkam, & Lee, 1999; Van Brummelen, 2002). In spite of the controversies, Christian educators must not deny current research, but must instead search the Scriptures to see if a biblical worldview supports or denies constructivist learning theories. This approach to evaluating current research in light of Scripture is supported by many including Saint Augustine (trans. 1982) who aptly said:

> When they [secularists] are able, from reliable evidence, to prove some fact of physical science, we shall show that it is not contrary to our Scripture. But when they produce from any of their books a theory contrary to Scripture . . . either we shall have some ability to

demonstrate that it is absolutely false, or at least we ourselves will hold it so without any shadow of doubt. And we will so cling to our Mediator, "in whom are hidden all the treasures of wisdom and knowledge," that we will not be led astray by the glib talk of false philosophy or frightened by the superstition of false religion.

This paper summarizes the negative aspects of constructivist philosophy and presents the positive outcomes of constructivist learning theory and classroom methodology. Finally, constructivist ideas are examined in relationship to a biblical perspective and Jesus' teaching to see how Christian educators can use constructivism in the classroom.

CONSTRUCTIVISM IN FAITH-BASED EDUCATION

Constructivist Philosophy of Education

Constructivism advocates that people learn better by actively constructing their own understanding and by reconciling new information with previous knowledge (Smerdon et al., 1999). Constructivists believe that "to arrive at meaningful knowledge, they [the learners] must learn through deep inquiry. As the unexamined life is not worth living, so the unexamined fact is not worth believing" (Perkins, 1999, p. 11).

According to some theorists, constructivism is more of a philosophical approach than a set of instructional practices (Smerdon et al., 1999). As a philosophy, constructivism assumes that "what constitutes 'knowledge' may be culturally constructed, rather than [absolute] truth or fact" (Smerdon et al., 1999, p. 4). Constructivism advocates the possibility of constructing world truth in many different ways. Those who support constructivist philosophy believe that current knowledge is no more valid than past beliefs (e.g., the belief that the world is round is no more true than the earlier belief that the world was flat) (Chrenka, 2001). Van Brummelen (2002, p. 32) suggests that Christian educators must be aware of the negative philosophical and theoretical basis of constructivist learning theory:

> Few teachers realize the theoretical basis of constructivism. . . . The theory breaks radically with the Western—and Christian— tradition that knowledge can be gained through the senses and thus leads to a picture of the real world. Constructivism holds that humans do not discover knowledge or read the book of nature. Rather, it claims that humans construct all knowledge either

individually or through social interaction. Knowledge does not discover or reflect a world that exists out there. Instead, humans make knowledge and impost it to help them cope with their experience. . . . No ultimate, true, objective knowledge exists. Knowledge is strictly subjective.

Constructivist Learning Theory and Classroom Methodology

The teacher-student relationship changes in constructivist education and puts the teacher in the role of facilitator and coach instead of the role of the classroom lecturer (Baines & Stanley, 2000; Olsen, 1999; Windschitl, 1999). Some constructivists advocate that even if a teacher *does* know the answer, the teacher is not supposed to communicate it to the students—"that would be a tyrannical imposition of the teacher's will upon the minds of the students" (Baines & Stanley, 2000, p. 3). The constructivist classroom teacher must motivate students, create "problem situations, foster retrieval of prior knowledge, and create a positive environment for learning" (Phye, 1997, as cited in Olsen, 1999, p. 2). "Teachers must ask themselves, 'Is my role to dispense knowledge or to nurture independent thinkers? How do I show respect for the ideas of the students? Am I here to learn from the students?' " (Windschitl, 1999, p. 3).

Constructivists believe that learners are capable of intellectual autonomy (Windschitl, 1999), and they acknowledge three *types* of learners: the active learner, the social learner, and the creative learner (Perkins, 1999; Piaget, 1950). The use of collaborative or cooperative learning often, although not always, fosters learning. Engaging in discovery and rediscovery energizes students and brings deeper understanding (Perkins, 1999).

There are multiple approaches to constructivist teaching methodologies, each encouraging active, social, and creative learning (Piaget, 1950). In turn, the constructivist classroom moves away from being teacher-centered to become student-centered in nature. Constructivist teaching practices include, but are not limited to: improving student thinking, using questions to allow students to identify their own theories, promoting classroom dialogue between and among students and teachers, encouraging student collaboration, enabling students to elaborate on their individual ideas, challenging thinking by presenting contradictions to students' ideas, promoting analysis and inquiry through questioning, allowing *wait time* during discussions and questioning, providing ample time for student thinking and processing of ideas, encouraging self-reflection and metacognition, and organizing classroom curriculum around real-life problems (Brooks, 1990, as cited in Olsen, 1999). In addition, Bruner (1973) suggested several additional constructivist concepts: Learners construct new ideas based upon their current and past knowledge; curriculum should be organized in a spiral manner so students can continually build upon what they have already learned; and, instruction should be concerned with experiences and contexts that make the student willing and able to learn (i.e., student readiness). Freire (1964) further promoted dialogue and collaboration in instructional methodology by advocating that through dialogue teachers and students are jointly responsible for the learning process.

Biblical Perspective of Constructivism in the Classroom

In contrast to the philosophical foundation of constructivism, a biblical philosophy of education acknowledges absolute truth (Byrne, 1977; Van Brummelen, 1998) and sees the teacher as the authority in the classroom, not simply a facilitator (Byrne, 1977; Zuck, 1998). In addition, the pupil is seen as a child with a sinful nature, and in need of redemption (Byrne, 1977). Finally, the purpose of education from a biblical view is righteous living and discipleship—bringing man into relationship with God in order to serve God ("Education," 1980; Van Brummelen, 1998), educating the pupil spiritually, socially, intellectually, emotionally, and physically (Byrne, 1977). Children are directed, nurtured, loved, and instructed in biblical truth from an early age, so that they can ultimately learn to make righteous choices regarding their lifelong relationships with God and others.

A biblical worldview also acknowledges that God is the author of all truth. All truth and knowledge ultimately come from God, so the Christian educator can say, like Saint Augustine, that wherever truth may be found, it is our Lord's (Augustine, trans. 1958). Although constructivist philosophy contradicts a biblical philosophy of education, there are several constructivist discoveries and methods that are true (e.g., inductive thinking, inquiry, and application) and can by used by the Christian teacher to God's glory.

If we view God as our teacher and biblical examples as God's instructional methodology, we will find that God uses a variety of instructional methods—many that could be labeled as *constructivist*. Although the Bible clearly disagrees with constructivist philosophy regarding the acquisition of knowledge and truth, the Bible supports the use of both traditional instructional methodologies and constructivist instructional methodologies.

The Bible clearly advocates that there is ultimate truth and knowledge that students should learn. In addition, students should learn lower-level knowledge—as seen in the admonishment to teach and know God's commands and actions (Deut 4:9). However, the Bible seems to advocate many ways of "teaching" core knowledge, and not all are through the "teacher-as-lecturer" approach advocated by traditionalists. For example, in the Garden of Eden, God used *choice* to teach Adam and Eve about good and evil and sin and redemption. God *challenged Cain's thinking* by presenting contradictions to Cain's ideas. Noah was allowed time for *self-reflection* as he spent over one hundred years building the ark. The same is true for Abraham, who waited decades for God's promise to come true. Joseph's trials can be viewed as life lessons that presented *conceptual clusters of problems* for him to resolve. God spoke to Moses by questioning and allowing *wait time* for Moses to process his thoughts.

Many of the prophets and apostles also used constructivist methods to teach. For example, although Moses presented great portions of the law to the Israelites, much of it was rehearsed and applied as the children of Israel wandered through the desert. The concept of learning while doing (versus rote memorization) is a Jewish concept that Moses instructed parents to use in teaching their children: "These commandments that I give you today are to be upon your hearts. Impress them on your children. Talk about them when you sit at home and when you lie down and when you get up" (Deut 6:6–8). Essentially, learning was to happen continuously, inside and outside of the formal classroom setting. Gideon's task was one of teaching through collaboration. Samson spoke in riddles and promoted inquiry through questioning. Samuel used questioning to confront Saul. Likewise, Nathan used questioning to confront David. Sometimes the messages presented by major and minor prophets were simple and sometimes they were quite complex—each prophet aligning curriculum according to students' levels of development.

CHRIST AND CLASSROOM INSTRUCTION

Jesus Christ is the master teacher. As traditional educators, Christians often mistakenly assume that Jesus' chief method of instruction was in the style of a classroom lecture, with all his pupils sitting in straight rows, practicing rote memorization. Yet the style and content of Jesus' teaching was unlike that which anyone had ever seen before (Mark 1:22; Luke 19:48). Jesus was effective because, as the master teacher, he deconstructed misconceptions (Luke 11:39–52) in order to reveal God's truth (John 14:6). Jesus spoke with authority (Matt 7:29), making each lesson applicable to individual students (Matt 9:36–37).

Jesus used a variety of methods to present God's truth:

Teaching with authority. Luke 4:32 says that because he taught with authority, Jesus' teaching was unlike the teaching of others. This example helps teachers today understand that teaching is more than facilitating and that the teacher's job is to impart new knowledge and learning for the student.

Teaching, preaching, and healing. Jesus' teaching style included several actions that promoted dialogue and student thinking. Matthew 4:23 says that Jesus went about teaching, preaching, and healing—exemplifying the need to align instructional methodology with the need and readiness of the learner.

Encouraging active learning. Much of Jesus' teaching required people to physically *do* something. Changing water to wine required servants to physically draw water (John 2:1–12). The fishermen were required to cast out nets. Peter learned a lesson about taxes by catching a fish. The then lepers walked and were healed. The woman with the issue of blood followed Jesus through the crowd. In addition, Jesus healed by making mud and requiring the blind man to wash in the pool of Siloam (John 9:6–7).

Teaching through parables. Parables required students to process new information. Jesus' use of parables constitutes over 90 percent of his recorded teaching in the gospels. Ironically, the multitudes often went away without having heard the explanation of the stories (Matt 13:34–35) thus *constructing* their own meaning to Christ's teaching.

Testing preconceived notions. Jesus' conversation with Nicodemus (John 3:3) tested Nicodemus's ideas about doctrine and spiritual birth. Jesus' willingness to converse with the Samaritan woman at the well (John 4:27) tested the disciple's notions about cultural propriety and tested the woman's notions about the Messiah. Both of these lengthy conversations also showed that Jesus provided time for individual student processing and thinking.

Several other passages show that Jesus' style of teaching was far from the traditional style of lecturing but was actually an example of what today's educators might label constructivist methodology. Some of these examples include:

- Applying old and new ideas (Mark 11:17)
- Using relevant demonstrations (Mark 12:13–17; Luke 9:46–48)
- Questioning students (Mark 12:16; Luke 20:3; John 14:9–10)
- Using wait time and leaving some questions unanswered (Luke 8:10)
- Speaking with love and respect (Mark 10:21)
- Teaching through discipline and correction (Luke 7:40–47)
- Encouraging pupils to elaborate on what they had learned (Luke 8:39)
- Promoting critical thinking skills (Mark 12:28–34)
- Opening students' minds to understanding (Luke 24:45)
- Teaching through example (Luke 14:1–4; John 13:15)

CONCLUSION

As Christian educators, we should purpose to use all of Christ's instructional methods in our classrooms, and a great majority of those methods support constructivist methodology. In addition, we should examine all educational philosophies and methods—secular and Christian—in light of the Scriptures (Col 2:8; Acts 17:11). We should always be willing to try new ways to bring students to a greater understanding of God's truth and academic knowledge (1 Cor 9:22).

> The pronouncement that one method of teaching is best seems dubious. In a constantly changing environment, a teacher must be eclectic, spontaneous, and highly adaptable. The insistence on a single strategy bears the hallmark of academic educators who are isolated in their own theoretical models. (Baines & Stanley, 2000, p. 4)

Christian educators should turn to Scripture to examine biblical principles of teaching and how Christ taught. From the Bible we see that the *best* methods include a variety of instructional approaches that are backed up by current research. For the Christian educator, Scripture supports the use of a constructivist methodology without supporting the philosophical premise upon which constructivism is based.

REFERENCES

Augustine. (trans. 1982). *Saint Augustine: The literal meaning of Genesis* (J. H. Taylor, S. J., Trans.). New York: Newman.

Augustine. (trans. 1958). *Saint Augustine: On Christian doctrine* (D. W. Robertson, Trans.) New York: Macmillan. (Original work published 427.)

Baines, L. A., & Stanley, G. (2000). We want to see the teacher: Constructivism and the rage against expertise. *Phi Delta Kappan, 82*(4), 327–330.

Bruner, J. (1973). *Going beyond the information given.* New York: Norton.

Byrne, H. W. (1977). *A Christian approach to education: Educational theory and application.* Milford, MI: Mott Media.

Chrenka, L. (2001). Misconstructing constructivism. *Phi Delta Kappan, 82*(9), 694–695.

Education. (1980). In *Webster's 1828 dictionary.* San Francisco: Foundation for American Christian Education.

Ellis, A. K. (2001). *Research on educational innovations.* Larchmont, NY: Eye on Education. (3rd ed.)

Freire, P. (1964/1993). *Pedagogy of the oppressed.* New York: Continuum.

Olsen, D. G. (1999). Constructivist principles of learning and teaching methods. *Education, 120*(2), 347–55.

Perkins, D. (1999, November). The many faces of constructivism. *Educational Leadership, 57,* 6–11.

Piaget, J. (1950). *The psychology of intelligence.* London: Routledge and Paul.

Smerdon, B. A., Burkam, D. T., & Lee, V. E. (1999). Access to constructivist and didactic teaching: Who gets it? Where is it practiced? *Teachers College Record, 101*(1), 5–34.

Van Brummelen, H. (1998). *Walking with God in the classroom: Christian approaches to learning and teaching.* Seattle, WA: Alta Vista College Press. (2nd ed.)

Van Brummelen, H. (2002). *Steppingstones to curriculum: A biblical path.* Colorado Springs, CO: Association of Christian Schools International. (2nd ed.)

von Glaserfeld, E. (1995). A constructivist approach to teaching. In L. Steffe & J. Gale (Eds.), *Constructivism in education* (pp. 3–16). Hillsdale, NJ: Erlbaum.

Windschitl, M. (1999). The challenges of sustaining a constructivist classroom culture. *Phi Delta Kappan, 80*(10), 751–755.

Zuck, R. B. (1998). *Spirit-filled teaching: The power of the Holy Spirit in your ministry.* Nashville, TN: Word Publishing.

4

Three Faces of Constructivism

HeeKap Lee

INTRODUCTION

CONSTRUCTIVISM IS IN OPERATION everywhere. It is a hot-potato issue at this time in the field of philosophy, education, technology, and even religion. Over the last few decades in the education field, constructivism has been readily accepted. Airasian and Walsh (1997) explain constructivism's popularity in three ways. First, constructivism is an educational renovation, as it criticizes the traditional education in which students passively receive information from teachers. Secondly, constructivism engages students through the active knowledge construction process, so that all students can learn and make educational successes. Finally, constructivism creates a new role for teachers as facilitators, rather than primary controllers of students' learning.

However, critical questions have been raised, including confusion over the term *constructivism* and the compatibility of the implicit assumptions of constructivism with those of faith-based education. Since constructivism was first introduced in education, it has evolved drastically. Many different forms of constructivism have been produced, which have contributed toward misunderstandings of the term by educational practitioners and teachers. Matthew (2000) once identified as many as eighteen different forms of constructivism being used.

Additionally, many arguments have appeared rejecting the notion of applying constructivist approaches towards faith-based education settings. For example, constructivists claim that "meaning is imposed on the world by individuals rather than existing in the world independently of us"

45

(Duffy and Jonassen, 1991, p. 8). Therefore, truth is relative to particular times, places, and people. That leads to the question, is truth changeable and constructible based on personal backgrounds or particular contexts?

The purpose of this chapter is to help clarify the term constructivism within three specific faces and to find possible connections between it and faith-based education. A discussion of the main features of constructivism will come first, followed by an explanation of the three faces: constructivism as a postmodern educational philosophy, constructivism as a post-positivist research paradigm, and constructivism as a pedagogical practice and instructional method that emphasizes active participation of learners. The chapter will culminate with the implications for constructivism in faith-based education in each face.

CONSTRUCTIVISM: THE MAIN FEATURES

Constructivism has a long history. Von Glaserfeld (1989) traced it back to the eighteenth century Italian philosopher, Giambattista Vico. However, the authentic constructivism in the field of education was introduced in the twentieth century by educational researchers and practitioners like Piaget, Vygotsky, Dewey, and Bruner. But what exactly is constructivism? Airasian and Walsh (1997) define constructivism as "an epistemology, a philosophical explanation about the nature of knowledge (p. 444)." Constructivism emphasizes that reality is a context bound so that each person constructs personal meaning in the learning process. Duffy and Jonassen (1992, p. 9–11) summarized it as a set of assumptions:

- The world is real, but structure is not a part of this reality;

- Meaning is imposed on the world by our experience;

- There are many ways to structure the world; many meanings or perspectives may be generated on the same data;

- None of the meanings is inherently correct; and

- Meaning is rooted in experience.

As it pertains to education, constructivism has evolved from dissatisfaction with traditional learning theories that were represented within the objectivism-positivism-dominated paradigm. Since its appearance in education, constructivism has been considered a panacea that brings educational innovation and reform to all levels of the educational systems (Pegues, 2007; Simpson, 2002; Bentley, 2003). Multiple approaches of constructivism have been presented. Matthew (2000) identifies at least eighteen different forms of constructivism, while Geelan (1997) classifies five forms (personal, social, critical, contextual, and radical constructivism). Oxford (1997) coins the term "shape-shifting" when he explains that constructivism has evolved to include contradictory concepts. According to Oxford, this confusing conglomeration of contradictions negatively influences how teachers apply "constructivism" in the classroom. Much confusion exist because researchers and educators apply the term at different levels, using varied principles in multiple ways. Some researchers use constructivism as an ontological and philosophical approach to education in the postmodern era; while other researchers adopt constructivism as a post-positivist research methodology in education. Some view it as a theory of learning; others consider it a theory of teaching, emphasizing student-centered pedagogical principles in classrooms. Three faces of constructivism will be presented: a postmodern philosophy, a research paradigm, and pedagogical practices, each addressing applicable ideas of how each face can be related to faith-based education.

THREE FACES OF CONSTRUCTIVISM

Constructivism as Postmodernism Philosophy

There have been three waves of enlightenments: premodernism, modernism, and postmodernism. The major characteristics of each historical enlightenment paradigm are documented in Table 4.1:

Table 4.1 Historical enlightenments

Premodernism: Greco-Roman era to the Middle Ages	Modernism: The Middle Ages to the twentieth century	Postmodernism: Present time
Thinking was influenced by dualism and rationalism.	Thinking was influenced by empiricism and logical scientific methodology.	Thinking is influenced by new age, constructivism, and multiculturalism.

| Faith and religion played central roles. | Scientific knowledge provided a unique image of objective reality, by identifying objective truths and showing their validity. The legitimate source of truth arose from scientific and professional knowledge. | The nature of meaning is relative and phenomena are context based. The creation of personal and social realities is emphasized. |
| To understand the world, people relied on prayer, faith, thinking, and reasoning. | Thinkers discovered truth via the logical process of science. | The process of gaining knowledge and understanding is social, inductive, hermeneutical, and qualitative. |

Postmodernism claims that there is no objective reality and denies absolute truth. Newton (2004) identified four characteristics of postmodernism. First, postmodernism sees flaws in the modernist enlightenment project and seeks to go beyond it and recover what was suppressed in modernism thinking. Second, postmodernists try to find the hole in every metanarrative; in particular, they focus on how metanarratives suppress opposite viewpoints and are used to control both nature and other people. Third, all truth claims must be seen as perspectives, influenced and biased by the cultural, political, and personal perspective of the person making the claim. Finally, postmodernism seeks new approaches to hermeneutics in which meaning is not in the text but in the interaction between the text and the reader.

Postmodernism permeates deeply as it pertains to education and how we come to understand and know the reality and the nature of truth (Savery & Duffy, 1995; Knight, 2006). Postmodern perspectives have become embedded in education, and they have influenced many to develop a new educational philosophy (English, 2003). Postmodernism opens up new opportunities to rethink the processes of knowing and the nature of pedagogy in unique ways. Savery and Duffy (1995, pp. 31–32) identify three ontological propositions that constructivists deal with in education: (1) "understanding is *in* our interactions with the environment"; (2) "cognitive conflict or puzzlement is the stimulus for learning and determines the organization and nature of what is learned"; and (3)

"knowledge evolves through social negotiation and through the evaluation of the viability of individual understandings."

How has constructivism affected education? Constructivism dictates that there can be no neutrality in education. In the modern era,
there was a hope to reach to the truth through human reasoning and
scientific power. The truth and knowledge has been considered as objective and universal, and all human beings share the same perceptions
about the reality and the truth. Education and schooling, especially
teachers, acted as the necessary push for students to acquire predefined
human truth and reality. However, in the postmodern era, the perception of the universal truth and reality are shaken, and the dominant educational approach has been questioned. Education theories, schooling,
and all instructional practices have been redefined and reconsidered.
Furthermore, the importance of affective and emotional domains are
recognized in education, which are also included in other theories such
as multiple intelligences, emotional intelligences, and learning styles
(Edlin, 2004). Newton (2004) summarizes the positive impacts of constructivism, including:

- Redefinition of educational terms or a questioning of their usefulness, often on a political basis

- Rewriting of history to restore the suppressed history of
  minorities

- Teachers openly promoting their political, moral or social views
  to students

- Promotion of values such as tolerance, intuition, diversity and
  multiculturalism above reason or strict moral absolutes

- Promotion of a constructivist view of truth or knowledge by which
  no answers are wrong, everything is relative to society (p. 183)

Based on the constructivist influence in education, several new approaches of educational philosophy have emerged. For example, Paulo
Freire (1972) created a new function of education to lead a liberation
movement from the oppressor. He coined the term *problem-posing
pedagogy* for the oppressed, in which lessons emphasize critical and liberating dialogue. He redefined the role of education for action against
dehumanized authority. In this book, he argues:

The problem-posing education, as a humanist and liberating praxis, posits as a fundamental method that men subjected to domination must fight for their emancipation. To that end, it enables teachers and students to become the subject of the educational process by overcoming authoritarianism and an alienating intellectualism; it also enables men to overcome their false perception of reality. The world—no longer something to be described with deceptive words—becomes the object of that transforming action by men which results in their humanization. (p. 74)

Can constructivism be evaluated as a philosophy of faith-based education? It is my contention that it can. Constructivism has made a positive impact on faith-based educational philosophies by providing new insights and values. However, some concerns should be recognized in constructivism as an educational philosophy. For example, even though all individuals construct their own knowledge, constructivists argue that individual constructions are not equal but depend upon an individual's viability (Savery & Duffy, 1995). That's why constructivists recommend social environments where people see whether their constructions can accommodate others'. Parker Palmer (1993) emphasizes the communal images of teaching, learning, and living in his book, *To Know as We Are Known*. He suggests a different kind of education where "we would be brought into the community of mutual knowing called truth" (p. 36). However, constructivism's tenets are contradictory because they argue that each individual has his/her social and cultural background and each person should be treated uniquely and specially.

The main criticism of teachers in faith-based settings is on the constructivists' argument that it is impossible to determine the objective truth. Constructivists claim that knowledge is constructed, not discovered. Palmer (1993) clearly mentions that "truth is personal, and all truth is known in personal relationships" (p. 48). However, the Bible clearly teaches us that truth is discovered and that revelation is the only way of knowing in Christian education, as opposed to the constructivist model of gaining knowledge through personal experiences. We know that God is the author of our knowledge and that God created all of reality and made all things perfect. Even though human beings are too imperfect to fathom all God's truth, we reach the truth with the help of the Holy Spirit. Gaeberlein (1968) believed that constructivism should not be accepted within a Christian worldview and stated:

> Revelation is the only sure ground for knowledge. Revelation be-
> gins in the creation itself. God made it the way He did in order to
> reveal Himself to us. But the knowledge found in the creation must
> conform to that revealed in the Bible. Again, the Bible's revelation
> must be centered in Jesus Christ, who is the Truth. (p. 123)

Therefore, care must be taken before adopting constructivism as a philosophy of faith-based education. Postmodernism certainly highlights
new features of educational venues; however, it can drive us to a radical
subjectivism in which we claim that there is no truth and reality. Edlin's
(2004) perspective is correct when describing how to deal with postmodernism in the educational philosophy for faith-based education.

> Through prayer, professional development and a vigorous debate,
> we must seize the opportunity and bring the hope and purpose of
> a Christian educational perspective into the mainstream public
> domain. (p. 208)

Constructivism as a Post-positivist
Research Paradigm in Education

Constructivism grew from attempts to address the problems associated
with positivist research models. When constructivism is considered as
a research paradigm, it underlies the epistemological questions such
as, What is knowledge? How do we know the knowledge? What is the
relationship between the knower and what is known? How do we know
what we know? and What counts as knowledge?

Over the past few decades, two contrasting epistemological perspectives have evolved in educational research (Pergues, 2007). One is a group
of researchers "seek explanations and predictions that will generalize to
other persons and places, while the other group of researchers deal with
multiple, socially constructed realities or qualities that are complex and
indivisible into discrete realities" (Glesne & Peshkin,1992, p. 6). The main
purpose of the former research paradigm is to uncover truth and facts
using the systematic scientific research process (Magon, 1977).

However, some researchers argue that the positivistic research
method has some fundamental limitations. For example, Guba and
Lincoln (1994) criticize that this research paradigm strips contexts from
meaning in the process of developing quantitative measures of phenomena, especially educational phenomena, which are too complicated

to define or simplify with a quantitative index. Therefore the goal of educational research is "not the traditional one of accurate prediction but instead the careful description and validation of a patterned set of interrelationships" (Magon, 1977, p. 668). Reeves (1997) identified this paradigm with four distinctive characteristics: constructivist; hermeneutic; interpretative; and qualitative. Research is the active construction process of educational phenomena and reality rather than passively reflected. The goal of this research is not to make a generalization or prediction based on the data analysis, but "instead explore the range of behavior and expand [our] understanding of the resulting interactions" (Glesne & Peshkin, 1992, p. 7). Ethnography, participant observation, interviews, conversational analysis, and case studies are methods used in this research paradigm. Table 2 lists the major features of the two research paradigms.

Table 4.2 Major features of positivism and constructivism

Main questions	Positivist research paradigm	Constructivist research paradigm
What is knowledge?	Verified truth and facts as quantitatively specified relations among variables	Abstract descriptions of meanings and members' definitions of situations produced in natural context
What is the relationship between the knower and what is known?	Separated into two independent entities	Interconnected, related, and integrated
How do we know the knowledge?	Through experiment, questionnaires, data gathering and analysis process	Through thick descriptions of phenomena via ethnography, participant observation, interviews, conversational analysis, case studies
What is the purpose of acquiring the knowledge?	Uncover truth and facts as quantitatively specified relations among variables	Describe meanings, understand members' definitions of the situation, and examine how objective realities are produced

Can constructivism be evaluated if considered as a research paradigm in education? Constructivism brings unique and intuitive perspectives to education by focusing on meaning making along with the construction of social and psychological worlds through individual cognitive processes (Schultheiss, 2005). This paradigm has included some critical issues such as gender, feminism, and multiculturalism as topics of research. The main method that constructivists usually take is an anthropological method of inquiry, especially human observation (Magoon, 1977). Such research emphasizes the criteria of trustworthiness including credibility, transferability, dependability, conformability, and authenticity (Guba & Lincoln, 1994).

However, some concerns and weaknesses are found in this research paradigm. For example, in this paradigm, truth is defined as the best informed and most sophisticated construction on which there is a consensus. The main concern of this research paradigm is to understand social phenomena rather than to discover truth through consensus of all stakeholders. But, in reality, it is hard to cocreate meaning among all stakeholders and the researcher. In addition, there is a tendency to downplay power relationships that privilege certain construction over others (Clark, 1999).

Despite these limitations, the constructivist research paradigm can be easily embraced in faith-based education. In this paradigm, the knower and the known are closely communicated and interdependent. The researcher is a part of the community under investigation, though the researcher is not solely responsible for the whole research process. During the research process, the researcher may grasp as much information related to the theme as possible, considering all individual educational phenomena, situations, and people uniquely and distinctively. Consider Jesus who treated each person he met as special and unique. He interacted with people in their reality full of empathy and compassion, helping them to construct their own meaning of their lives. The main goal of constructivist research is to describe the educational phenomena thickly and with detail, so that everybody can understand the situation. By doing so, the researcher may form a community in which all stakeholders and researchers appeal to a large sense of community responsibility.

Constructivism as Pedagogical Practices

The popular concept of constructivism is to view it as a theory of teaching and pedagogical practice. Reigeluth (1999) identifies constructivism as an instructional design theory that is concerned with "what an effective instruction should be like," and with "what its effective instructional practices and strategies are." Many researchers and educational practitioners proclaim that constructivism provides useful pedagogical methods on how to help students construct their knowledge (Yilmaz, 2008; Kinnucan-Welsch & Jenlink, 1998; Richardson, 2003; Windschiti, 1999).

Savery and Duffy (1995, pp. 32–34) suggested a set of constructivist instructional principles including:

1   Anchor all learning activities to a larger task or problem.

2. Support the learner in developing an ownership for the overall problem or task.

3. Design an authentic task.

4. Design the task and the learning environment to reflect the complexity of the environment they should be able to function in at the end of learning.

5. Give the learner ownership of the process used to develop a solution.

6. Design the learning environment to support and challenge the learner's thinking.

7. Encourage testing ideas against alternative views and alternative contexts.

8. Provide opportunity for and support reflection on both the content learned and the learning process.

Brooks and Brooks (1993, p. ix) suggested five constructivism-based overarching instructional principles:

1. Teachers seek and value their students' point of view.

2. Classroom activities challenge students' suppositions.

3. Teachers pose problems of emerging relevance.

4. Teachers build lessons around primary concepts and big ideas.

5. Teachers assess students learning in the context of daily teaching.

Brown (1992, pp. 149–152) suggested a set of constructivist teaching techniques that included:

1. Students as active researchers, teachers, and self-monitors
2. Teachers as guides of discovery and as models of inquiry
3. Thinking as a basic literacy
4. The emphasis of depth, themes, coherence, and the understanding of content taught
5. Use of technology for reflection and collaboration
6. Authentic assessment through performance, projects and portfolios

From the principles listed by various proponents of constructivism, several instructional models have arisen. A few will be presented based on the learner responsibility levels: limited, moderate, and full learner responsibility. The idea of the three levels of learner responsibility was originally from Fay and Bretz (2008). Their ideas, although slightly modified, are presented in Table 4.3.

Table 4.3 Characteristics of each level of learner responsibility

Level	Description	Method
1 (Limited learner responsibility)	The problem and procedure are provided to the learner. The learner interprets the data in order to propose viable solutions.	Inquiry-based learning, 5 *e*'s (engagement, exploration, explanation, elaboration, and evaluation)
2 (Moderate learner responsibility)	The problem is provided to the learner. The learner develops a procedure for investigating the problem, decides what data to gather, and interprets the data in order to propose viable solutions.	Discovery learning

3 (Full learner responsibility)	A raw phenomenon is provided to the learner. The learner constructs the problem to explore, develops a procedure for investigating the problem, decides what data to gather, and interprets the data in order to propose viable solutions.	Problem-based learning

Level 1 refers to inquiry-based learning that requires limited learner responsibility. Inquiry-based learning (IBL) is open-ended, learner-centered, hands-on activities with directed assistance of the teacher. To lead a successful inquiry process, the teacher's role is essential; the teacher guides questions that challenge the learners in the inquiry process. Colburn (2000) identifies the teacher's behaviors that promote IBL, such as:

- Asking open-ended, divergent, questions

- Waiting a few seconds after asking the questions, giving students time to think

- Responding to students by repeating and paraphrasing what they said without praising and criticizing

- Avoiding telling students what to do, praising, evaluating, rejecting, or discouraging student ideas and behaviors

- Maintaining a disciplined classroom (p. 44)

The emphasis on inquiry was first emphasized by Dewey (1938) in his book, *Experience and Education*. In this book, Dewey stresses the active role of educator to lead inquiry. He said:

> The educator is responsible for a knowledge of individuals and for a knowledge of subject matter that will enable activities to be elected which lend themselves to social organization, an organization in which all individuals have an opportunity to contribute something. (p. 61)

There are two methods of inquiry: guided and unguided. In the former case, the teacher plays a key role in asking the questions, promoting responses, and structuring the materials, while in the latter the teacher acts as the classroom clarifier (Orlich et. al, 1985). However, in both methods of the inquiry-based learning, the teacher is the key element in the inquiry process (Colburn, 2000). That makes a primary difference between inquiry-based learning (IBL) and a problem-based learning (PBL). In an IBL approach, the teacher facilitates learners by guiding inquiry through learning materials; however, in PBL, the whole learning process depends on the learners, and they are the ones who are responsible for acquiring information to solve the problem (Savery, 2006). Borich (2007) formulated an inquiry-based learning cycle that consisted of five stages: ask, investigate, create, discuss, and reflect.

Level 2, discovery learning, is an effective intervention for a higher level of learning. In order to lead successful discovery learning, both teacher and learners need to be committed to learning process. The teacher presents a set of instances and examples while learners develop and formulate a rule in the discovery learning process (Driscoll, 2005). Therefore, identifying learners' readiness and background knowledge before engaging in the discovery process is critical. Bruner (2004) suggests a set of discovery procedures that includes: students identify problems; brainstorm solutions; formulate questions; investigate, analyze and interpret results; discuss; reflect; make conclusions; and present results. Lee (2006) also identifies a discovery learning model that consists of four stages: (1) inspiring learners by identifying teachable moments; (2) guiding inquiry with intriguing questions; (3) allowing learners to explore hypotheses; and (4) encouraging application.

The highest level of the constructivism-based instruction model requires full learner responsibility. In this method, learners have full responsibility for their own learning. In problem-based learning (PBL), the teacher "does not teach students what they should do/know and when they should do/know it. Rather the teacher is there to support the students in developing their critical thinking skills, self-directed learning skills, and content knowledge in relation to the problem" (Duffy & Cunningham, 1996, p. 191). Therefore, in PBL, the key to the learning process is coming up with a problem to investigate because it guides the whole learning process.

Wood (2003, pp. 328–330) identifies a seven-step process for PBL:

Step 1: Identify and clarify unfamiliar terms presented in the scenario, and list those that remain unexplained after discussion.

Step 2: Define the problem(s) to be discussed.

Step 3: Initiate a brainstorming session to discuss the problem(s), suggesting possible explanations on the basis of prior knowledge. Students draw on each other's knowledge and identify areas of incomplete knowledge; scribe records all discussion.

Step 4: Review steps 2 and 3 and arrange explanations into tentative solutions.

Step 5: Formulate learning objectives though consensus. The learning objectives are focused, achievable, comprehensive, and appropriate.

Step 6: Private study. (All students gather information related to each learning objective.)

Step 7: Sharing the results of private study. Students identify their learning resources, share their results, and a teacher checks their understanding and assesses the group's achievement.

How can we evaluate constructivism as an instructional theory in faith-based education? Archer (1998) points that the constructivist instructional methodology is consonant with Christian teaching. Constructivism-based instructional models are compatible with faith-based education by encouraging students to be self-reflective thinkers through being actively involved in the learning process. Actually, Jesus used many constructivist methods when he taught the disciples and audiences. He asked questions that allowed people to think deeply. His teaching did not simply asking audiences to recite a simple fact or recognize a law code, but encouraged audiences to inquire, discover and problem-solve. The result? The crowds were amazed at his teaching (Matt 7:28).

Yount (1996) summarizes that constructivism can be useful when teaching in Christian education with the following suggestions.

- Use explanations, demonstrations, and pictures to help students understand concepts.

- Learning should be flexible and exploratory, allowing students to solve problems on their own.

- Arouse curiosity, minimize risk of failure, and maximize relevance of the subject to students.

- Periodically return to important concepts.

- Encourage informed guessing.

- Use a variety of materials and games.

- Let students satisfy their own curiosity, even if the ideas are not directly related to the lesson.

- Use examples that compare and contrast the subject matter to related topics.

DISCUSSION: THREE FACES OF CONSTRUCTIVISM AND THEIR COMPATIBILITY WITH FAITH-BASED EDUCATION

Constructivism has three faces (a postmodern educational philosophy, a post-positivist research paradigm, and a set of pedagogical practices and instructional methods that emphasize active participation of learners). All three faces give unique and useful insights to review faith-based education and schooling in the postmodern era.

Constructivism as a postmodern educational philosophy allows us to rethink the truth and reality through the subject dimension. Constructivism as a research paradigm helps us to understand complicated educational phenomenon in the postmodern era by using interpretive and qualitative methodology. Finally, constructivism as an instructional practice strengthens the faith-based education by emphasizing learners' active participation and engagement in the learning process. All three faces have contributed to faith-based education; however, we need to be careful not to fall away or to slide toward extreme constructivism, which denies objective truth and reality.

Table 4.4 Three faces of constructivism

Faces of constructivism	Main questions and answers		Compatibility with faith-based education
	Questions	Answers	
Philosophy	What is the nature of knowledge?	There is no objective reality. Knowledge is not discovered, but constructed.	We need to be very careful when we adopt constructivism as a philosophy of faith-based education.
Research paradigm	What is knowledge? How do we acquire knowledge? What is the relationship between the knower and what is known?	The purpose of research is meaning making and the constructing of social and psychological worlds through individual, cognitive processes. It emphasizes the criteria of trustworthiness including credibility, transferability, dependability, conformability, and authenticity.	Even though some concerns exist, the many benefits that constructivism offers as a research method in faith-based education heavily outweigh the disadvantages.
Pedagogical practices	What is effective instruction like? What are effective teaching strategies?	Learning is effective when it places value on the students' unique experiences. Learning is inseparable from the context of the activity in which the learning takes place.	Constructivist instructional methodology is consonant with Christian teaching. It is highly compatible with faith-based education.

CONCLUSION

Constructivism has many faces. In this chapter, the three faces of constructivism were presented: (1) constructivism as an educational philosophy in the postmodern era; (2) constructivism as a post-positivist research paradigm in education; and (3) constructivism as a collection of pedagogical practices. In addition, the compatibility of the three faces of constructivism with faith-based education was reviewed. This is very tricky idea. Originally I criticized the idea of constructivism as an educational philosophy in faith-based education because constructivists argue the existence of objective truth and reality. However, I changed my stance to embrace all three faces with caution.

REFERENCES

Airasian, P. W., & Walsh, M. E. (1997). Constructivist cautions. *Phi Delta Kappan, 78*(6), 444–449.

Archer, A. C. (1998). *Constructivism and Christian teaching*. Presented at the 23rd International Faith and Learning Seminar. University of Eastern Africa, Baraton, Kenya.

Bentley, M. L. (2003, October 29–November 2). *Critical consciousness through critical constructivist pedagogy*. Presented at the annual meeting of the American Educational Studies Association, Mexico City, Mexico.

Bridges, E. M. (1992). *Problem-based learning for administrators*. Eugene, OR: ERIC Clearinghouse on Educational Management.

Brooks, J. G., & Brooks, M. G. (1999). *In search of understanding: The case for constructivist classrooms*. Alexandria, VA: Association for Supervision and Curriculum Development.

Brown, A. L. (1992). Designing experiments: Theoretical and methodological challenges in creating complex interventions in classroom settings. *Journal of the Learning Science, 2*, 141–178.

Bruner, J. S. (1961). The act of discovery. *Harvard Educational Review, 31*, 21–32.

Bruner, J. S. (2004). *Toward a theory of instruction*. Cambridge, MA: Belknap.

Clark, L. S. (1999). *Learning from the field: The journey from post-positivist to constructivist methods*. Paper presented to the International Communication Association, San Francisco, CA. Retrieved from http://www.colorado.edu/Journalism/mcm/qmr-const-theory.htm

Colburn, A. (2000, March). An inquiry primer. *Science Scope, 23*(6), 42–44.

Dewey, J. (1938). *Experience and education*. New York: Macmillan.

Driscoll, M. P. (2005). *Psychology of learning for instruction*. Boston: Pearson. (3rd ed.)

Duffy, T. M., & Cunningham, D. (1996). Constructivism: Implications for the design and delivery of instruction. In D. H. Jonassen (Ed.). *Handbook of research for educational communications and technology* (pp. 170–198). New York: Macmillian Library.

Duffy, T. M., & Jonassen, D. H. (1991, September). Continuing the dialogue: An introduction to this special issue. *Educational Technology*, 9–11.

Duffy, T. M., & Jonassen, D. H. (1992). Constructivism: New implications for instructional technology. In T. M. Duffy & D. H. Jonassen (Eds.), *Constructivism and the technology of instruction: A conversation* (pp. 1–16). Hillsdale, NJ: Erlbaum.

Edlin, R. J. (2004). Postmodernism and education. In J. Ireland (Ed.), *Pointing the way: directions for Christian education in a new millennium* (pp. 201–208). Blacktown, Australia: National Institute for Christian Education.

English, F. W. (2003). *The postmodern challenge to the theory and practice of educational administration*. Springfield, IL: C. C. Thomas.

Fay, M. E., & Brentz, S. L. (2008, Summer). Structuring the level of inquiry in your classroom: A rubric helps teachers compare experiments and plan inquiry trajectories. *Science Teacher, 75*(6), 38–42.

Fosnot, C. T. (1996). Constructivism: A psychological theory of learning. In C. T. Fosnot (Ed.), *Constructivism: Theory, perspectives, and practice* (pp. 8–33). New York: Teachers College Press.

Fox, R. (2001). Constructivism examined. *Oxford Review of Education, 27*(1), 23–35.

Freire, P. (1972). *Pedagogy of the oppressed.* New York: Herder & Herder.

Gaebelein, F. (1968). *The pattern of God's truth: Problems of integration in Christian education.* Colorado Springs, CO: Association of Christian Schools International.

Geelan, D. R. (1997). Epistemological anarchy and the many forms of constructivism. *Science and Education, 6*(1), 15–28.

Gephart, R. (1999, Summer). Paradigms and research methods. *Research Methods Forum, 4.* Retrieved from http://division.aomonline.org/rm/1999_RMD_Forum_Paradigms_and_Research_Methods.htm

Glesne, C., & Peshkin, A. (1992). *Becoming qualitative researchers: An introduction.* New York: Longman.

Guba, E. G., & Lincoln, Y. S. (1994). Competing paradigms in qualitative research. In N. K. Denzin & Y. S. Lincoln (Eds.), *Handbook of qualitative research* (pp. 105–117). Newbury Park, CA: SAGE.

Hammer, D. (1997). Discovery learning and discovery teaching. *Cognition and Instruction, 15*(4), 485–529.

Jonassen, D. (1999). Designing constructivist learning environment. In C. M. Reigeluth (Ed.), *Instructional-design theories and models: A new paradigm of instructional theory* (Vol. 2, pp. 215–239). Hillsdale, NJ: Erlbaum.

Kinnucan-Welsch, K., & Jenlink, P. M. (1998). Challenging assumptions about teaching and learning: Three case studies in constructivist pedagogy. *Teaching and Teacher Education, 14*(4), 413–427.

Knight, G. (2006). *Philosophy and education: An introduction in Christian perspective.* Berrien Springs, MI: Andrews University Press. (4th ed.)

Krauss, S. E. (2005, December). Research paradigms and meaning making: A primer. *Qualitative Report, 10*(4), 758–770.

Lee, H. (2006). Jesus teaching through discovery. *International Christian Teachers Journal 1*(2). Retrieved from http://icctejournal.org/ICCTEJournal/past-issues/volume-1-issue-2/jesus-teaching-through-discovery

Magoon, A. J. (1977, Fall). Constructivist approaches in educational research. *Review of Educational Research, 47*(4), 651–693.

Matthew, M. R. (1993). Constructivism and science education: Some epistemological problems. *Journal of Science Education and Technology, 2*(1), 359–370.

Matthew, M. R. (2000). Appraising constructivism in science and mathematics. In D. Phillips (Ed.), *Constructivism in education* (pp. 161–192). Chicago, IL: University of Chicago Press.

Niglas, K. (2001, September). *Paradigms and methodology in educational research.* Paper presented at the European Conference on Educational Research, Lille, France.

Newton, J. (2004). The challenge of postmodernity. In J. Ireland (Ed.), *Pointing the way: Directions for Christian education in a new millennium* (pp. 175–200). Blacktown, Australia: National Institute for Christian Education.

Orlich, D. C., Harder, R. J., Callahan, R. C., Kravas, C. H., Kauchak, D. P., Pendergrass, R. A., & Keogh, A. J. (1985). *Teaching strategies: A guide to better instruction.* Lexington, MA: D. C. Heath. (2nd ed.)

Oxford, R. L. (1997). Constructivism: Shape-shifting, substance, and teacher education applications. *Peabody Journal of Education, 72*(1), 35–66.

Palmer, P. (1993). *To know as we are known.* San Francisco: Harper Collins.

Pegues, H. (2007, Summer). Of constructivism wars: Constructivism, objectivism, and postmodern stratagem. *Educational Forum, 71*(2), 316–330.

Reigeluth, C. M. (1999). What is instructional-design theory. In C. M. Reigeluth (Ed.), *Instructional-design theories and models: A new paradigm of instructional theory* (Vol. 2, pp. 5–29). Hillsdale, NJ: Erlbaum.

Reeves, T. C. (1997). Established and emerging evaluation paradigms for instructional design. In C. Dills & A. J. Romiszowski (Eds.), *Instructional development paradigms* (pp. 163–178). Englewood Cliffs, NJ: Educational Technology Publications.

Richardson, V. (2003). Constructivist pedagogy. *Teacher College Record, 105*(9), 1623–1640.

Riegler, A. (2001). Toward a radical constructivist understanding of science. *Foundation of Science, 6*(1), 1–30.

Savery, J. R. (2006, Spring). Overview of problem-based learning: Definitions and distinctions. *Interdisciplinary Journal of Problem-Based Learning, 1*(1), 9–20.

Savery, J. R., & Duffy, T. M. (1995). Problem-based learning: An instructional model and its constructivist framework. *Educational Technology, 35*(5), 31–38.

Schultheiss, D. E. P. (2005, November). Qualitative relational career assessment: A constructivist paradigm. *Journal of Career Assessment, 13*(4), 381–394.

Simpson, C. D. (2002). Dare I oppose constructivist theory? *Educational Forum, 66*(4), 347–354.

Tiene, D., & Ingram, A. (2001). *Exploring current issues in educational technology.* Boston: McGraw Hill.

von Glaserfeld, E. (1989). Cognition, construction of knowledge and teaching. *Synthese, 80,* 120–141.

Windschiti, M. (1999, June). The challenges of sustaining a constructivist classroom culture. *Phi Delta Kappan, 80*(10), 751–755.

Wood, D. F. (2003, February). ABC of learning and teaching ion medicine: Problem-based learning, *British Medical Journal, 326,* 328–330.

Wright, N.T. (2002). *The New Testament and the people of God* (vol. 1). London, England: Society for Promoting Christian Knowledge.

Yount, W. R. (1996). *Created to learn: A Christian teacher's introduction to educational psychology.* Nashville, TN: Broadman & Holtman.

Yager, B. (1991). The constructivist learning model: Toward real reform in science education. *Science Teacher, 51,* 52–57.

Yilmaz, K. (2008, Spring). Constructivism: Its theoretical underpinnings, variations, and implications for classroom instruction. *Educational Horizons, 86*(3), 161–172.

Constructivism in Faith-Based Education

Introduction

PART 2 PROVIDES PRACTICAL applications for applying constructivist principles and strategies to faith-based education. The writers present various constructivist-based learning methods, including constructivist course and lesson design, problem-based learning (PBL), discovery learning, and instructional strategies. Chapter 5 discusses the teaching methods of Jesus from the lens of constructivism. The author argues that the constructivism inherent in Jesus' teaching method contributed to the effectiveness of the message's meaning. After explaining the basic tenets of constructivist learning methods and their relationships to Jesus' teaching, the author introduces Jesus' teaching model, which was embedded with constructivist principles.

Chapter 6 describes the application of constructivism as a curriculum design process that results in learning activities where students are able to engage in the construction of meaning through their learning experiences. The author proposes a constructivist course design model based on Jesus' teaching process. It provides a basis for interest, a motivation to learn, and student engagement/ownership in the learning process. Highlighted in this chapter is the application of two constructivist, research-based practices, understanding by design (UbD) and differentiated instruction (DI), which provide simple and yet comprehensive methods for teachers to engage students in the learning process and guide them in multiple learning opportunities to construct meaning and develop learning strategies that engender life-long learning. Integration of faith is incorporated into the curriculum development process. In addition, a practical application of constructivism is included to meet the needs of Christian teachers in designing standards-based instruction.

In constructivist learning, questioning is one powerful learning strategy because questioning provides a cognitive approach to motivation, whereby the teacher challenges students' thinking and learning. Scripture reveals over one hundred questions that Jesus asked; for example, Matthew's gospel contains forty-five of Jesus' questions. Chapter 7 uses Bloom's taxonomy to analyze Jesus' questions and concludes that most his questions can be categorized in comprehension and analysis.

Was Jesus a constructivist? You may find the answer after you read chapter 8. The author and her students analyzed the teaching method of Jesus in Mark and concluded that Jesus used many constructivist teaching practices but also adopted other methods from other theories of learning.

Chapter 9 shows that constructivism in education has become a preferred pedagogical process and an emerging instructional metanarrative furthered by the language and terms that define it. The author proposes a new definition for constructivism, and she encourages further engagement regarding the use of children's picture books as tools to explore grand narratives behind constructivist and Biblical perspectives in educational training.

Chapter 10 examines how three Christian public school teachers at the elementary and middle grade levels perceived their own practice in light of constructivism. Not only did these teachers face a theological challenge to their practice, they also faced the constraints of external controls and limited time, which often work against collaborative, student-centered, and experiential learning. Despite their focus on active, student-centered learning, these pedagogies are often viewed as too time consuming to employ. This study was to explore whether and how Christian educators, who see their work as a calling, continue to use these learning approaches and how they perceive their faith to relate to these professional decisions.

Chapter 11 focuses on of powerful constructivist learning format: discovery learning. Based on Jesus' teaching process using guided discovery, the author suggests several guided discovery instructional principles and introduces ideas that might apply to practical educational settings.

Chapter 12 presents an interactive constructive approach to instruction that is informed by a view of the human being as an interactive processer and constructor of meaning. The interactive view has emerged out of cognitive science and the cognitive developmental view of Piaget, and although the same foundational sources of constructivist theories exist within these perspectives, there are still some potential differences. The author addresses the characteristics of three modes of learning theories and then introduces a teaching model from an interactive constructivist point of view.

Chapter 13 suggests a constructivist science lesson from a Christian perspective by reviewing Colburn's three aspects of constructivism: philosophical, theoretical, and methodological. The author warns Christian educators to exercise caution when using the constructivist method because of the inconsistency between the constructivist methodology and the features of faith-based education.

Building a community is another key component of constructivism. Chapter 14 deals with how to foster community among learners in the online learning environment, a community that requires conscious and concerted effort by the instructor and the institution. The author also presents how to include an element of faith among the course participants in an online setting.

Chapter 15 is a case study in which the author implemented project-based learning in multicultural education in her teaching for early education students. The author designed her class based on constructivist principles and found that it enhanced students' learning as well as promoted students' intrinsic motivation to learn.

Chapter 16 deals with one of critical issues of education, assessment. The author connects total quality management (TQM) with Biblical assessment models of constructivism. This connection leads to a discourse on assessment as a foundational component of academic change in general, particularly from Vygotsky's social constructivism and from Christian perspectives. In addition, the author presents a framework for a healthy use of assessment in faith-based schools, from presecondary to secondary education.

5

Jesus' Teaching Model and Its Embedded Constructivist Principles

HeeKap Lee

INTRODUCTION

Jesus' teaching always brought huge success. The listeners of his teaching opened their eyes and ears as he touched their inner insights and intuitions. "After He taught, the crowds were amazed" (Matt 7:28). What made his teaching so successful? Lee (2006) analyzed Jesus' teaching as the following set of principles: Jesus identified the perfect teaching moment, facilitated inquiry by asking inspiring questions, enabled audiences to formulate hypotheses through insights, and encouraged his audiences to apply their gained knowledge to practical situations. His teaching strategy modeled constructivist learning. Like constructivists, Jesus recognized that learning is not the same as memorizing facts or reciting the law but rather the organization of new facts into existing schema or the creation of a new schema altogether, resulting in changed lives through the application. To Jesus, the process was as important as the content to change one's life. He proclaimed, "The truth will set you free." From a constructivist perspective, this chapter identifies a model consisting of five stages that Jesus used.

THE CONSTRUCTIVIST METHOD THAT JESUS USED

The power of teaching can be seen in Jesus' earthly ministry. Though he only taught for three short years, his teaching resulted in instantaneous and explosive responses from audiences (Minear, 1982). He taught ordinary, unschooled disciples (Acts 4:13) for three years and made an immense impact on the Jewish society. It was not uncommon that a great multitude would quickly be drawn from a wide area and that crowds listened in awe of his teachings (Matt 7:28; 22:33). How can we characterize the methods of Jesus' teaching? Several principles that Jesus used when he taught can be identified. For example, Pazmino (2001) points out the following five principles of Jesus' teaching practice: (1) "Jesus' teaching was authoritative"; (2) "Jesus' teaching was not authoritarian"; (3) "Jesus' teaching encouraged people to think"; (4) "Jesus lived what he taught"; and (5) "Jesus loved those whom he taught" (pp. 72–73).

First of all, his teaching was sometimes very unclear and allowed certain levels of uncertainty and ambiguity (Lee, 2006). His teaching is not simply pouring new information or facts into his audiences' head like the Jewish leaders taught. Rather, he intrigued his audiences by giving them a puzzling problem or situation. He challenged them to reflect their ways of thinking to reflect deeply. In such cases, it was not always what Christ said, but what he did not say that made such a profound effect. Why? Because as the "aha" light appeared, the listeners knew exactly, from the heart, what was true.

Secondly, his teaching was casual and contextualized. He did not follow a systematic reaction to situations or a coherent program (Newell, 2009). However, his teaching was powerful because he always gained his audiences' attention by establishing points of contact with various persons and groups and by his involvement with them. Jesus' teaching was adapted to his audience, and he differentiated the main focus of his teaching based on his audiences' situations and contexts (Pazmino, 1992). This aspect is the key to his teaching. The process of learning is not simply accepting the teachers' idea or explanation. It is active knowledge construction.

Thirdly, he was very enthusiastic to change society through teaching. Before he got arrested in Gethsemane, he said to the crowd, "Am I leading a rebellion, that you have come out with swords and clubs to capture me? Every day I sat in the temple court, teaching, and you did not arrest me" (Matt 26:55). He truly believed that teaching was the essential way to spread the truth. Full of enthusiasm and knowledge, he proved to be a competent teacher. Mainly his teaching was oral, using many questions, although he sometimes created projects (e.g., two-by-two evangelizing projects) and utilized natural settings in order to capture the larger contexts of a problem. This made a huge impact on his audiences.

Reflecting on his teaching methods, it is amazing that he used various ideas and tactics that constructivists have proven to be effective instructions. Was Jesus a constructivist? Although this debatable issue remains unresolved, I am sure that he used many constructivist methods. However, we need to keep in mind, in terms of his method, that even if nowadays they are called constructivist methods, the constructivism Jesus employed is totally different than the purpose and focus of today's constructivism. In table 5.1, key differences are addressed between the constructivist ideas today (pragmatic constructivism) and those of Jesus.

Table 5.1 Two paradigms of constructivism

Two paradigms	Pragmatic constructivism	Constructivism as practiced by Jesus
Motivation for teaching	Professional duty Expanding a learner's intellectual capacity	Loving spirit Restoring our relationship with our Creator
Focus area	Physical and cognitive domains	The whole range of human domains (physical, cognitive, emotional, and spiritual)
Target audience	All learners	Only those who are ready to learn
Methods used	Zone of proximal development, scaffolding, inquiry, problem-based learning, discovery, authentic tasks, and evaluation	Questioning, inductive reasoning (using contrast, enigma, hyperbole, metaphor, paradox, simile)
End goals	Strengthening learners' cognitions to master a given task	Renewing mind and spirit as God created

The purpose of Jesus' teaching was to renew and restore the broken relationships between humanity and God, and individuals and their neighbors. This redemptive, restorative, and reconciling goal of his teaching is embedded throughout his ministry. He always focused on the true relationship between God and humans, between humans and their fellows, and between humans and the physical universe (Pazmino, 2008; Graham, 2003; Giles, 1981).

In line with his purpose, his target audience was only those who were ready to learn. As he said in Matt 11:15, "He who has ears let him hear." Jesus did not focus on all who were there, rather he only focused on those who listened carefully. However, Jesus focused on the total aspects of human lives including physical, moral, and spiritual, as well as emotional dimensions, while pragmatic constructivism focuses on strengthening learners' cognitions by providing a toolbox for learning in order to master a given task (Perkins, 1999).

JESUS' TEACHING PROCESS OF EMBEDDED CONSTRUCTIVIST PRINCIPLES

The teaching method that Jesus used involved a set of constructivist principles consisting of five phases: (1) inspiring learning by asking essential questions; (2) facilitating situational learning experiences that are relevant to learners' contexts and needs; (3) allowing the learner to explore hypotheses; (4) encouraging the learner to transfer the application; and (5) transforming society in a community. Throughout these five phases of teaching, the main intention is to change the whole lives of the disciples, including visible as well as invisible domains.

Figure 5.1 The five phases of Jesus' teaching

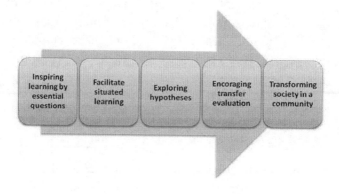

Phase 1: Inspiring Learning by Asking Essential Questions

Jesus was not afraid to ask questions when he taught. He did not always expect a response, but he knew the value of asking a question that would cause his audiences to stop and contemplate their beliefs and positions. His questions neither tended to be directive nor were they answered with simplistic ideas but penetrated the essence of his teaching. Educational researchers call these kinds of questions *essential questions* (Jacobs, 1997; Wiggins & McTighe, 2008, 2005). Essential questions are not usually answered by remembering a simple fact or recite information with a mere sentence; rather, they require higher order thinking skills such as analysis, synthesis, or evaluation according to Bloom's taxonomy. Brown (2009, p. 26) identified some benefits of essential questions, such as

- Essential questions encourage multiple perspectives.
- Essential questions connect learning with personal experience.
- Essential questions address overarching themes.
- Essential questions foster lifelong learning.

The New Testament is filled with many cases of Jesus' essential questions to his disciples, and Jewish religious leaders, as well as Gentiles. The following is a couple of examples of essential questions asked by Jesus in the Bible.

- Didn't you know that I had to be in my Father's house? (Luke 2:49)
- Who do you say that I am? (Matt 16:15)
- How long should I stay with you? (Matt 17:17)
- Where is your faith? (Luke 8:25)
- Do you believe this? (John 11:25–26)
- Who touched my clothes? (Mark 5:30)
- Do you still not see or understand? (Mark 8:17)
- John's baptism—where did it come from? Was it from heaven or from men? (Matt 21:24)
- Who is my mother and who are my brothers? (Matt 12:48)
- Judas, are you betraying the son of man with a kiss? (Luke 22:48)
- What are you discussing together as you walk along? (Luke 24:17)

A question-based approach helps implement constructivist theory in many useful ways. Students become more invested as they apply their judgments and conclusions to the situation. Using essential questions helps implement constructivist theory in many useful ways. As Brown (2009) clearly pointed out, essential questions "focus on the development of students' ability to sustain inquiry and critical thinking, which is also at the heart of the skills, dispositions, responsibilities, and self-assessment" (p. 26). Using essential questions brings huge educational benefits. First, throughout the question and answer process, learning is viewed as a dynamic process in which learners actively participate in the question-and-answer session. Second, learners gradually become more reflective, critical, and high-order thinkers by connecting the learning topics to their real-life situations. Finally, the learners become more invested as they apply their judgments and conclusions to solve their problems (Richetti & Sheerin, 1999).

The essential questions that Jesus asked challenged his audiences and their thinking. Throughout these essential questions, he helped the listeners effectively consider and make sense of important ideas that they did not yet grasp or see as valuable.

Phase 2: Facilitating Situated Learning Experiences

"Situated cognition is a theory of instruction that suggests learning is naturally tied to authentic activity," such as culture, language, and learners' backgrounds (Brown, Collins, & Duguid, 1989). Learning is effective when it connects to the learners' contexts, real lives, and environments. Brown, Collins, and Duguid (1989, p. 32) found that:

> Recent investigations of learning challenge this separating of what is learned from how it is learned and used. The activity in which knowledge is developed and deployed, it is now argued, is not separable from or ancillary to learning and cognition. Nor is it neutral. Rather, it is an integral part of what is learned. Situations might be said to co-produce knowledge through activity. Learning and cognition, it is now possible to argue, are fundamentally situated.

Jesus knew that his teaching would greatly impact his hearers when he used common resources, objects, and tools that were relevant to the audiences' lives and their social and cultural contexts. His teaching message was always the same; however, the delivery methods were different based on the audiences' situations. As a member of a first-century agricultural society, he quoted a story of casting seeds. He pointed out birds, lilies, vineyards, and fig trees. When he met Peter and Andrew by the Sea of Galilee as they were casting a net into the sea, Jesus said to them, "follow me and I will make you fishers of men" (John 21:17). He taught the audiences by describing shepherds because shepherding was a common job to the first-century Israelites. In addition, he loved to share stories that delivered important messages. Pentecost (1982) says that Jesus conveyed and pointed out the life-changing pedagogical strategy and benefits from using authentic, contextual stories. The stories themselves were so plain, although ironically, understanding the hidden message was quite challenging. That's why Jesus said in Mark 8:18, "Do you have eyes but fail to see, and ears but fail to hear?"

Collins, Brown, and Newman (1998) stress that situated cognition is the key factor to lead an effective instruction. In order to do that, the teacher needs to know the learners' backgrounds and their cultural and contextual information. Jesus was so comfortable in meeting all kinds of people. He met prostitutes, farmers, fishermen, shepherds, children, a Samaritan woman, a soldier, and Jewish leaders. As a perfect man, Jesus grew in the same environment with other Jews in the first-century Hellenistic Palestinian culture under the Roman authority. He spent thirty years of his life working as a carpenter. He clearly saw the people's agony, difficulties, and life stories. Whenever he met with the people, the audiences were changed. Why? Because he knew them by name. Jesus approached them personally and connected with them individually. Using constructivist terms, Jesus' teaching was situated and contextualized to people living in the first-century agrarian society (Wanak, 2009; Pazmino, 1992).

Therefore, Jesus never used the same method to different situations with different kinds of people. Sometimes, he criticized the arrogant, showed anger to the money changers, but at the same time, he also peacefully wrote a letter on the ground upon meeting the adulteress woman, even weeping at the tomb of the dead. He taught servant leadership when the disciples disputed and welcomed the children when his disciples rebuked them not to come to Jesus. When Peter sank into the sea, he instructed him to have faith. When the disciples were struggling with the winds and waves of the sea, Jesus was sleeping. The message was always the same, but, his delivery was situated based on the audience's context. That's why his teaching was memorable to whoever listened to his message.

Phase 3: Allowing Learners to Explore Hypotheses

Jesus allowed his audiences to discover deeper meanings, insights, and intuitions of the truth. This was a big difference between Jesus' teaching strategies in comparison with the strategies of various Jewish religious leaders. Jewish religious leaders primarily focused on repetition and recitation of the law, so learners could recall their teachings verbatim (Warden, 1998). However, Jesus' teaching was primarily focused on the learners' need to search for a new way of seeing that would renew their consciousness, which was dominated by the hegemony of conventional wisdom (Wanak, 2009). Jesus knew that learning is gained through deep insights and reflections in which learners review underlying principles and assumptions. Pazmino (1992, p. 127) characterizes the teaching of Jesus this way:

> Jesus stimulated serious thought and questioning in his teaching, and he expected his hearers to carefully consider their personal commitment to the truths he shared. In response to many inquiries, he did not supply simple, ready-made answers to every problem of life. Jesus expected his students to search their minds and hearts in relation to his teachings and to consider the realities of life.

Jesus did not simply make declarative statements about the truth. Hence, His teaching allowed those who heard to distinguish many levels of cognitive dissonances, challenging them to realign their thinking and cultural patterns to lead them to the kingdom of God. Mezirow (1991) calls this process perspective transformation, while Piaget (1985) explains this as disequilibrium. Disequilibrium is a state in which the mind mentally notes discontinuity, which causes a strong motivator to learn. Learners can regain equilibrium by either adding new information and facts into their present schema, or by accepting new ideas and changing their prior schema. Jesus' teaching methods, such as contrast (Matt 6:19–20), enigma (Matt 24:28), humor (Matt 19:24), hyperbole (Matt 5:29), hypocatastasis (Matt 16:6b), metaphor (Matt 5:14b), metonymy (Matt 5:14b), paradox (Matt 10:39), personification (John 3:8), pun (John 3:3), and simile (Matt 4:30–32) often placed people's minds into disequilibrium, thus requiring them to formulate new modified schema to return to equilibration. They changed the old principles and beliefs that prevented them from accepting new ideas and new learning by reasoned faith. Wanak (2009, p. 169) clearly points out:

> Jesus invites his listeners to distance themselves from the rules and roles of conventional wisdom. Jesus consciously and purposefully taught in a manner designed to transform his listeners' acculturated consciousness.

Jesus believed knowledge can be gained only through deep insight and reflection in which learners review underlying principles and assumptions (Lee, 2006). However, this kind of approach was not to be understood by everyone (Matt 13:35); only those who truly hungered for righteousness learned his spiritual messages and grew. He often stated, "He who has ears to hear let him hear" (Matt 11:15; 13:9, 43; Mark 4:23; Luke 14:35).

Phase 4: Encouraging Learners to Transfer Applications

How do we define learning? Learning is simply accepting at a heart level something such as the truth, that has an impact on subsequent behavior (Graham, 2003). The ultimate goal of learning is the learners changing their behaviors or performance after they apply the lesson gained. In order to do that, three academic goals may be necessary in education. First, the learners need to learn important knowledge and skills. Then, they need to make meaning of the content they learned. Finally, the learners are encouraged to transfer their learning to a new situation (Wiggins & McTighe, 2008). Kirkpatrick (1994) also emphasizes the importance of transferring the learning to other situations. However, he suggests going one stage further than the level of application. Kirkpatrick states the final level of evaluation would be to measure the effects on the classroom and the educational environment resulting from the students' application. The table below depicts the key ideas of Kirkpatrick's added four levels of evaluation model.

Table 5.2 Four levels of evaluation

Levels	Evaluation description
Level 1 (Reaction evaluation)	What students thought and felt about the training or education program they attended
Level 2 (Learning evaluation)	The resulting increase in knowledge or capability
Level 3 (Transfer evaluation)	The extent of behavior or capability for improvement and application
Level 4 (Result, impact evaluation)	The effects on the classroom and environment resulting from the students' performance

Jesus' primary concern did not include that his listeners acquired knowledge, but rather that they changed the way they thought, that they were transformed from a life in the world of conventional wisdom to a life centered around God (Wanak, 2009). Pedagogy of praxis is the key of the teaching process of Jesus. After explaining the parable of the good Samaritan, Jesus encouraged the expert of the law to apply the learning by saying, "Go and do likewise" (Mark 10:37). In addition, when Jesus forgave an adulterous woman, he instructed, "Go now and leave your life of sin." He emphasized action more than memorizing facts and stressed long-term rather than short-term results (Yount, 1996). He always encouraged applying the lesson learned to the learners' practical situations. That is why Jesus harshly criticized Jewish leaders for being hypocrites. They taught by their words and focused on the outward observation of the law, while they themselves did not follow as Christ commanded (Matt 23:3). The Jewish leaders thought they were effective in teaching the law to fellow Jews, but without practicing it themselves, they were only misleading the people (Powell, 1995). In Matt 23:2–7, Jesus criticized the teachers of the law and Pharisees because they did not practice what they preached. In his Sermon on the Plain (Luke 6:20–49), Jesus spoke as a teacher who challenges and encourages his students to apply what they have learned in the halls of life, not just in the halls of a classroom.

Phase 5: Transforming Society in a Community

Jesus knew that learning is a participation in communities of practice. Learning is a co-constitutive process in which all participants are transformed through their actions in community. From the moment he started his public ministry, Jesus knew that he would stay with his disciples only a limited time. He knew that the task of evangelism would be entirely upon his disciples. Therefore, his top priority was to choose twelve to be trained as apostles, who would be carrying on the evangelism work after he left. Throughout a three-year journey, Jesus established close relationships with them. The relationship between Jesus and his disciples was not one of teacher to student, rather it was a relationship between instructor to apprentice (Harkness, 2001). When Jesus called his disciples, they left their homes and immediately followed after him. They lived together, learned from him, and witnessed his many miracles. Through life-long relationships, Jesus empowered his disciples to continue his work. After a three-year training session, all of his disciples grew up to their full potential and finally became fishers of men.

The ultimate end of teaching is to prepare or disciple students for the same task. Palmer (2009) calls this a community of congruence. This kind of community exists "to help people [disciples] develop language that can represent the movement's vision, giving that language the strength it will need to survive and thrive in the rough-and-tumble of the public realm" (p. 179).

The relationship between Jesus and his disciples remains permanent. Even after Jesus ascended, all the disciples remembered his teaching as they continued to preach the example of the Christ, based on their prior experiences. It is a commitment unto death, and stands as a commitment to change society as a whole. Peter, no longer a coward who disowned his master, now boldly spoke in front of the Sanhedrin. John, once the son of thunder, totally transformed to proclaim love as the essence of God's character. Jesus knew teaching was a calling from God. It was not just passing information or knowledge to his disciples in a cognitive sense alone. How was this possible? This tremendous result was produced when the disciples of Jesus participated together with Jesus in ministry.

Some constructivists coined the term "community of practice" as an important learning principle (Wenger, 1998; Jonassen & Land, 2000). It involves a group of people who share a concern or a passion for something they do, learning it better as they interact regularly (Lava & Wenger, 1998). In fact, the three years of the public ministry of Jesus with his disciples shows the typical example of community of practice, where his disciples became knowledgeable and competent through life-long experience.

CONCLUSION

Jesus' teaching made a huge impact on his audiences, including his disciples. The unschooled and commoners were changed drastically, and they started to transform the whole world. What made his teaching so effective? Reflecting on his teaching methods, it is amazing that he used various ideas and tactics that constructivists have found to be effective for instruction. In this chapter, I focused on two issues. First, I reviewed the basic tenets of constructivist learning methods and their relationships to Jesus' teaching. Then, I presented Jesus' teaching model and its embedded constructivist principles, which consists of a five-stage-teaching process. The five stages are:

1. Inspiring learning by asking essential questions

2. Facilitating situated learning experiences

3. Allowing learners to explore hypotheses

4. Encouraging learners to transfer applications

5. Transforming society in a community

The disciples stayed with Jesus for a short three years. His teaching methods were effective, so the disciples were fully trained and applied what they learned, thus turning the world upside down for Christ, as they proclaimed his message of salvation for all (Luke 6:40).

REFERENCES

Brown, J. S., Collins, A., & Duguid, P. (1989). Situated cognition and the culture of learning. *Educational Researcher, 18*(1), 32–42.

Brown, K. (2009, September/October). Questions for the 21st century learner. *Knowledge Quest, 38*(1), 24–27.

Collins, A., Brown, J. S., & Newman, S. E. (1988). Cognitive apprenticeship: Teaching the craft of reading, writing, and mathematics. In L. B. Resnick (Ed.), *Knowing, learning and instruction: Essays in honor of Robert Glaser* (pp. 453–494). Hillsdale, NJ: Erlbaum.

Giles, K. N. (1981). Teachers and teaching in the church. *Journal of Christian Education, 70*, 5–17.

Graham, D. L. (2003). *Teaching redemptively: Bringing grace and truth into your classroom.* Colorado Springs, CO: Purposeful Design.

Harkness, A. G. (2001). De-schooling the theological seminary: An appropriate paradigm for effective ministerial formation. *Teaching Theology and Religion, 4*(3), 141–154.

Jacobs, H. H. (1997). *Mapping the big picture: Integrating curriculum and assessment K–12.* Alexandria, VA: Association for Supervision and Curriculum Development.

Jonassen, D. H., & Land, S. M. (Eds.). (2000). *Theoretical foundations of learning environments.* Hillsdale, NJ: Erlbaum.

Kirkpatrick, D. L. (1994). *Evaluating training programs.* San Francisco: Berrett-Koehler.

Lee, H. (2006). Jesus teaching through discovery. *International Christian Teachers Journal, 1*(2). Retrieved from http://icctejournal.org/issues/v1i2/v1i2-lee/

Mezirow, J. (1991). *Transformation dimensions of adult learning.* San Francisco: Jossey-Bass.

Minear, P. S. (1982). *Matthew: The teacher's gospel.* New York: Pilgrim.

Newell, T. (2009). Worldviews in collision: Jesus as critical educator. *Journal of Education and Christian Belief, 13*(2), 141–154.

Palmer, P. (2009) *Courage to teach: Exploring the inner landscape of a teacher's life.* New York: John Wiley & Son. (10th ed.)

Pazmino, R. W. (1992). *Principles and practices of Christian education: An evangelical perspective.* Grand Rapids, MI: Baker Book House.

Pazmino, R. W. (2001). *God our teacher: Theological basics in Christian education.* Grand Rapids, MI: Baker Academic.

Pazmino, R. W. (2008). *Foundational issues in Christian education: An introduction in evangelical perspective.* Grand Rapids, MI: Baker Academic. (3rd ed.)

Pentecost, J. D. (1982). *The parables of Jesus: Lessons in life from the master teacher.* Grand Rapids, MI: Kregel.

Perkins, D. (1999, November). The many faces of constructivism. *Educational Leadership, 57*(3), 6–11.

Piaget, J. (1985). *The equilibrium of cognitive structures: The central problem of intellectual development.* Chicago, IL: University of Chicago Press.

Powell, M. A. (1995). *God with us: A pastoral theology of Matthew's gospel.* Minneapolis, MN: Fortress.

Richetti, C., & Sheerin, J. (1999, November). Helping students ask the right questions. *Educational Leadership, 57*(3), 58–62.

Vygotsky, L. S. (1978). *Mind in society: The development of higher psychological processes.* Cambridge, MA: Harvard University Press.

Wanak, L. (2009). Jesus' questions. *Evangelical Review of Theology, 33*(2), 167–178.

Warden, M. D. (1998). *Extraordinary results from ordinary teachers: Learning to teach as Jesus taught.* Loveland, CO: Group.

Wenger, E. (1998). *Communities of practice: Learning, meaning, and identity.* New York: Cambridge University Press.

Wiggins, G., & McTighe, J. (2005). *Understanding by design.* Alexandria, VA: Association for Supervision and Curriculum Development. (2nd ed.)

Wiggins, G., & McTighe, J. (2008, May). Put understanding first. *Educational Leadership, 65*(8), 36–41.

Yount, W. R. (1996). *Created to learn: A Christian teacher's introduction to educational psychology.* Nashville, TN: Broadman & Holtman.

6

Constructivist Curriculum Design

Harry Hall

When I hear, I forget.
When I see, I remember.
When I do, I understand.

—ancient Chinese saying

INTRODUCTION

IT WAS CLEAR FROM the earliest days that students learned best through engagement, doing. You have learned in previous chapters that constructivism is an instructional process where students are able to engage in the construction of meaning and understanding of their world through their learning experiences. This constructed meaning and understanding of reality that God and Jesus have modeled can provide a basis for interest, a motivation to learn, and student engagement and ownership in the learning process. It speaks to a student-centered teaching with a focus on learning through engagement that also draws heavily from the foundational works of Piaget and Vygotsky. What does it look like in a classroom and how does it influence curriculum design, teaching, and learning?

In a fifth grade classroom in Allen Elementary, a public school in Marion, Indiana, the students recently completed a learning unit on the Revolutionary War. A traditional, teacher-centered classroom would have the students reading from a text book and listening to lectures over the issues that the teacher felt were most important. The assessment would be multiple choice, or short answer, or perhaps an essay. That is how most of us were taught and how many classrooms (from kindergarten to college) operate today. However, in this constructivist classroom, students assumed roles of revolutionary figures, and, after conducting research that involved not only the textbook but also internet resources, they acted out their roles in a loosely defined experience. The politicians, teachers, children, cobblers, painters, ministers, news reporters, and so on viewed the period and events through their roles and were able to interact with each other. Leveled character readings and books were assigned by the teacher but with student input. These multiple sources provided a social and historical context to events that enabled students to construct meaning and achieve a depth of understanding far beyond that found in a traditional classroom. In this student-centered learning activity, they learned by active engagement and were able to *construct* meaning in the process.

Clearly, the learning activity on the Revolutionary War did not take place by chance; the teacher purposefully planned and organized the unit based on the constructivist concepts using understanding by design (UbD) (Wiggins & McTighe, 2005) and differentiated instruction (DI) (Tomlinson, 2001) for curriculum design and teaching. Students had specific guidelines to follow and were taught the rules of classroom social engagements. There were small-group and individual assignments and projects that centered on the required learning outcomes and appropriate standards. Students were engaged, creative, and played an active role in their learning process and outcomes. Although the Revolutionary War took place several hundred years ago, this learning activity brought it to life and connected these students with events in that period of American history. This is a far cry from the traditional "sage on the stage" model of teacher-centered instruction and represents a significant improvement in learning opportunities for those students. This unit was "student-centered" learning where the students were in the center ring and the teacher was the supportive "ring-master" coordinating and facilitating the learning experiences. This constructivist experience was another clear example where students were able to connect with reality and thereby bring meaning and clarity to this learning opportunity. These students developed a sense of ownership of this learning activity because they were active participants. They will tell their children and their grandchildren about this unit where they brought the American Revolutionary War to life.

WHAT IS IMPORTANT?

What really matters in education? It is that students, just as those fifth graders at Allen Elementary, master not only the prescribed learning outcomes but that they find meaning during the process. That learning process will lay the foundation for them to become life-long learners who value education and the knowledge, skills, and dispositions that come with it. Learning should be a collaborative, learning adventure where everyone has an active role to play.

Far too often comments can be heard in the teachers' lounge as teachers lament that, although they do their job (teaching the material), students fail to learn (their jobs) because they are lazy and their parents are not involved in or supportive of the school. One can even hear suggestions that test scores will improve only when the school has better students. This failure to assume responsibility for learning stretches from preschool to doctoral programs. There is a common saying that applies here: "parents send the best students they have and students come to the best school available from the best homes and families that they have." Obviously, we must successfully teach whoever walks in the school house door (that door could be a home, elementary, middle, or high school, or even a college or university)—no excuses!

There are three essential elements to remember about education. The first one is motivation. The second one is motivation. The third one is motivation. (This statement has been attributed to Dr. Terrell H. Bell, former U.S. secretary of education, 1981–1984.) Can unmotivated students learn? Maybe, but Dr. Bell believed that motivation is the critical factor. If you agree that motivation is a pivotal consideration in the learning process, then the next questions would be, how are students motivated? and who is responsible? Look in the mirror, and you will see the person that has that job (you, as a parent, teacher, administrator, or community member); it truly takes a community to raise a child.

One has to only go to a kindergarten class, ask who is going to college or who wants to fly to the moon, and then see all of their hands shoot up (often they jump up as well) to appreciate that most students begin their school careers highly motivated (intrinsically self-motivated), but there is evidence to suggest that intrinsic motivation wanes the longer they stay in school. Ask those same questions to a ninth grade class and the results would differ significantly: many of those students would know that they were not going to college and some would be considering not even finishing high school. Our high school dropouts and under-educated high school graduates (who are unable or unmotivated to attend college) represent a significant burden both financially and socially to our country. Why are we in this situation? One very possible factor could be that their (our) community has directly or indirectly convinced those young people that they are not smart enough to be successful in school and, consequently, they quickly lose their intrinsic motivation to succeed. Parents and schools usually apply a variety of extrinsic incentives (such as grades, rewards, etc.). But, as evidenced by our high dropout rate, extrinsic motivation is a weak and overused method to encourage students: candy, money, cars, and other rewards by themselves will never be sufficient. Intrinsic motivation is tremendously more powerful and effective than extrinsic. If we want to motivate our students intrinsically then we must find ways to make the learning process an enjoyable, relevant (meaningful), and, at the same time, effective and successful learning experience. One of the strengths of constructivism is that those students are intrinsically motivated to learn because they see real-world value in the learning process and find the instruction interesting; they develop a love for learning and a feeling of confidence about their future!

ROLE OF THE TEACHER

The way of a fool seems right to him,
but a wise man listens to advice.

—Proverbs 12:15

Efficacious teachers truly believe that all students can learn and assume responsibility for student learning; they do not seek to blame others (Ashton, 1984). They believe that their students can learn, and they can effectively teach them (Guskey & Passaro, 1994; Hall, 1999). This means that they do not limit their duties to presenting or teaching the material. Additionally, they consider motivating and engaging the students in the learning process and the eventual learning outcomes as integral components of their teaching (Edwards, Green, & Lyons, 1996). Great teachers inspire (motivate) their students to learn and succeed. They do not depend on candy or bribes (extrinsic motivation) but on lighting a bright flame of student interest and engagement (intrinsic motivation).

And, as you would expect, if their students do not learn the material, then they assume responsibility for the failure and do not blame their students or parents. Great teachers hold themselves accountable for not only teaching but also learning.

So, as they used to say many years ago, the sixty-four-thousand-dollar question (now with inflation it is the million-dollar question) is, how do teachers motivate students to learn? It represents the greatest challenge to teachers, and unfortunately it is one of the greatest failures in far too many classrooms in the United States and across the world. Far too often, teachers teach as they were taught, and the most common form of teaching is lecturing because it is easy and direct. Usually, curriculum is dictated by "coverage"— covering all of the material in a textbook. However, it is usually extremely boring because students are passive learners (not playing an active role in the learning process) with little motivation to actually achieve the desired learning outcomes. That is not to say that direct instruction does not play a role in the process since there are some situations where new knowledge needs to be introduced and shared with students. Nevertheless, we must do better if we expect our students to learn what they need to be successful in our global community.

The teacher is also responsible for developing an effective learning community. My memories of elementary were of rows of desks where children kept their feet flat on the floor, did not fidget, doodling or daydreaming were forbidden, and everyone did the same thing at the same time. I guess that is why I enjoyed recess so much—I could be a real, individual, human being then. However, an effective learning community should be a classroom where

- Everyone feels accepted and welcome regardless of their outward appearance (clothes, color of skin, gender, or ethnicity);
- Everyone feels safe and loved;
- Teamwork is the norm, not the exception;
- Fairness is the rule;
- Character and social-skills development are important;
- Diverse learning needs are accommodated;
- The expectation is that everyone will succeed; and
- Growth is the primary measure of success.

INTEGRATING FAITH

Another significant challenge for Christian educators is how they can integrate their faith into their teaching. One can easily find how to teach based on Biblical principles, but there is very little guidance or support for Christian teachers who must adapt a secular curriculum to their faith. This would also apply to Christian home-school educators who want to follow a secular curriculum but want to ensure that their message of faith is clear and evident. One does not have to be of this world to teach about it, and our children must learn about this world standing on the solid moral and ethical foundation provided by the Word and the model of Jesus Christ.

Jesus was a model constructivist: he taught his disciples through the use of parables (real world connections and meaning) and active engagement. He clearly demonstrated that learning is a team activity that is meant to be shared. It could be said that Jesus was modeling the lessons demonstrated by God. The book of Exodus contains numerous examples of God teaching his people lessons of faith and righteous living as they journeyed through the desert. For example, in chapter 20, God defined the responsibilities of the Israelites. The Bible is an almost endless source of Christian concepts, models, and principals that can be used to demonstrate God's wisdom and justice in relation to any subject.

DEVELOPING CURRICULUM AND TEACHING

Two constructivist, research-based practices are the application of understanding by design (UbD) (Wiggins & McTighe, 2005) and differentiated instruction (DI) (Tomlinson, 2001). Additionally, these two practices can be joined in "Integrating Differentiated Instruction + Understanding by Design" (Tomlinson & McTighe, 2006). In simplistic terms, UbD is a system or methodology for developing what is taught while DI focuses on the students, the environment (classroom), and how we teach. Said in another way, UbD is primarily the curriculum design guide while DI serves as the instructional design guide. These two constructivist approaches to teaching provide simple and yet comprehensive methods that engage students in the learning process and guide them in multiple learning opportunities to construct meaning and develop learning strategies that engender life-long learning.

Great teachers and coaches in one's life are remembered not so much as for what was learned but by why and how it was learned: they inspire us to learn and be better human beings. Constructivist teachers inspire their students and construct meaning in the process of learning as Jesus did with his disciples. That is why we can remember them and the lessons they taught us.

Understanding by Design

In order to teach something, one must first consider what is to be taught. UbD posits that in order to effectively plan curriculum we must begin with the end in mind. It is what the students should be (character: attitudes, values, and beliefs), know (knowledge and understanding), and do (skills: the ability to apply knowledge) after the lesson. We must begin with the end in mind and ensure that we are making progress toward that goal once we begin teaching.

Step 1: Begin with the end in mind: What are the students expected to learn?

What determines the learning objective for a lesson? In these days of accountability for outcomes, learning objectives are based on standards that are defined for preschool to university. If you are a home-school teacher in Ghana, or even the United States for that matter, then you will probably depend on a commercial curriculum (there are many) that defines at least the scope and sequence of learning expectations. Just as classroom teachers must be focused on the learning standards by grade and discipline, home- and private-school teachers should ensure that those same standards drive their curriculum planning if they expect their students to be successful in standardized tests, which are required in many states and for college entrance tests. Most programs at the university level have learning outcomes based on state and/or national standards. Standards represent the end game but by themselves are not workable: they must be unpacked into big ideas and essential questions.

Unpacking standards is a critical skill because it provides clear and understandable learning expectations upon which teachers can design effective curriculum. The best way to help you understand this concept is to demonstrate it. For example, an art standard reads: "Students will recognize how technical, organizational, and aesthetic elements contribute to the ideas, emotions, and overall impact communicated by works of art." If you were the art teacher and wanted to prepare lesson plans that addressed these expectations, you could start by determining the big ideas and essential questions. For this standard, a big idea could be: artists' cultures and personal experiences inspire the ideas and emotion they express. The essential question serves to frame and guide the process of teaching and assessment. For the previous big idea, several essential questions seem appropriate such as, where do artists get their ideas? or, in what ways do culture and experience inspire artistic expression? So, the big idea is unpacked from the standard and defines what we want our students to learn. The essential question gives purpose and direction to teaching, learning, and assessment. The student must be able to answer the essential question and understand the big idea for effective, standards-based learning to be successful. How was this accomplished in our Revolutionary War unit?

At Allen Elementary, the fifth-grade team of teachers looked at Indiana Social Studies Standard 5.1: "Students will describe the historical movements that influenced the development of the United States from pre-Columbian times up to 1800, with an emphasis on the American Revolution and the founding of the United States." One of the big ideas that can be unpacked from standard 5.1 is: the causes and effects of the Revolutionary War impacted the lives of the colonists. Several essential questions were developed from that big idea such as:

- What were the causes and consequences of the Revolutionary War and the quest for independence?
- How did colonial men, women, and children contribute to the Revolutionary War?
- When is it justified to revolt and rebel against authority and government?
- Did all of the colonists have the same point of view concerning independence?
- Are there similar conflicts in the world today?

During this process of identifying big ideas and essential questions, a constructivist teacher could also consider standards from other disciplines such as language arts. Also, since we want our faith to be integrated early in the curriculum development process, could you think of some relevant Biblical events or lessons that would apply? Several come to mind; for example, God directed Moses to rebel against and defy the authority of the pharaoh who was certainly as powerful as our King George of the Revolutionary War. Is there a parallel between the suffering of the colonialist under the burden of heavy taxes and the Israelites being treated as slaves and required to make more bricks as punishment? How did the Bible explain the rationale for resisting the authority of Pharaoh? Unpacking standards by identifying big ideas and essential questions and integrating other disciplines and faith all serve to guide the constructivist teacher in developing standards-based curriculum that is designed to meet the learning needs of students.

Clearly, defining the learning outcomes in an organized and consistent manner is an important and necessary first step. If we can identify the big ideas and essential questions then we are ready for the next step.

Step 2: How will you know when they have learned the desired results?

As you would expect, this step points toward assessment, which must be planned from the beginning instead of treated as an afterthought. It considers assessment from several perspectives: what do your students already know, how will you know they are learning the expectations as you are teaching, and how will you ensure they met the learning outcomes at the completion of the learning activity? Assessment must be planned from the beginning since the most effective measure of learning is one that is an integral part of the learning process. Rick Stiggins has written extensively on how assessment must be "for learning" instead of just a measure "of learning." In addition to determining if students learned the material, constructivist teachers assess learning during the activity as well. When your students' eyes glaze over and they get that "deer in the headlights" look, it is time to change what you are doing. It is a waste of everyone's time to continue teaching if no learning is taking place. Ensuring that assessment is part of the learning process is a fundamental component in effective curriculum design.

In planning the unit on the Revolutionary War unit, what assessments would help the teacher

- Understand the readiness level of the students?

- Monitor their learning during the unit?

- Ensure that they achieved the expectations of the appropriate standards?

The first bullet addresses a fundamental of teaching; we must know what the students know about a topic or subject before we can effectively teach them. Otherwise, we could bore them to tears if they already know the material or overwhelm them if they have no understanding of early American history. Also, we want to find "anchor points" so that we can attach and relate new information to previous knowledge. There are several ways to do this. The most common is a simple class discussion about the Revolutionary War where the teacher leads the discussion using probing questions about that period to expose student knowledge, identify prior knowledge to support new learning, and to generate interest in the material. Another method could be a simple multiple choice quiz that addresses the major topics of the period such as a timeline, identifying main characters, describing causes, etc. This could even serve as the basis for a post-test as another means of assessing learning.

The second bullet speaks to ensuring that learning is taking place during the learning activity. It could be addressed in journals, graphic organizers, and vocabulary assessments. These assessments would be designed to be an integral component of the learning activity and would guide learning instead of just measuring it (assessing for learning instead of assessing of learning).

Finally, how could you assess learning near the end of the unit? To do that, we must determine if the students can answer the essential questions and understand the big ideas. How they demonstrate that knowledge and understanding can be in many forms such as a presentation or an essay. Giving students options allows them to adapt their learning style to demonstrate academic achievement and growth. Just as students have different learning styles, they also have different forms of expression or abilities to demonstrate learning. The teacher must define the quality indicators (most commonly a rubric) but should also provide students with options that will allow them to demonstrate that quality using forms of expression that are aligned with their readiness skills, interests, intelligences, and learning profiles. The critical task is to define the expectation as to what should have been learned without limiting how it is demonstrated (such as a rubric that defines the "what" without the "how").

Beginning with the end in mind, monitoring that learning is taking place, and ensuring that students have achieved the learning outcomes: these are the fundamental components of effective curriculum development in constructivist terms. From the constructivist view, teaching and learning must be focused on what the student needs to be, know, and do; it must value formulative more than summative assessments; and it must have real-world relevance. For the next step we will begin the transition from curriculum design based on UbD to planning the actual teaching (DI).

Differentiated Instruction

Step 3: Developing the learning plan or lesson

Have you heard the overused and little understood expression "all children can learn"? It is certainly true but it is not that simple: Children can learn provided that they have the necessary readiness skills and knowledge, are motivated to learn, and the learning activity accommodates their particular learning preference or style. As constructivist teachers, we must understand and apply these concepts to the learning plan if we expect our students (children) to achieve their learning potential. In other words, we must learn to differentiate our teaching or instruction based on the students that are sitting in front of us.

As an illustration of how not to teach, a third-grade teacher in an elementary school where I was principal comes to mind. She was notorious for her file cabinets that bulged with "pilgrim" lessons that she had used for almost thirty-five years. The dog-eared and faded lesson plans were numbered by week. Beginning in mid-September, she started with lesson number one. This continued through Christmas and into January. Most students loved the candy corn, the pilgrim hats and belt buckles, the Indian headdresses, and stories about how the Indians saved the pilgrims who then invited them to share their bounty at Thanksgiving. Most parents enjoyed the constant stream of student work that came home every day. However, there were several flies in that ointment: the premade lesson plans did not necessarily fit the learning needs of the students, and the learning outcomes did not follow the pacing guides or address all of the subjects, such as mathematics or current learning standards. Consequently, there were constant behavior problems, particularly from students who were bored or confused. Each year, there were complaints from parents who expressed concern that their children were not learning enough. The fourth grade teachers regularly complained that her (the third-grade teacher) former students lacked the readiness skills needed for subjects like mathematics (it was impossible to teach long division without being able to multiply) and when her former students took standardized tests, their scores where consistently below what they should have been. Granted, they knew more about the pilgrims than anyone else, but there is more to learning and life than just that segment of our history. It did not matter who walked in her classroom door, special needs or just nontraditional learners, they were all expected to fit the learning requirements of her lesson plans that she had used (successfully she would tell you) for years. In fact, there were some very talented and successful teachers and administrators in that school system who were her former students. Some students did well in her class despite the lack of mathematics simply because they were very traditional learners. However, more than a few students suffered a difficult year where they felt disenfranchised from the learning process and began the dropout spiral of academic failures and often compensated with misconduct in an attempt to hide their perceived and eventually real inadequacies. She was a classic nondifferentiated teacher who taught focused on the peak of her student learning bell-curve, and those students who were at either end of the curve simply were on their own. What is the lesson for us? If you are teaching your children at home, just because one child did well with a particular lesson, do not expect that younger siblings will have the same, positive learning experience. We must meet the learning needs of students instead of students being required to adjust their learning needs to our lessons.

So, how do we meet those needs? The answer is that we must differentiate our learning activities in order to accommodate the learning needs of our students. I have heard teachers say, "Differentiated instruction, oh, we did that back in the 1970s, and it did not work then." Just for clarity, differentiated instruction is not individualized instruction, another name for homogenous grouping, asking harder questions or giving more work, teacher centered, or more chaotic (Tomlinson, 2001). Differentiated instruction focuses on the student by recognizing and accepting different interests, learning styles, intelligences, knowledge, and skills. It applies research-based best instructional practices; blends of whole-class and small group instruction; involves planning from start to finish; includes assessment that is on-going and is a blend of formative and summative; and is a constant "work in progress" that is constantly being improved upon with experience (Tomlinson, 2001).

DIFFERENTIATING INSTRUCTION

As a teacher, take a moment and look across the pond of faces looking (or in some cases should be looking) back at you. What do you see? In most cases you see a group of young people who vary in so many ways. In outward appearance, they vary by gender, dress, cleanliness, posture, facial expression, skin tone and coloring, and person (their image). They also vary by conduct and attentiveness. What you do not see may be just as, if not more so, important as those obvious external characteristics: their families; culture; faith; neighborhood/community; knowledge and skills learned in previous classes; desire to learn; age; previous successes and failures; potential juvenile criminal record (yes, I have had a third grader with a parole officer); gifts or special abilities (intelligences); passion (what excites them); fears (perhaps of you); ability to read, write, and understand American English; and emotional and social maturity.

The more that a teacher knows about and is able to relate to students' characteristics (particularly internal), the better that teacher can provide effective instruction that supports their learning. Does this mean that a teacher must meet the individual learning needs of every student all of the time? The answer is obvious, no. However, you can provide a variety of instruction and assessment thereby making it clear to them that there is hope and that you recognize and acknowledge that not everyone learns in the same way, has different interests, and has different levels of readiness to learn.

There are many ways to look at providing learning experiences that cater to the similarities and differences of students. Carol Ann Tomlinson (2001 and 2003) uses four student considerations or traits:

Readiness: a student's knowledge, skills, and understandings of a particular topic or subject. As a former math teacher, I know how difficult it is to teach division if students do not know their math facts such as the multiplication table.

Interest: what captures a student's attention and causes them to be engaged in the learning process? Most young boys are more interested in cars, trucks, and airplanes than reading about Dick, Jane, and Spot running up a hill, so we must provide appropriate subject readers if we expect to capture their interests and foster a love of reading.

Learning profile: what is the student's preference for learning style? This could cover many differences such as brain-based learning, multiple intelligences, culture, or even gender. It also applies to products that are used to support and verify learning (assessments).

Affect: how a student feels about themselves, their place in the classroom, and their relationships with others (school and home). Affect could be viewed as the interaction of the three other student considerations (readiness, interest, and learning profile) but it also includes the impact of social interactions within the classroom and larger community. For Christians, this would be the obvious connecting point for faith and dispositional considerations.

There is no single recipe that provides a balanced, "one-dish meal" for learning. It is a process of knowing your students and ensuring that you acknowledge their differences by providing them with a variety of learning experiences. One cannot address every difference in every lesson, but one can provide differing options during the semester or school year. These considerations should influence the lesson design where we seek to ensure that our students will be able to answer the essential questions and understand the big ideas of learning activities.

Readiness, interest, learning profile, and affect influence how we plan the learning activity; more specifically, the learning environment (the classroom), what is taught (content), the process (the actual teaching), and the products (how students demonstrate and support learning) influence curriculum development.

Readiness can influence content such as in the social studies class at Allen Elementary where the teacher provides leveled readers to compensate for the variety of reading readiness. Another example could be in a French class where the teacher uses magazines in French but some are written for French adolescents and others for nonnative speakers. An example of when readiness can influence process would be when the teacher assigns more difficult problems to more advanced students or even uses more-advanced students to tutor or mentor less-advanced students. Assigning products should also be influenced by student readiness such as by assigning different rubric levels for homework based on student readiness. The essential consideration for readiness is that all students deserve and rich, engaging, and appropriately challenging learning experience.

Interests, or what is it that captures their attention, should influence lesson planning since it directly influences the level of student engagement in the learning process. It can influence content by varying the topics selected for a given subject such as allowing students to select their character in the Revolutionary War unit. The process (actual learning activity) can be differentiated by giving students choices in what aspects or elements of the subject they will focus on and thereby link to their interests. Lessons influenced by student interests also involve allowing them to make sense (study) of a particular idea in a manner that is aligned with their preferred method of learning. Product differentiation again implies that teachers should give students choices concerning how they demonstrate knowledge, skills, and understand of the subject. For example, some students might want to do a dramatic presentation while others might prefer to use a PowerPoint presentation. Having said that, teachers are also obligated to occasionally teach their students how to be successful in product assignments that are outside their comfort zone. In all cases, the teacher must clearly define the product expectations. Choice does not mean assignments are without quality boundaries and guidelines.

Learning profile is an acknowledgement that we all learn differently based factors such as our intelligences, gender, and even cultural influences. The critical prerequisite is to know, understand, and accept your students. Also, many students do not understand their learning profile and consequently can be unhappy and disappointed at their inability to accomplish what others seem to do so easily. Since there are so many variations in learning profiles it is impossible to address all of them in every component of a learning activity. Teachers should consistently address the three primary groups of intelligences (analytical, practical, and creative), gender-based preferences, and cultural preferences such as whole-to-part or part-to-whole, group or individual, etc. Kathleen Butler (1999) has developed a useful planning chart that can help teachers design quality learning activities that accommodate varied learning styles, levels of thinking, and performance. If students understand their learning profile and the teacher provides options, usually there will be opportunities for students to make choices that will suit their needs and support active learning.

Affect involves how the students feel about themselves, their classroom, and their teacher. In order to be successful, students need

- To feel affirmed, accepted, acknowledged, and safe

- To feel like they are contributing—that their presence makes a difference, their gifts are valued, and they help others and the class as a whole

- To feel a sense of control over their classroom environment—that it is a good fit, that they are able to make choices, and that they understand what quality looks like and how to be successful

- To understand the purpose for school—its relevance, significance, and connection to the real world

- To feel a sense of challenge through work is difficult and a stretch, to feel accountable, and to believe that their accomplishments are meaningful

CONCLUSION

Constructivism is a student-centered philosophy and method of teaching that encourages students to see relevance and meaning in the learning process. It the same process that God used and is recorded in the Bible. His son, Jesus, used these principles to teach his twelve disciples, who became the church as we know it today. Using backwards planning (beginning with the end in mind), integrating faith, and differentiating the learning process are primary components that will lead to engaged students who play an active role in their learning. Instead of trying to adopt all of these concepts, take small steps and build on your successes. We are all a "work in progress," and your teaching improvements will continue throughout your entire career if you are a reflective, life-long learner.

REFERENCES

Ashton, P. (1984). Teacher efficacy: A motivational paradigm for effective teacher education. *Journal of Teacher Education, 35*(5), 28–32.

Butler, K. (1999). *Strategy chart for learning styles, levels of thinking and performance.* Columbia, CT: Learner's Dimension.

Edwards, J. L., Green, K. E., & Lyons, C. A. (1996). *Teacher efficacy and school and teacher characteristics.* ERIC document ED 397055

Guskey, T. R., & Passaro, P. D. (1994). Teacher efficacy: A study of construct dimensions. *American Educational Research Journal, 31*(3), 627–643.

Hall, H. D. (1999). A comparison of alternatively and traditionally certified teachers. *Dissertation Abstracts International, 60*(30), 707. (UMI No. 072699)

Tomlinson, C. A. (2001). *How to differentiate instruction in mixed-ability classrooms.* Alexandria, VA: Association for Supervision and Curriculum Development. (2nd ed.)

Tomlinson, C. A. (2003). *Fulfilling the promise of the differentiated classroom: Strategies and tools for responsive teaching.* Alexandria, VA: Association for Supervision and Curriculum Development.

Tomlinson, C. A., & McTighe, J. (2006). *Integrating differentiated instruction and understanding by design: Connecting content and kids.* Alexandria, VA: Association for Supervision and Curriculum Development.

Wiggins, G., & McTighe, J. (2005). *Understanding by design.* Alexandria, VA: Association for Supervision and Curriculum Development. (2nd ed.)

Appendix

Constructivist Planning Template

Here is a simple template to help you think through and apply the constructivist principles that have been discussed. It also describes the final stage (reflection and change) that is essential for growth and improvement. Remember that we climb great mountains and accomplish seemingly impossible tasks (like changing how we teach) by taking one step at a time.

STEP 1: BEGINNING AT THE END: WHAT ARE THE DESIRED OUTCOMES?

1. What should the students be able to *know, understand, and do*? (What are the standards?)

2. What are the *big ideas*?

3. What are the *essential questions*?

4. What is the message of *faith* that complements the essential questions and can be incorporated?

STEP 2: HOW WILL YOU KNOW THAT THEY HAVE LEARNED THE DESIRED RESULTS? (ASSESSMENT)

1. What is acceptable *evidence* of their learning? (What are the products of their learning?)

2. What *other evidence* can be used to collaborate?

3. How can I provide options for assessments that will encourage diverse learners?

STEP 3: DEVELOPING THE LEARNING PLAN OR LESSON

1. Pre-assessment: What can we learn about their

    a. Readiness skills? What do they already know? What skills and knowledge do they need in order to learn this new material?

    b. Interests? How can we to link to their interests, engage them in learning, and make them active participants?

    c. Learning preferences/styles? If you do not know, then just provide alternatives—tiered/varied learning activities and assessments.

2. Learning activities: What activities, sequence, and resources are appropriate to accomplish the goals (answering the essential question using the acceptable evidence)? How can we provide a variety of learning activities that allow options according to readiness, interests, and learning styles?

3. Sanity checks: how will you know that they are learning, and what will you do if this is not working?

STEP 4: REFLECTING AFTER THE LESSON

1. Did we accomplish our goals and how could this have been done more effectively?

7

Jesus and Bloom: How Effective Was Jesus in Requiring People to Think Critically?

HeeKap Lee and Calvin G. Roso

INTRODUCTION

M ANY CHRISTIAN EDUCATORS ARE quick to say that Jesus Christ was not only a great teacher, but that Jesus was the master teacher. One reason why Jesus' teaching was so powerful and the crowds were so amazed (Matt 7:28) was because of his questioning skills. A simple review of the Gospel of Matthew shows that Jesus used questions during the majority of his teaching and conversations (75 percent of the time). As the master teacher, how would Jesus' questioning style perform when assessed according to critical thinking theories? This study analyzes Jesus' questions in the Gospel of Matthew according to the critical thinking skills addressed in Bloom's Taxonomy (1956) and effective questioning techniques (Christenbury & Kelly, 1983; Paul & Elder, 2008; Walsh & Sattes, 2005, Wilen, 1987).

STATEMENT OF THE PROBLEM

Up to 75 percent of classroom teaching is done via questions and an-swers (Doyle, 1986; Goodlad, 1984; Stevens, 1912)—this could mean three hundred to four hundred questions asked each day (Leven & Long, 1981). However, most questions asked by teachers in classrooms are convergent or knowledge-level ones.

> In machine-gun fashion, [teachers] pose an average of 40–50
> questions in a typical 50-minute class segment. However, most of
> these questions are not well-prepared and do not serve the pur-
> pose of prompting students to think. (Appalachia, 1994, p. 1)

With the majority of teacher-time spent on questioning, and with
the on-going need for understanding effective questioning techniques,
it is helpful for educators to analyze the style and effectiveness of Jesus'
questioning techniques.

REVIEW OF THE LITERATURE

Because constructivism promotes the use of questions (Brooks & Brooks,
1993, 1999; Vygotsky, 1978), it is important for constructivist teachers to
learn how to question effectively (McKeown & Beck, 1999; Richetti &
Sheerin, 1999). For example, questions that focus on ideas rather than
facts better enable students to move toward understanding. Developing
open-ended questions to elicit student's insights and opinions are a
strong method in constructivist teaching.

> To question well is to teach well. In the skillful use of the question
> more than anything else lies the fine art of teaching; for in [the
> question] we have the guide to clear and vivid ideas, the quick
> spur to imagination, the stimulus to thought, the incentive to ac-
> tion. (Degarmo, as cited in Wilen, 1991, p. 5)

Critical thinking, through the use of questions, encourages students to consider not only their own experience(s) but also other resources and experiences beyond their own world (Christenbury & Kelly,
1983). Effective questioning involves several approaches that must be
considered. One approach to consider is the *effective use of wait time*
(Appalachia, 1994). Most teachers ask students to respond immediately to questions. However, research shows that when teachers wait
three to five seconds, students give longer and more thorough answers
(Appalachia, 1994).

Another approach to effective questioning is asking questions at
multiple cognitive levels. Ironically, nearly 80 percent of questions asked in
K–12 classrooms are at the knowledge or recall level of learning (Dillon, as
cited in Appalachia, 1994). Chuska (2003) suggests a checklist of characteristics that lead higher-order thinking questions. Such questions:

- Have no one "right" answer
- Are open-ended
- Call for reflection
- Can be answered based on students' knowledge
- Are interesting to students
- Motivate or stimulate thinking
- Demonstrate a search for understanding
- Allow for individual input based on prior knowledge
- Provoke more questions
- Raise students' curiosity
- Challenge preconceptions (Chuska, 2003, p. 101)

Redirecting questions are also effective for teachers to use. Typically, when students do not answer questions, teachers answer the question themselves. However, redirecting questions to another student encourages more interaction between and among students (Ornstein, as cited in Appalachia, 1994).

Christenbury and Kelly (1983) suggest a *questioning circle* (see figure 7.1) to show how effective questioning is nonsequential and overlaps "the matter, personal reality, and external reality" (p. 13). *Matter* focuses on the lower level of factual information within a subject. *Personal reality* includes an individual's "experiences, values and ideas." *External reality* presents questions about universal experience, history, values, and concepts. They suggest that:

> The area where all thee circles intersect, the dense area, represents the most important questions, the questions that subsume all three areas and whose answers provide the deepest consideration of the issue. The order of questions depends upon the material under consideration, upon the teacher, and upon the students. (Christenbury & Kelly, 1983, p. 14)

Figure 7.1 The questioning circle (Christenbury & Kelly, 1983)

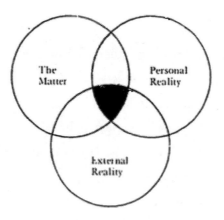

Discussion by Walsh and Sattes (2005) synthesizes research on questioning practices into a clear and concise list of what makes a quality question. Walsh and Sattes, developers of the Questioning and Understanding to Improve Learning and Thinking (QUILT) framework, have spent much time researching and applying how quality questions can impact student learning. They suggest that teachers who believe questioning is an effective instructional tool need to be willing to take extra time to develop quality questions. Their analysis suggests quality questions are purposeful, have a clear content focus, engage students at varied and appropriate cognitive levels, are clear and concise, and are seldom asked by chance. From this analysis, Walsh and Sattes (2005) have developed a Rubric for Formulating and Assessing Quality Questions. This rubric focuses on the areas of purpose, content focus, cognitive level, and wording and syntax while including an assessment scale for teachers.

METHODOLOGY

We analyzed the questions posed by Jesus in the Gospel of Matthew and categorized them according to their level of difficulty and effectiveness. Bloom's original taxonomy (1956) was chosen to assess the difficulty level of Jesus' questions asked in the Gospel of Matthew. Although a revision of Bloom's taxonomy does exist (Anderson & Krathwohl, 2001), the original version of Bloom (1956) was used for this study because a majority of current research evaluating the practice of cognitive thinking skills continues to use Bloom's original version (Crowe, Dirks, & Wenderoth, 2008; Elser & Rule, 2008; Griffin, Mitchell, & Thompson, 2009; Halawi, McCarthy, & Pires, 2009; Manton, English, & Kernek, 2008; Oliver & Dobele, 2007; Tomlinson & McTighe, 2006; Vosen, 2008). Because Bloom's taxonomy was originally intended for evaluating "degrees of cognitive complexity of assessment" (Tomlinson & McTighe, 2006), it works well as a tool for evaluating the level of critical thinking in discussion questions.

We began by listing verbatim every question Jesus asked that is included in the book of Matthew. These questions included questions to groups of people (e.g., disciples, the multitudes, Pharisees, etc.), questions asked to individuals (e.g., Peter, the rich young ruler), and questions that were rhetorical in nature. After listing the questions, each question (with consideration of its context) was read and analyzed to see which categories of difficulty and effectiveness were used. Because questions can include several parts, each question was often included in more than one category in Bloom's taxonomy. Questions and their corresponding categories were listed in a table of difficulty and a table of effectiveness to observe possible patterns or themes.

The following is a brief explanation of each level of Bloom's taxonomy.

1. Knowledge questions prompt factual recall of information. Question stem examples include *who, what, when, why, where, name, list, define,* and *identify.*

2. Comprehension questions help determine whether or not students understand the meaning of the content presented.

3. Application questions prompt students to solve problems or situations stated in the question by using the information they have learned.

4. Analysis questions ask students to look carefully at the organizational structure of the information presented to formulate ideas.

5. Synthesis questions give students an opportunity to come up with something new with the information they have learned.

6. Evaluation questions ask students to make a judgment about two ideas or concepts using a predetermined set of criteria.

In addition to evaluating Jesus' questions according to Bloom (1956), a modified Rubric for Formulating and Assessing Quality Questions (Walsh & Sattes, 2005, p. 24), was also used for question evaluation. We chose the Walsh and Sattes rubric because the developers are highly respected in the area of discussion question assessment due to their development of and participation with the QUILT research. The rubric was slightly modified, taking into consideration that Jesus' audience were "listeners," and not the traditional classroom students. This modification is valid when one notes the following statement in the Walsh and Sattes text: "This scoring rubric . . . is generic and may be adapted by individual teachers to specific content areas and/or grade levels" (2005, p. 24). Each of the forty-five questions in the Gospel of Matthew (see appendix 1) was analyzed according to the Walsh and Sattes rubric, and questions were scored in each category: purpose, focus, cognitive level, and communication. After analyzing the questions using the Walsh and Sattes rubric, we compared and contrasted the findings from both evaluation tools.

ASSESSING JESUS' QUESTIONS USING BLOOM'S TAXONOMY

The research shows that Jesus' questioning in the Gospel of Matthew is consistently filled with higher-order thinking questions that are relevant and engaging. The questions consistently ranked high on both Bloom's taxonomy (1956) and the Rubric for Formulating and Assessing Quality Questions (Walsh & Sattes, 2005). In addition to asking questions at multiple cognitive levels, Jesus' questions met other approaches recommended by researchers (Appalachia, 1994), including the effective use of wait time and redirecting questions.

Jesus Used All Levels of Questions

Jesus was the master teacher, using all levels of penetrating questions to cause his audiences to think deeply and creatively. With a possible 100 percent in each category, Jesus' questions were distributed as follows: knowledge questions (16 percent), comprehension (73 percent), application (33 percent), analysis (76 percent), synthesis (38 percent), and evaluation (47 percent) respectively. Below are the examples of his questions based on Bloom's taxonomy.

1. Knowledge
   - Haven't you read that at the beginning the Creator made them male and female? (Matt 19:4)
   - Whose portrait is this? And whose inscription? (Matt 22:20)

2. Comprehension
   - Are not two sparrows sold for a penny? (Matt 10:29)
   - How can anyone enter a strong man's house and carry off his possessions unless he first ties up the strong man? (Matt 12:29)

3. Application
   - Why do you look at the speck of sawdust in your brother's eye and pay no attention to the plank in your own eye? (Matt 7:3)
   - Who is my mother and who are my brothers? (Matt 12:48)

4. Analysis
   - What good will it be for a man if he gains the whole world, yet forfeit his soul? Or what can a man give in exchange for his soul? (Matt 17:26)
   - John's baptism, where did it come from? Was it from heaven or from men? (Matt 21:24)

5. Synthesis
   - Why do you ask me about what is good? (Matt 19:17)
   - Which is greater: the gold or the temple that makes the gold sacred? ... Which is greater: the gift or the altar that makes the gift sacred? (Matt 23:17-19)

6. Evaluation
   - If you love those who love you, what reward will you get? (Matt 5:46)
   - Do you believe that I am able to do this? (Matt 9:28)

Jesus Used Comprehension and Analysis Questions Frequently

Nearly 87 percent of Jesus' questions were constructed to require thinking that moved across multiple levels of Bloom's taxonomy (1956). In the forty-five questions that Jesus asked in the book of Matthew, the great majority of these questions focused on higher-level thinking skills as identified in Bloom's taxonomy. Seventy-three percent of the questions can be categorized in Bloom's second level—comprehension, with all but five (Matt 17:25, 19:4, 21:42, 22:20, 22:32) of these thirty-three questions also requiring higher-level thinking skills. Interestingly, the five questions that focused only on Bloom's two lowest level skills were either directly or indirectly aimed at the Pharisees and lawyers. Perhaps Jesus knew that those who were accusing him were often unable to think at higher levels?

Why did he use questions at the comprehension level frequently? He pictured that education is a level beyond recalling or reciting facts. Jesus knew that knowledge or information is not very useful unless it is understood, and the most useful way that a teacher checks whether students comprehend the information they possess is to have them state that information in their own words rather than recall what they have read or heard (Hunter, 2004). That's why Jesus used to ask his disciples, "Have you understood?" after he taught something.

Jesus also loved to ask analysis questions (76 percent) to his audiences. In the analysis category, listeners are asked to "identify the parts or concepts and describe the relationships between the parts." Jesus' analysis questions required people to distinguish, inspect, appraise, question, examine, differentiate, categorize, solve, analyze, debate, calculate, and compare. Analysis was an important stage in which his audiences recognized the interrelationships between facts and knowledge so that they could reorganize information into a new pattern and apply creative interpretations to that information (Hunter, 2004). The purpose of Jesus' questioning was not to teach something in order to remember the laws or Jewish customs that usually became the primary educational purpose of Jewish leaders. Jesus believed that learning is gained through deep insights and reflections in which learners review underlying principles and assumptions by focusing on the internal side of human beings rather than the outward observation of the law. Analysis questions call for students to identity causes and motives, as well as the internal structure of a subject (Yount, 1996).

The next highest number of questions asked was in the category of evaluation (Bloom's highest level) where 46 percent of Jesus' questions were asked. These questions asked people to judge, measure, estimate, evaluate, choose, select, estimate, value, and appraise. Thirty-seven percent of Jesus' questions could be categorized in Bloom's second-highest level, synthesis. Thirty-three percent of the questions fell in the application category (the third highest level). These questions asked people to distinguish, examine, solve, analyze, employ, dramatize, practice, interpret, illustrate, apply, use, or translate.

ASSESSING JESUS' QUESTIONS USING WALSH AND SATTE'S QUALITY QUESTIONING RUBRIC

All of Jesus' questions also ranked high in the Walsh and Sattes quality questioning rubric (2005), specifically in the areas of purpose, content focus, and cognitive level. All but three questions (6 percent) ranked high in the wording and syntax category. Each of these questions earned two out of three points (medium rank) in wording and syntax because some words were perceived as potentially misleading and/or ambiguous. These questions were: But if the salt loses its saltiness, how can it be made salty again? (Matt 5:13), Who is my mother, and who are my brothers? (Matt 12:48), and How many loaves do you have? (Matt 15:34). In analyzing these questions, however, we believe the ambiguity of the wording is not a weakness because it actually causes the listener to apply even higher thinking skills. For example, How can [salt] be made salty again? requires the listener to deduce that salt cannot be made salty again and, therefore, believers must not lose their distinct "flavor" if they wish to remain effective. Likewise, How many loaves do you have? does not refer to literal loaves of bread, but requires the listener to think more abstractly than it might initially appear.

CONCLUSION

Jesus knew the power of a question. One right question asked at the right situation could change the whole direction of his audience's thinking. His questions transformed his followers' lives by challenging their image of God, by reconciling them in true relationship with the God Father. Jesus showed the power of questions. Just by being asked the question, "Who do you say that I am?" (Matt 16:13), Peter recognized the true being of Jesus. When confronted by a question from an opponent, Jesus responded skillfully with a question for the opponent that required him to move to another plateau in his thinking. He proved that the effective use of questions is the key to good teaching.

By studying the teaching style of Jesus, we see that his effective use of questions correlates with what current research recommends and, therefore, offers an excellent model for teachers to emulate. After analyzing Jesus' questioning style, we found that Jesus' questions offer several recommendations for classroom teachers:

- Increase the frequency of questioning

- Focus on higher-level thinking skills

- Focus on practical knowledge

- Focus on application to real-life situations

- Ask questions at multiple levels of thinking

- Ask questions that are aligned to the purpose and content of the lesson

- Ask questions that are clearly stated

While Jesus asked good questions, his questions were not easy to answer. His questions neither tended to be strongly leading nor answerable with simple ideas (Lee, 2006). Jesus asked questions to review general principles and to inspire deep thinking. That's a big difference between Jesus' teaching and other Jewish religious leaders. Jewish religious leaders' teaching primarily focused on repetition so their learners would remember their teachings verbatim. Jesus' questions are mainly focused on learners to help them uncover principles or relationships that were hidden under the surface level of the question. Jesus certainly believed that some audiences were not open to his teaching, and he did not spend much time with them, especially Pharisees and the teachers of the Law.

In analyzing Jesus' questioning techniques, 46 percent of his questions were asked at the highest level of Bloom's taxonomy (1956), and nearly 87 percent of Jesus' questions were constructed to require thinking that moved across multiple levels of Bloom's taxonomy—this is in contrast to studies that show 80 percent of K–12 questioning is at the two lowest levels of Bloom's taxonomy (Dillon, as cited in Appalachia, 2004).

Similar trends were found when forty-five questions asked by Jesus in the Gospel of Matthew were analyzed using the Rubric for Formulating and Assessing Quality Questions (Walsh & Sattes, 2005). For example, 46 percent of Jesus' questions are purpose oriented, and 70 percent are at a high cognitive level according to Bloom. All of Jesus' questions (100 percent) ranked in the high cognitive level according to Walsh and Sattes. Because both evaluative methods showed that Jesus' questioning techniques were highly challenging, therefore, Jesus' questions could be used as models for training current educators in improving their own questioning techniques.

REFERENCES

Anderson, L. W., & Krathwohl, D. R. (2001). *A taxonomy for learning, teaching, and assessing: A revision of Bloom's taxonomy of educational objectives.* New York: Addison Wesley Longman.

Appalachia Education Laboratory. (1994). *Questioning and understanding to improve learner thinking (QUILT): The evaluation results.* Charleston, WV: Appalachia Education Laboratory.

Bloom B. S. (1956). *Taxonomy of educational objectives, Handbook I: The cognitive domain.* New York: David McKay.

Brooks, J. G., & Brooks, M. G. (1993, 1999). *In search of understanding: The case for constructivist classrooms.* Alexandria, VA: Association for Supervision and Curriculum Development.

Chuska, K. (2003). *Improving classroom questions.* Bloomington, IN: Phi Delta Kappa.

Christenbury, L., & Kelly, P. (1983). *Questioning: A path to critical thinking.* Urbana, IL: ERIC Clearinghouse on Reading and Communication Skills and the National Council of Teachers of English. ERIC document ED226372

Crowe, A., Dirks, C., & Wenderoth, M. P. (2008, Winter). Biology in bloom: Implementing Bloom's taxonomy to enhance student learning in biology. *CBE: Life Sciences Education, 7*(4), 368–381.

Doyle, W. (1986). Classroom organization and management. In M. C. Wittrock (Ed.), *Handbook of research on teaching* (3rd ed., pp. 392–431). New York: Macmillan.

Elser, C. F., & Rule, A. C. (2008, April). *A menu of activities in different intelligence areas to differentiate instruction for upper elementary students related to the book "Because of Winn-Dixie."* Paper presented at the Annual Graduate Student Research Symposium, University of Northern Iowa, Cedar Falls, IA. ERIC document ED501255

Goodlad, J. I. (1984). *A place called school.* New York: McGraw-Hill. ERIC document ED 236137

Griffin, D. K., Mitchell, D., & Thompson, S. J. (2009, September). Podcasting by synchronizing PowerPoint and voice: What are the pedagogical benefits? *Computers & Education, 53*(2), 532–539.

Guilford R. D. (July 1956). The structure of intellect. *Psychological Bulletin, 53,* 267–293.

Halawi, L., McCarthy, R., & Pires, S. (2009, July/August). An evaluation of e-learning on the basis of Bloom's taxonomy: An exploratory study. *Journal of Education for Business, 84*(6), 374–380.

Hunter, M. (2004). *Mastery teaching: Increasing instructional effectiveness in elementary and secondary schools.* Thousand Oaks, CA: Corwin.

Lee, H. (2006). Jesus' teaching through discovery. *International Christian Teachers Journal, 1*(2). Retrieved from http://icctejournal.org/issues/v1i2/v1i2-lee/

Levin, T., & Long, R. (1981). *Effective instruction.* Alexandria, VA: Association for Supervision and Curriculum Development.

Manton, E. J., English, D. E., & Kernek, C. R. (2008, December). Evaluating knowledge and critical thinking in international marketing courses. *College Student Journal, 42*(4), 1037–1044. ERIC document EJ817019

McKeown, M. G., & Beck, I. L. (1999, November). The constructivist classroom. *Educational Leadership, 57*(3), 25–28.

Oliver, D., & Dobele, T. (2007). First year courses in IT: A Bloom rating. *Journal of information technology education, 6,* 347–360. ERIC document EJ807676

Paul, R., & Elder, L. (2008). Critical thinking: The art of Socratic questioning, Part 3. *Journal of Developmental Education, 31*(3), 34–35.

Richetti, C., & Sheerin, J. (1999, November). Helping students ask the right questions. *Educational Leadership, 57*(3), 58–62.

Stevens, R. (1912). *The question as a means of efficiency in instruction: A critical study of classroom practice.* New York: Teachers College, Columbia University.

Tomlinson, C. A., & McTighe, J. (2006). *Integrating Differentiated Instruction and Understanding by Design.* Alexandria, VA: Association for Supervision and Curriculum Development.

Vosen, M. A. (2008, July). Using Bloom's taxonomy to teach students about plagiarism. *English Journal, 97*(6), 43–46.

Vygotsky, L. (1978). *Mind in society: The development of higher psychological processes.* London: Harvard University Press.

Walsh, J. A. & Sattes, B. D. (2005). *Quality questioning: Research-based practice to engage every learner.* Thousand Oaks, CA: Corwin.

Wilen, W. (1987). *Questions, questioning techniques, and effective teaching.* Washington, DC: National Education Association.

Wilen, W. (1991). *Questioning skills for teachers: What research says to the teacher.* Washington, DC: National Education Association. (3rd ed.). ERIC document 332983

Yount, W. R. (1996). *Created to learn: A Christian teacher's introduction to educational psychology.* Nashville, TN: Broadman & Holman.

Appendix 1

Jesus' Questions in the Gospel of Matthew

1. But if the salt loses its saltiness, how can it be made salty again? (Matt 5:13)

2. If you love those who love you, what reward will you get? (Matt 5:46)

3. Is not life more important than food and the body more important than clothes? . . . . Are you not much more valuable than they [the birds]? Who of you by worrying can add a single hour to his life? And why do you worry about clothes? (Matt 6:25–28)

4. Why do you look at the speck of sawdust in your brother's eye and pay no attention to the plank in your own eye? (Matt 7:3)

5. Which of you, if his son asks for bread, will give him a stone? . . . . If you, then, though you are evil, know how to give good gifts to your children, how much more will your Father in heaven give good gifts to those who ask him? (Matt 7:9, 11)

6. Why do you entertain evil thoughts in your hearts? Which is easier to say, "Your sins are forgiven," or to say, "Get up and walk"? (Matt 8:4–5)

7. How can the guests of the bridegroom mourn while he is with them? (Matt 9:15)

8. Do you believe that I am able to do this? (Matt 9:28)

9. Are not two sparrows sold for a penny? (Matt 10:29)

10. What did you go out into the desert to see? A reed swayed by the wind? (Matt 11:7)

11. Haven't you read what David did when he and his companions were hungry? (Matt 12:3)

12. If any of you has a sheep and it falls into a pit on the Sabbath, will you not take hold of it and lift it out? (Matt 12:11)

13. If Satan drives out Satan, he is divided against his kingdom. How then can his kingdom stand? (Matt 12:26)

14. How can anyone enter a strong man's house and carry off his possessions unless he first ties up the strong man? (Matt 12:29)

15. You brood of vipers, how can you who are evil say anything good? (Matt 12:34)

16. Who is my mother, and who are my brothers? (Matt 12:48)

17. Have you understood all these things? (Matt 13:51)

18. You of little faith, why did you doubt? (Matt 14:31)

19. And why do you break the command of God for the sake of tradition? (Matt 15:3)

20. Are you still so dull? (Matt 15:16)

21. How many loaves do you have? (Matt 15:34)

22. You of little faith, why are you talking among yourselves about having no bread? Do you still not understand? Don't you remember . . . ? How is it that you don't understand that I was not talking to you about bread? (Matt 16:8–11)

23. Who do people say that the Son of Man is? . . . . What about you? Who do you say I am? (Matt 16:13–15)

24. O unbelieving and perverse generation, how long shall I stay with you? How long shall I put up with you? (Matt 17:17)

25. From whom do the kings of the earth collect duty and taxes—from their own sons or from others? (Matt 17:25)

26. What good will it be for a man if he gains the whole world, yet forfeits his soul? Or what can a man give in exchange for his soul? (Matt 17:26)

27. What do you think? If a man owns a hundred sheep, and one of them wanders away, will he not leave the ninety-nine . . . to look for the one that wandered off? (Matt 18:12)

28. Haven't you read that at the beginning the Creator made them male and female? (Matt 19:4)

29. Why do you ask me about what is good? (Matt 19:17)

30. What is it you want? (Matt 20:21)

31. John's baptism—where did it come from? Was it from heaven, or from men? (Matt 21:24)

32. What do you think? There was a man who had two sons. . . . Which of the two did what his father wanted? (Matt 21:31)

33. Therefore, when the owner of the vineyard comes, what will he do to those tenants? (Matt 21:40)

34. Have you never read in the Scriptures . . . ? (Matt 21:42)

35. Whose portrait is this? And whose inscription? (Matt 22:20)

36. Have you not read what God said to you, "I am the God of Abraham . . ."? (Matt 22:32)

37. What do you think about the Christ? Whose son is he? (Matt 22:42)

38. How is it then that David, speaking by the Spirit, calls him "Lord"? . . . . If then David calls him "Lord," how can he be his son? (Matt 22:43–45)

39. Which is greater: the gold, or the temple that makes the gold sacred? . . . . Which is greater: the gift, or the alter that makes the gift sacred? (Matt 23:17–19)

40. Why are you bothering this woman? (Matt 26:10)

41. Could you men not keep watch with me for one hour? (Matt 26:40)

42. Are you still sleeping and resting? (Matt 26:45)

43. Do you think I cannot call on my Father, and he will at once put at my disposal more than twelve legions of angels? But how then would the Scriptures be fulfilled that say it must happen in this way? (Matt 26:53–54)

44. Am I leading a rebellion that you have come out with swords and clubs to capture me? (Matt 26:55)

45. My God, my God, why have you forsaken me? (Matt 27:46)

Appendix 2

Bloom's Taxonomy Assessment of Jesus' Questions in the Gospel of Matthew

	Knowledge	Comprehension	Application	Analysis	Synthesis	Evaluation
5:13		Interpret	Analyze Distinguish Examine Solve			Estimate Judge
5:46			Employ Dramatize Illustrate Practice	Analyze Distinguish Examine Experiment	Formulate Set up	Estimate Judge Measure
6:25–28		Recognize	Illustrate Interpret	Analyze Calculate Compare Distinguish Examine Inspect	Formulate Propose	Estimate Evaluate Choose Judge Measure Rate Select
7:3		Explain Express Identify	Demonstrate Illustrate	Analyze Appraise Calculate Examine Inspect Solve	Formulate Propose	Estimate Judge Measure
7:9, 11		Explain Express Identify	Dramatize Employ Illustrate Practice	Analyze Distinguish Examine Experiment	Construct Formulate Propose	Choose Estimate Evaluate Judge Measure Select
8:4–5		Identify Recognize		Analyze Appraise Examine Question Solve	Formulate	Assess Choose Compare Judge Select

9:15		Explain Express Identify	Dramatize Illustrate	Analyze Appraise Examine Question Solve	Formulate Propose	Assess Evaluate Judge
9:28						Appraise Assess Evaluate Judge Rate Score Value
10:29		Identify Report Review	Apply Dramatize Shop Use	Appraise Calculate Distinguish Inspect Inventory Solve	Formulate	Appraise Evaluate Measure Value
11:7						Appraise Assess Evaluate Judge Measure Value
12:3	Recall	Identify Locate	Interpret			
12:11		Explain Express Tell		Examine Relate		
12:26			Illustrate	Debate Diagram Distinguish Examine Solve	Formulate	
12:29		Explain Express Tell	Apply Illustrate	Debate Solve	Formulate	
12:34		Explain Express Tell	Apply Illustrate	Debate Solve		
12:48	List Name Recall	Identify Locate	Interpret	Distinguish Examine	Formulate Propose	Appraise Compare Select Value
13:51		Discuss	Apply Demonstrate Employ Illustrate Translate	Examine Relate		

14:31		Discuss Identify Review		Analyze Appraise Examine		
15:3		Discuss Identify Review		Analyze Appraise Examine		
15:16		Discuss		Debate Distinguish		
15:34		Identify Report		Calculate		
16:8–11		Discuss Explain	Illustrate	Analyze Appraise Distinguish Examine		
16:13–15		Identify Recognize Report Restate	Interpret	Appraise		Assess Judge
17:17				Analyze Appraise	Formulate	
17:25		Identify Report				
17:26				Analyze Distinguish Examine	Formulate Propose	Assess Choose Compare Evaluate Measure Value
18:12				Analyze Distinguish Examine		
19:4	Recall	Discuss Tell				
19:17		Explain		Examine	Formulate Propose	Appraise Evaluate
20:21		Express Identify Report Tell		Distinguish Examine		
21:24				Analyze Appraise Differentiate Distinguish Debate		Assess Evaluate Judge Measure

21:31				Analyze Appraise Differentiate Distinguish Debate		Assess Evaluate Judge Measure
21:40				Analyze Appraise Differentiate Distinguish Debate		Assess Evaluate Judge Measure
21:42	Recall	Explain Identify Recognize				
22:20	Name Recall	Identify Recognize Report				
22:32	Recall	Report				
22:42	Recall	Identify Report		Distinguish		Appraise Choose Judge Value
22:43–45				Analyze Debate Differentiate	Formulate Propose	Assess Compare
23:17–19				Compare Examine Inspect	Propose	Assess Evaluate Judge Score
26:10		Report		Appraise Debate Examine		
26:40		Express Tell		Appraise Examine		
26:45		Express Tell				
26:53–54		Express Tell		Appraise Examine	Propose	
26:55		Express Tell				
27:46		Express Tell		Distinguish Examine	Formulate Propose	Appraise Assess

Appendix 3

Walsh and Sattes's Quality Questioning Assessment of Jesus' Questions in the Gospel of Matthew (3 = high, 2 = medium, 1 = low)

	Purpose	Content Focus	Cognitive Level	Communication
5:13	3	3	3	2*
5:46	3	3	3	3
6:25–28	3	3	3	3
7:3	3	3	3	3
7:9, 11	3	3	3	3
8:4–5	3	3	3	3
9:15	3	3	3	3
9:28	3	3	3	3
10:29	3	3	3	3
11:7	3	3	3	3
12:3	3	3	3	3
12:11	3	3	3	3
12:26	3	3	3	3
12:29	3	3	3	3
12:34	3	3	3	3
12:48	3	3	3	2*
13:51	3	3	3	3
14:31	3	3	3	3
15:3	3	3	3	3
15:16	3	3	3	3
15:34	3	3	3	2*
16:8–11	3	3	3	3
16:13–15	3	3	3	3

17:17	3	3	3	3
17:25	3	3	3	3
17:26	3	3	3	3
18:12	3	3	3	3
19:4	3	3	3	3
19:17	3	3	3	3
20:21	3	3	3	3
21:24	3	3	3	3
21:31	3	3	3	3
21:40	3	3	3	3
21:42	3	3	3	3
22:20	3	3	3	3
22:32	3	3	3	3
22:42	3	3	3	3
22:43–45	3	3	3	3
23:17–19	3	3	3	3
26:10	3	3	3	3
26:40	3	3	3	3
26:45	3	3	3	3
26:53–54	3	3	3	3
26:55	3	3	3	3
27:46	3	3	3	3

*These questions received 2s because some words might be perceived as ambiguous.

8

Did Jesus Utilize Constructivist Teaching Practices?

Rhoda Sommers-Johnson

INTRODUCTION

IN SEVERAL UNDERGRADUATE COURSES, teacher education students spent a semester studying excerpts from the gospels to discover the teaching methods Jesus used, drawing conclusions about his attitude towards students, reviewing his interactions with individuals, and applying his methods to their lives as teachers. After gaining an understanding of the behavioral, cognitive, and constructivist theories of learning, the students drew conclusions about the teaching theory Jesus used. They concluded that while Jesus did utilize many constructivist teaching practices as described by Brooks and Brooks (1993) and Kim (2005), he also implemented aspects of other learning theories.

DID JESUS UTILIZE CONSTRUCTIVIST TEACHING PRACTICES?

The story of this research began a number of years ago when I was looking for a way to challenge my preservice teachers, sophomores and juniors, in several educational psychology and curriculum courses to think seriously and intentionally about Jesus as the master teacher. At the time, I was not intending to look at Jesus' teaching methods through the lens of any particular learning theory; I was focused on intentionally integrating faith and learning in my courses. Granted, I already valued the constructivist theory and designed much of my curriculum to reflect this theory because I believe constructivist practices honor students as created in the image of God to be thinking individuals. It also helps create the atmosphere of reciprocal learning that I so value in my classroom. My teacher education students and I were truly on a journey to learn about Jesus' teaching methods, look at his interactions with and attitudes toward students, and apply them to our lives as teachers.

Though the findings of our study are not intended to be a theological, philosophical, or conclusive statement about Jesus as the master teacher, they have left an indelible mark in the personal and professional lives of my students and me. We discovered that in many teaching situations Jesus taught in ways consistent with the constructivist theory of learning in both his methodology and the classroom environment he created, but he also drew from other learning theories given differing objectives, students' needs, learners' receptivity, and contexts.

I framed our study of Jesus, the master teacher, by selecting excerpts from the gospels and asking my students three questions:

1. What methods is Jesus using to teach his students?

2. What conclusions can you draw about Jesus' interactions with and attitudes toward his students?

3. What application would you like to make to your life as a teacher?

Each day of class, I read an excerpt from the gospels, posed the questions, and asked the students to record their answers to the questions. We then, as a class, discussed the students' ideas, and I collected their written responses. These responses were later typed into a document and organized according to the selections studied. At the end of the semester when my students had an understanding of the behavioral, cognitive, and constructivist learning theories, I asked two summary questions:

1. Which learning theory did Jesus use when teaching? Explain your answer.

2. What difference has looking at Jesus' teaching methods made in your process of becoming a teacher?

Again, the students recorded their answers, we discussed them, I collected their responses, and the students' observations were compiled as raw data. Before I discuss the findings and conclusions of our study, however, it is important to first review the constructivist theory and teaching practices that reflect this theory.

CONSTRUCTIVIST THEORY AND TEACHING PRACTICES

There is agreement in the literature that constructivism is a learning theory in which the students are active, social learners who construct their own knowledge by building on or revising what they already know or have experienced (Bertrand, 2003; Johnson, 2004; Rakes, Fields, & Cox, 2006; Schnuit, 2006; Underhill, 2006). The focus is on what the student does and brings into the learning environment. Students are tasked with creating personal meaning while also creating a shared meaning with others during the learning process (Gagnon & Collay, 2001).

The constructivist theory does not see the teacher as the focus in the learning process; rather, the teacher is a facilitator of the learning experience and assists students in creating both a personal and shared knowledge. The teacher creates an environment and designs experiences that challenge learners' previously held knowledge and understanding. This is often a difficult shift for teachers who are accustomed to performing in the classroom and shaping learning experiences in which they play an active role and the students' are passive receptors of knowledge. Instead, in the constructivist approach students are active thinkers, capable of shaping their knowledge and understanding in ways that allow them to use it and make sense of it.

McKeown and Beck (1999) point out, "the teacher in a constructivist classroom works as hard as one who uses a recitation or lecture mode, but differently" (p. 27). Someone not acquainted with the teaching-learning process may observe a constructivist classroom and conclude that this theory is merely a way for teachers to do less; however, this is far from the truth. Yuen and Hau (2006) note that "constructivist teaching usually [requires] extra time in comparison to . . . teacher-centered teaching" (p. 288).

In reflecting on my own teaching methods, I find that creating a constructivist classroom requires thoughtful planning as well as a level of confidence in and humility about my own knowledge and understanding not required with a more teacher-centered approach. When lecturing, the teacher is more in control of the knowledge that gets discussed, and this knowledge becomes a self-contained box in the possession of the teacher with the goal of direct transfer to students. When students are invited to be cocreators of knowledge, there are many boxes in the room with the goal of shared transfer of the boxes so that each individual's box, including the teacher's, becomes larger. Facilitating this growth and transfer process requires incredible attention, listening, openness, critical thinking, prob-ing, energy, humility, and wisdom. On the other hand, it also allows the teacher to model life-long learning and eliminates the pressure of being the sole source of knowledge in the classroom. This does not negate the need for "expert knowledge," but this knowledge is merely used differently (Educational Broadcasting Corporation, 2004, para. 6).

While constructivist teachers are not generally found at the tradi-tional front and center of the classroom, according to Brooks and Brooks (1993) and Kim (2005), they:

- Encourage and accept student autonomy and initiative (p. 103)

- Use raw data and primary sources, along with manipulative, inter-active, and physical materials (p. 104)

- When framing tasks, . . . use cognitive terminology, such as clas-sify, analyze, predict, create (p. 104)

- Allow student responses to drive lessons, shift instructional strat-egies, and alter content (p. 105)

- Inquire about students' understandings of concepts before shar-ing their own understandings of those concepts (p. 107)

- Encourage students to engage in dialogue, both with the teacher and with one another (p. 108)

- Encourage student inquiry by asking thoughtful, open-ended questions and encouraging students to ask questions of each other (p. 110)

- Seek elaboration of students' initial responses (p. 111)

- Engage students in experiences that might engender contradic-tions to students' initial hypotheses, and then encourage discus-sion (p. 112)

- Allow wait time after posing questions (p. 114)

- Provide time for students to construct relationships and create metaphors (p. 115)

- Nurture students' natural curiosity through frequent use of the learning-cycle model (p. 116)

- [Assess] student learning in the context of teaching (Kim, 2005, p. 10)

In reviewing this list, it becomes clear that being a constructivist teacher is not only about what a teacher does, but also who that teacher is in the classroom. It becomes a way of thinking, being rather than do-ing, and participating in a culture with distinctive beliefs, norms, and practices (Akar & Yildirim, 2006).

While one can find lists of constructivist teaching methods (Wiggins & McTighe, 2005; Woolfolk, 2004), Beswick (2005) warns against creating a prescriptive list or to equate constructivism with a specific set of teach-ing strategies. He suggests that a constructivist classroom is more of an environment that the teacher creates rather than the teaching practices the teacher uses, and he goes so far as to suggest that "any teaching strategy could be part of a constructivist learning environment" (p. 43). McKeown and Beck (1999) also address the issue of classroom environment as part of the constructivist theory. They note that teachers must create a class-room environment that supports constructivist teaching methods and provides emotional safety for students as they explore and share their for-mative thoughts. The culture created by the teacher must be one in which "learners can interact with peers, relate to the teacher, and experience the subject" (Akar & Yildirim, 2006, p. 6). According to Beswick, not only is the teacher responsible for shaping the learning environment, but stu-dents' attitudes and values also play a role in the atmosphere that is created in the classroom. While Gagnon and Collay (2001) focus on designing constructivist learning experiences, they too highlight the importance of classroom environment when they emphasize the

> absolute necessity of establishing a positive, affective climate. . . . A sense of trust, safety, and community in the class and school must be wrapped around and woven through [constructivist learning design] for deep student learning to take place. . . . Students and teachers must build a culture of social support and mutual helpful-ness complemented by an appreciation of diversity. (pp. xi–xii)

Did Jesus subscribe to the constructivist theory of learning or are we putting him in a box when we attempt to label his beliefs about learning? While Jesus did not explicitly articulate his educational philosophy, we are able to catch glimpses of his values and beliefs through his interac-tions with his students and the stories found in the gospels about the learning experiences from his classroom.

THE MASTER TEACHER

While my students and I looked at passages from all four of the gospels, given the length of this chapter, I have chosen to focus only on passages from the Gospel of Mark. For each passage we studied, I will give a brief overview or summary along with my students' responses and observations regarding Jesus' teaching methods and interactions with his students. The passages are discussed here chronologically as recorded in the Gospel of Mark, though my students and I did not necessarily study them in chronological order.

Mark 4:26–32: Kingdom of God Parables

Jesus chose to tell his students stories in the hope that they would begin to understand the kingdom of God. Instead of creating a well-organized lecture, in this instance Jesus used metaphors to inspire his students to think about the kingdom he was establishing. At this point in time, many of Jesus' students were thinking he would create an earthly kingdom that would result in the liberation of the Jews, not the spiritual kingdom Jesus was actually establishing. After giving his students time to think about the metaphors, Jesus then explained them to the students who were ready to understand.

According to my students, Jesus "used stories to teach his students" and "spoke using parables to the people [in general] but with his disciples, he explained everything." Jesus "wanted [his students] to come to a deeper [understanding] of the subject," and he gave them time to think about the truths before explaining to them what he meant. While I personally have felt that Jesus' use of parables seems somewhat unfair and exclusive, a number of my students observed that "he wanted his students to understand" and "he cares because he made sure they all understood." One student even noted that Jesus' approach allowed him to interact individually with his students and in small groups, which enabled him to reach students at their individual levels.

Mark 4:35–41: Calming the Sea

In this story, Jesus and his disciples were in a boat when "a furious squall came up, and the waves broke over the boat, so that it was nearly swamped" (Mark 4:37). In the midst of this storm, Jesus was sound asleep and the disciples were in charge of getting across the sea safely.

When the disciples asked for help, Jesus dramatically calmed the storm and asked them, "Why are you so afraid? Do you still have no faith?" (Mark 4:40).

My students interpreted this passage by writing that Jesus "let them try and solve the problem by themselves . . . , but he was also there when they needed him." Jesus helped his students "after they asked for it." While Jesus answered his students' cry for help, he ended the episode by asking questions. His students in turn asked each other a question about who Jesus was, but Jesus opted to allow the disciples to continue looking for answers to their question and did not immediately answer it.

Though Jesus was asleep when the storm hit the boat, he obviously cared deeply about the safety of his students and addressed their fear. He was patient even though he was disappointed that they did not trust him fully. We do see, however, that Jesus' students knew they could turn to him for help when the problems they were facing were beyond their means of solving.

Mark 6:30–44: Feeding Five Thousand People

Jesus and his students went to a place where they were hoping to find solitude and refreshment. Instead, a huge crowd followed them, wanting to hear Jesus teach. By the end of the day, everyone was tired and hungry, so Jesus' students suggested he send the people to the nearby villages to find food. To the disciples' surprise, Jesus suggested that they provide food for the crowd.

Jesus' was asking his students to solve a problem. He created a situation and asked them to find a solution to the need; however, Jesus is not the one who first initiated the problem that was at the heart of the lesson. The disciples came to him and noted that the people needed food. He followed their initiative and ended up teaching a powerful lesson while meeting both physical and spiritual needs and demonstrating compassion.

We again see that Jesus did not abandon his students, but he paved the way, which enabled them to be successful. A number of my students noted that Jesus' strategy expressed confidence in his students. He was compassionate and did not totally leave them on their own because he wanted them to be successful, but he expected them to take the lead in solving the problem and meeting the people's needs. Jesus allowed his students' responses to drive the lesson. The possibility of actually providing enough food (plus leftovers) for five thousand people was so far removed from the disciples' thinking that Jesus' directions to find food for all of them created a contradiction in their initial hypothesis for meeting the crowd's needs.

Mark 8:27–30: Peter's Confession

Jesus taught this entire lesson through the use of questioning. It came after many other lessons and experiences that were important preparation for this use of questioning. While this can be seen as an entire lesson, I also see it as a time of assessment in which Jesus was gauging what his students had learned and what they still needed to learn (Brooks & Brooks, 1993; Gagnon & Collay, 2001; Kim, 2005). Maybe he was also using it to help his students discover their tacit understandings and beliefs and help this understanding to become explicit.

The timing of this conversation is key. Jesus gave his students time to observe him, experience miracles, and in essence to discover the relationship between his ministry and what was prophesied about him in the Old Testament. Had Jesus asked these questions earlier, the disciples, and especially Peter, may not have been as confident in their responses. While Jesus was interested in the disciples' initial responses about what others were saying about him, he probed and allowed them to discover and be affirmed for finding the truth.

This lesson began with a global, safe question in which Jesus appeared to be asking what others were saying about him. He then made it personal and asked the disciples whom they thought he was. His response to Peter's answer was a warning not to tell others the truth; Jesus never did tell Peter whether or not his answer was correct, though the implication was there.

Jesus asked questions that required his students to think for themselves and made it clear that he wanted to hear his students' ideas, not what his students thought he wanted them to say. My students noted that Jesus also "respected their opinions and answers" to his questions. Jesus' response to Peter's answer indicated that "he trusted them with his identity." Jesus trusted and respected his students enough to share his deepest secret with them.

Mark 10:13–16: Jesus and the Little Children

In the midst of Jesus' busy day, adults decided to bring little children to him in hopes that he would bless them. The disciples wanted to protect Jesus' time and energy so they decided that blessing children was not an important activity for their teacher. Jesus, however, valued the children and wanted to bless them.

A student observed that Jesus used "gentle correction [and] taught the lesson without making the disciples feel dumb." He not only corrected the misinformation, but he also showed them what was right (Wiggins & McTighe, 2005). The whole incident must have created disequilibrium in the disciples' minds as they tried to understand that Jesus valued everyone equally. They certainly had to alter their initial hypothesis about whom Jesus considered important. Jesus in turn was able to demonstrate that no one was insignificant in his classroom.

Mark 10:35–45: Request of James and John

James and John wanted to be sure they served prominently in Jesus' kingdom, so they asked him for important positions. Jesus immediately recognized that they did not understand what they were asking and shifted the conversation so they would reconsider their request. Somehow the other ten disciples heard about James and John's request and were irritated. Jesus used the entire incident to teach his disciples about the need to serve rather than to be served.

Jesus must have been very approachable in order for James and John to come to him with their request. He quietly listened to them, allowed their responses to drive the lesson, but then he probed their thinking. My students noted that "Jesus wanted them to think about things on their own" though he did take initiative to ensure that the disciples understood the real meaning behind the lesson. Most likely, Jesus' disciples were curious about how his kingdom would be organized and who would hold what positions. Jesus used their natural curiosity to teach a deep lesson about true leadership.

Mark 11:27–33: Questioning Jesus' Authority

All the excerpts to this point have centered around Jesus and his disciples. This story describes an encounter with the religious leaders who came to Jesus with a question. Jesus responded with his own question. The religious leaders then discussed how best to answer Jesus' question and eventually decided it was unanswerable. Jesus ended the encounter by telling them that he would not answer their initial question either. Most likely the religious leaders were hoping to trap Jesus by the answer he might give to their question, and Jesus knew this. However, he treated them with respect and did not create an aversive environment in his classroom. He treated them like the critical thinkers God created them to be.

Jesus again modeled the use of questioning as a teaching strategy, but he did not facilitate the actual answering of his questions. He appeared to differentiate between students who were ready to learn and students who were not, but even with students who were not yet ready to draw conclusions, he generated thinking. He wanted his students to "figure it out themselves."

Mark 12:13–17: Paying Taxes

Here again the religious leaders placed themselves in the role of Jesus' students. While they were trying to trap Jesus by what he said, he orchestrated the lesson so he was able to have them learn. He initially answered their question with a question and then used a familiar object, a coin, to promote further thought. Even the religious leaders who had chosen to be Jesus' enemies "were amazed at him" (Mark 12:17) because Jesus' response was not an answer they expected.

In this scene, Jesus used an object to promote thinking in his students, asked them to analyze the markings found on the object, and encouraged dialogue. As one of my students wrote, Jesus' "students were trying to distract him [from his true mission], but he stayed on task." Jesus also knew his students' hearts, which allowed him to teach them effectively; he used this knowledge to facilitate valuable learning.

Mark 14:17–26: The Lord's Supper

Jesus and his disciples shared the traditional Passover meal from the Jewish religion, but Jesus was intent on taking the tradition further and helping his students understand new things. Using simple objects like bread and wine, Jesus foreshadowed things to come.

According to my students, Jesus "used bread and wine as visual . . . metaphors" and "had his students reflect . . . to see if they were capable of betraying him." Jesus also chose not to "single out [Judas], but instead he spoke to everyone, and [Judas] knew he was speaking to him." By using familiar objects as metaphors, Jesus shaped the lesson so his students could comprehend his intent at differing levels. Because of student differences in existing prior knowledge and varying levels of motivation and interest, Jesus' students had the opportunity to construct different understandings from the same experience.

During this gathering, Jesus was sharing his heart with his students. He and his students developed a deep level of trust, which is an essential element in creating a classroom environment in which students are willing to take risks with their learning (Gagnon & Collay, 2001). Jesus also demonstrated that he was not naïve about his students; he was very aware of what was in their hearts. While we need to believe in our students and expect the best of them, we also need to be wise and honest about their hearts.

COMPARING CONSTRUCTIVIST TEACHING PRACTICES AND JESUS' METHODS

To summarize Jesus' teaching practices, the chart below lists again the practices of constructivist teachers from Books and Brooks (1993) and Kim (2005) along with the incidents from Jesus' teaching where my students and I found each of them to be evident.

Table 8.1 Jesus' use of constructivist teaching practices

Constructivist teaching practices	Incidents in Jesus' classroom
Encouraging and accepting student autonomy and initiative	Calming the sea (Mark 4:35–41) Feeding five thousand people (Mark 6:30–44) The request of James and John (Mark 10:35–45) Questioning Jesus' authority (Mark 11:27–33) Paying taxes (Mark 12:13–17)
Using raw data and primary sources, along with manipulative, interactive, and physical materials	Feeding five thousand people (Mark 6:30–44) Paying taxes (Mark 12:13–17) The Lord's Supper (Mark 14:17–26)
Framing learning tasks using cognitive terminology such as classify, analyze, predict, and create	Feeding five thousand people (Mark 6:30–44) Paying taxes (Mark 12:13–17)

Allowing student responses to drive lessons, shift instructional strategies, and alter content	Calming the sea (Mark 4:35–41) Feeding five thousand people (Mark 6:30–44) Jesus and the little children (Mark 10:13–16) The request of James and John (Mark 10:35–45) Questioning Jesus' authority (Mark 11:27–33)
Inquiring about students' understanding of concepts before sharing one's own understanding of those concepts	Peter's confession (Mark 8:27–30) The request of James and John (Mark 10:35–45)
Encouraging students to engage in dialogue, both with the teacher and with each other	Calming the sea (Mark 4:35–41) Peter's confession (Mark 8:27–30) The request of James and John (Mark 10:35–45) Questioning Jesus' authority (Mark 11:27–33) Paying taxes (Mark 12:13–17) The Lord's Supper (Mark 14:17–26)
Encouraging student inquiry by asking thoughtful, open-ended questions and encouraging students to ask questions of each other	Calming the sea (Mark 4:35–41) Feeding five thousand people (Mark 6:30–44) Peter's confession (Mark 8:27–30) The request of James and John (Mark 10:35–45) Questioning Jesus' authority (Mark 11:27–33) The Lord's Supper (Mark 14:17–26)
Seeking elaboration of students' initial responses	Peter's confession (Mark 8:27–30) The request of James and John (Mark 10:35–45)
Engaging students in experiences that might engender contradictions to their initial hypotheses or prior knowledge and then encouraging discussions	Kingdom of God parables (Mark 4:26–32) Calming the sea (Mark 4:35–41) Feeding five thousand people (Mark 6:30–44) Jesus and the little children (Mark 10:13–16) Paying taxes (Mark 12:13–17)
Allowing wait-time after posing questions	Kingdom of God parables (Mark 4:26–32) Questioning Jesus' authority (Mark 11:27–33) The Lord's Supper (Mark 14:17–26)
Providing time for students to discover relationships and create metaphors	Kingdom of God parables (Mark 4:26–32) The Lord's Supper (Mark 14:17–26)

Nurturing students' natural curiosity	The request of James and John (Mark 10:35–45)
Assessing student learning in the context of teaching	Peter's confession (Mark 8:27–30)

At the end of our study, I asked my students, "Which learning theory did Jesus use when teaching? Explain your answer." The results were mixed. Many students decided that Jesus was a constructivist teacher for the following reasons:

- He "had [students] think for themselves and investigate to find their own answers."

- "He did not want to feed [students] the answers."

- He "guided everyone and let his students voice their opinions."

- "He would tell different parables and [the students] would have to derive their own meaning from his stories."

- He used "inquiry, problem-based learning, cooperative learning, dialogue, and instructional conversations."

- He "involved students in teaching."

- Other students noted that Jesus did not exclusively use the constructivist theory, but that he also used other learning theories:

- "When teaching students, he expected a change in their behavior."

- He taught them the "right way to change their [behavior]."

- He told "them what he wanted them to do."

I must agree with my students. While there is clear evidence that Jesus used teaching practices that come out of the constructivist theory, I also find by looking at the gospels in their entirety that there were times Jesus used direct instruction and clearly pointed out knowledge to his students. Not all of the learning that occurred reflected his students' interests; sometimes Jesus selected topics that were painful for his students to consider, ones that would probably not have been a natural outgrowth of his students' prior knowledge and experiences. Yet Jesus knew what was ultimately best for his students, and he knew how best to reach them given the content he was teaching.

While my bias is that many times the constructivist approach is the best way to engage students in learning and it reflects an underlying belief that students are created in the image of God to be independent, critical thinkers, we are not looking at the total picture if we place Jesus in the constructivist box. He was much more than that. As the master teacher, he knew what methods to use when, with what content, and with which students. As Christian teachers, we are called to imitate him and seek wisdom in knowing how best to use all the learning theories we have. Each theory reflects a part of the learning process, but in themselves they are inadequate to paint the whole picture.

This study raises additional questions for me to address as a Christian teacher educator since constructivism is essentially a philosophy that purports that truth is relative (Yuen & Hau, 2006). Am I modeling and challenging my students to think through the implications of the various theories and what they say about one's philosophical beliefs? Am I teaching them to divorce teaching practices from a given theory's underlying philosophy when I advocate for the constructivist learning theory? How do I help them reconcile the fact that utilizing postmodern teaching practices contradict belief in absolute truth?

REFERENCES

Akar, H., & Yildirim, A. (2006). *Learners' metaphorical images about classroom management in a social constructivist learning environment.* Paper presented at the annual meeting of the American Educational Research Association, San Diego, CA. ERIC document ED492054

Bertrand, Y. (2003). *Contemporary theories and practice in education.* Madison, WI: Atwood Publishing. (2nd ed.)

Beswick, K. (2005). The beliefs/practice connection in broadly defined contexts. *Mathematics Education Research Journal, 17*(2), 39–68.

Brooks, J. G., & Brooks, M. G. (1993). *In search of understanding: The case for constructivist classrooms.* Alexandria, VA: Association for Supervision and Curriculum Development.

Educational Broadcasting Corporation (2004). Concept to classroom. *Thirteen Online.* http://www.thirteen.org/edonline/concept2class/constructivism/index.html

Gagnon, G. W., & Collay, M. (2001). *Designing for learning: Six elements in constructivist classrooms.* Thousand Oaks, CA: Corwin.

Johnson, G. M. (2004). Constructivist remediation: Correction in context. *International Journal of Special Education, 19*(1), 72–88.

Kim, J. S. (2005). The effects of a constructivist teaching approach on student academic achievement, self-concept, and learning strategies. *Asia Pacific Education Review, 6*(1), 7–19.

McKeown, M. G., & Beck, I. L. (1999). Getting the discussion started. *Educational Leadership, 57*(3), 25–28.

Rakes, G. C., Fields, V. S., & Cox, K. E. (2006). The influence of teachers' technology use on instructional practices. *Journal of Research on Technology in Education, 38*(4), 409–424.

Schnuit, L. (2006). Using curricular cultures to engage middle school thinkers. *Middle School Journal, 38*(1), 4–12.

Sommers, R. C. (2002). [Jesus, Master Teacher]. Unpublished raw data.

Underhill, A. F. (2006). Theories of learning and their implications for on-line assessment. *Turkish Online Journal of Distance Education, 7*(1), 165–174.

Wiggins, G., & McTighe, J. (2005). *Understanding by design.* Alexandria, VA: Association for Supervision and Curriculum Development. (2nd ed.)

Woolfolk, A. (2004). *Educational psychology.* Boston, MA: Allyn and Bacon. (9th ed.)

Yuen, K., & Hau, K. (2006). Constructivist teaching and teacher-centred teaching: A comparison of students' learning in a university course. *Innovations in Education and Teaching International, 43*(3), 279–290.

9

Beyond Constructivism:
Exploring Grand Narratives and Story Constructively

E. Christina Belcher

THE INFLUENCE OF CONSTRUCTIVISM

CONSTRUCTIVIST PRINCIPLES ARE EMBEDDED in the educational theory of John Dewey and social behaviorism (as found in the work of Edward Thorndike and B. F. Skinner); in social learning theory (as noted in the work of Maria Montessori, Jean Piaget, Lev Vygotsky, and Jean-Jacques Rousseau); in action research (which finds its voice in the philosophical work of Kenneth Gergen, Karl Marx [critical theory], and, although lesser known in the Canadian context, Pierre Bourdieu). Currently, educators are moving beyond viewing constructivism as "a process or methodology of teaching" to recognizing it as inherent in varied disciplines of postmodern phenomenology. This includes research in the areas of discourse (MacLure, 2003), Bourdieuian methodology (Mills & Gale, 2007), and the problematizing of knowledge (Moore, 2007).

As a professor working in Christian higher education, I have observed differences in students educated from different educational "fields"—public or private—and have identified patterns based on what students believe education is for. Many of these patterns mirror the constructivist teaching they had experienced prior to university. Since the majority of students coming into the education program have been "schooled" publically, they may be Christians in faith yet be thoroughly unprepared to discuss educational perspectives, public or private, in Christian higher education. Even the title of this paper, "Beyond Constructivism: Exploring Grand Narratives and Story Constructively," may suggest different understandings to the reader. Does the word *con-structively* refer to constructivism, the pedagogical act of constructing ways of imparting content information in a particular discipline, such as language arts? Or does the word *constructively* refer to exploring story and language in ways that are constructive to different perspectives and overarching narratives? For the purposes of what you are now reading, the answer is not either-or, but both.

Constructivism in education is becoming a preferred pedagogical process and an emerging instructional metanarrative, assisted by the language and terms that define it. Thus, my definition of constructivism will differ from definitions seen in educational textbooks. " I define constructivism for the purpose of this chapter as follows: *Constructivism is an interdisciplinary and religious view of teaching and learning that uses language and story as a means to promote and deliver critique in a specific way and for a specific end, resulting in an overarching educational metanarrative."*

I shall expand on this definition as I discuss the two themes that have emerged from my own professional practice as an educator over the last couple of decades. The first theme, *constructivism, knowledge, and wisdom are all linked*, considers the impact of defining language in relation to philosophical and pedagogical foundations within a liberal arts education and explores "disequilibrium" in philosophy and faith.

The second theme, *constructivism creates a new way of interpreting story, and a new way of being or not being a child*, considers the use of modern and postmodern story and the intentionality of teaching from a biblical worldview.

THE PEARLY GATES OF CONSTRUCTIVISM

The first theme, *constructivism, knowledge, and wisdom are all linked*, considers the impact of defining language in relation to pedagogy within a liberal arts education and explores philosophy and faith perspectives. Education is driven not only by language, but also by intent. This realization can be noted in this quote from Neil Postman's book, *The End of Education.*

> What makes public schools public is not so much that the schools have common goals, but that the students have common gods. The reason for this is that public education does not serve a public. It *creates* a public. And in creating the right kind of public, the schools contribute toward strengthening the spiritual basis of the

American creed. This is how Jefferson understood it, how Horace Mann understood it, how John Dewey understood it. And, in fact, there is no other way to understand it. The question is not, Does or doesn't public schooling create a public? The question is, What kind of public does it create? (Postman, 1995, pp. 17, 18; [italics in original]).

Postman notes that "isms" or cultural narratives (which he terms gods with a small *g*), rely on "cultural language" that incorporates broad, culturally accepted principles. As these principles become popular, they become accepted and revised (often uncritically) as grand narratives, or large communal stories that eventually emerge within pedagogy. From a revised pedagogical story, educational instruction in any discipline can be delivered. Postman's book presents narratives as an avenue that could lead the public into new ways of thinking, educating, and being human.

In one sense, this idea of narratives constructing and reconstructing reality is at the heart of constructivism. To accept constructivism without thought would assume that it has no intent behind the theory, which is not true. Because of this, the first thing one must consider about constructivism is the assumptions that underpin it.

Constructivist preferences and Christian preferences are not the same. Different language embodies different perspectives. Different educational fields produce different "stories" or grand narratives about education, which are not always taken seriously. N. T. Wright (1996) reminds us of this when he says:

> In our modern culture, we sometimes imagine that stories are kids' stuff: little illustrations, while abstract ideas are the real thing. So Jesus' stories, people say, were just "earthly stories with a heavenly meaning," but that's rubbish! Stories are far more powerful than that. Stories create worlds. Tell the story differently and you change the world. And that's what Jesus aimed to do. . . . People in Jesus' world knew that stories meant business; that stories were a way of getting to grips with reality. (p. 36)

Difference between a constructivist and a Christian perspective can be explored in regard to what Kieran Egan (2002; Egan & Judson, 2008) describe as "binary opposites." Binary opposites can be understood as theoretical systems of meaning that fundamentally organize philosophy, language, and culture to reveal paradox or polarity. The binary opposites explored in this chapter are between Western humanist philosophy and other theoretical views.

In the subsequent paragraphs I explore binary opposites arising from definitions and understandings that have been compiled from student responses and conversations. In the first interactive session of one core course that I teach annually, I question students about their definitions and understanding of key words essential to the task of teaching and learning from cultural and Christian perspectives, and we then chart the responses. The key words used in this exercise are knowledge, experience, constructive learning, assessment, student, teacher, and story. I chose these key words because they are prolific in course text books in teacher education. The chart used here includes the most common answers provided from my personal teaching experience over twelve years to form the content of table 9.1. From this, the themes for this paper have emerged.

In the first column of the chart, definitions flow from cultural experience and formerly "schooled" understandings of these terms prior to this course. In the second column of the chart, the definitions flow from a Biblical understanding of these same concepts. The results are then compared and discussed in light of educational perspectives that may be otherwise left unconsidered.

The following pages explore student understanding of key terms related to a constructivist and a Christian perspective. Granted, there are many perspectives, but I have selected the broadest binary opposites for this paper. These observations will then be discussed in the context of grand narratives. Grand narratives are sometimes referred to in current public educational texts as "worldviews," which are seen as common cultural preferences or lenses from which knowledge is viewed[1] (Naested, Potvin, & Waldron, 2004). Christian institutions also use the word "worldview" to explain what Postman (1995) has called grand narratives and their perspectives. David Naugle notes:

> [The concept of] worldview offers . . . a fresh perspective on the holistic nature, cosmic dimensions, and universal applications of faith. Plus, the explanatory power, intellectual coherence, and pragmatic effectiveness of the Christian worldview make it exceedingly relevant for believers personally, but also establish a solid foundation for vigorous cultural and academic engagement. (2002, pp. 4, 5)

1. Mary Poplin, who became a Christian while within the public university system, notes in her book *Finding Calcutta* (2009), that from a Christian worldview one can understand any other worldview; but no other worldview will help to understand the Christian one.

For the purposes of this paper, the term *grand narratives* will be used rather than the term *worldview*. It is helpful to remember that the boundaries between public and Christian grand narratives are not "pure." What I mean by *pure* is that it would be rare to find anyone who only expresses the definitions of one side of the chart. There are variances. It is also prudent to remember that perceptions for table 9.1 were founded in the youthful responses of early university students entering an education program at a private liberal arts institution and were in many ways representative of an noncritiqued or unexplored educational imprint—regardless of whether this educational imprint was public, private, home, Catholic, or Protestant. Theories do not teach; people do. It is in relational activity and spirited discussion that students explore and became aware of educational narratives and their perspectives. In the following table, I first present the most common student definitions of terms. Below each definition is what the students think is the consequence, or long term perspective, of this definition. The chart was compiled in the first third of a course that introduced topics of teaching, learning, and philosophy, which followed a course on introduction to the teaching profession.

Table 9.1: Language, definition, and binary opposites within fields of educational teaching and learning

Educational term		Common cultural definitions	Common scriptural definitions
Knowledge and teaching	Student definition	Knowledge comes from experience, personal interest and from knowing the political and vocational expectations for teaching. To teach is to partake in a vocation.	Knowledge comes from knowing God, knowing oneself and being known by God. To teach is to fulfill a call to serve God and man truthfully in whatever vocation you are in by deed and word.
	Consequence of definition	Knowledge involves skill that results in individual success or employment within a global society as outlined in educational ministry documents.	Knowledge is folly without wisdom. Wisdom unites truth, understanding, and knowledge to "further what is good and repress what is evil" within community for God's glory and for the benefit of the next generation.

Experience and learning	**Student definition**	Experience is part of an individual journey of learning from mistakes.	Experience is how life equips someone to learn to become mature in order to become more like the character of Jesus.
	Consequence of definition	Personal life experiences form the basis for skill acquisition and further learning.	Life experience assists wise decision making when considering consequences to the individual and to community.
Constructive learning	**Student definition**	Constructive learning builds upon individual learning.	Constructive learning develops character so that the student may use learning to wisely serve others.
	Consequence of definition	Constructive learning moves from the known to the unknown in cognitive, social, and behaviorist domains and is based on the educational psychology and philosophy taught in teacher education programs.	To be a constructive member of society requires learning from experience mentally, physically, and spiritually in ways that result in becoming a wise and mature servant-leader.
Assessment	**Student definition**	In assessment, individuals are evaluated and ranked for future advancement in a profession.	Assessment is only of value if coupled with integrity, humility, and justice in our walk with God and others.
	Consequence of definition	Assessment considers the ways in which cognitive knowledge has been understood in graded classroom contexts in accordance with assessment rubrics, evaluations, or models.	Assessment involves the way in which learned skills are embodied over time based on what is done with what has been learned, and the outcomes and consequences of such application.

Student	**Student definition**	A student is a member of society enrolled in an educational institution.	A student "studies" in order to become wiser.
	Consequence of definition	A student is facilitated by a teacher and gains the required learning outcomes valued in current society.	A student is mentored by a teacher in order to be a wise steward in living life within community before and in relationship with God.
Teacher	**Student definition**	A teacher is someone who teaches something.	A teacher is a "professor" of belief who leads from behind and develops a love of wisdom and learning in others.
	Consequence of definition	A teacher designs pedagogy and facilitates curricular knowledge that is valued by culture and society as outlined in educational textbooks and other media.	A teacher is a mentor, who desires to reconcile God and humans in scholarly knowledge and lifestyle.
Story and educational example	**Student definition**	A story is a myth or tale to be individually explored and enjoyed.	A story describes a way of sharing language as "living history" that gets to grips with reality.
	Consequence of definition	A cultural representation of experience written in story form for the interpretation of the reader. Story is mostly about the interpretation of the recipient or revision of it by the teacher (Johnson, 1999).	Story is a relational dance (Palmer, 1998) between the teller, who has a reason for the story, and the recipient, who engages with the life of the teller.

A grand narrative with the individual being central to knowledge undergirds the first column. This is juxtaposed with a Christian grand narrative in the second column.

If each column in the above chart is read in a linear manner, it is evident that each column suggests a different context that is foundational to future pedagogy. The implementation of such pedagogy may result in a different kind of teacher or student. In the current cultural public grand narrative, the knowledge that is valued in constructivism is content based. It is largely pragmatic, subjective, and relativistic in scope. Because of its pragmatic, subjective, and relativistic nature, this type of knowledge is the kind that one can "assent" to without needing to believe it. However, from a Christian grand narrative, Parker Palmer (1993) notes that the truth must be done to be known; to educate requires creating a space to explore what truth is and how one can live in obedience to it. This expectation is linked to the wisdom literature of the Bible, which is not the same as knowledge from a constructivist perspective. A Christian is called to not only "assent" to knowledge, but to embody that knowledge in wise ways coherent with Biblical faithfulness and precepts that mirror the character of Christ. Because the second column focuses on "intent," while the first column focuses on "content," it leads to a more embodied than intellectual view. Addressing this view of "embodied" knowledge, Eisner (2002) identifies that learning is to be more than cognitive:

> Teachers have what some call lived experience (Connelly & Clandinin, 1988). The body is now considered a source of understanding: Some things you can understand only through your ability to feel. Knowledge, at least a species of knowledge, has become embodied. It is intimate. (p. 381)

Bev Norsworthy (2008) adds to this understanding in her doctoral thesis, in reference to the belief that theory, epistemology, and practice can never be separated. Bullough (2008) supports this view when he states:

> However, viewed from a Biblical epistemological perspective, theory and practice can never be separated. Theory must be done, that is, practiced to be known. The known and the knower are inextricably intertwined and related. The knowledge and actions within teaching are both expressions of self. (p. 52)

Both sides of table 9.1 contain "truths" about education that flow from different starting points. Adherents value some more than others in accordance with their larger grand narrative that underpins the definitions. Educational theory is delivered not only rationally, but also relationally, and any teacher may implement any perspective of the chart above, based on personal worldview and spiritual life decisions.

Exploring Disequilibrium

Nicholas Wolterstorff (2002) urges Christians to be "lovingly dissatisfied" with life in ways that create disequilibrium in the world. The Christian mind and the thinking of society generally are not in step in many areas. It is not hard to see in table 9.1 that Christian definitions and perspectives in a postmodern context could create such a concept of disequilibrium, but the opposite is also true. It must be remembered that people habitually fail to live fully in either perspective. Just as there are binary opposites, there are also similarities and places for common ground. There are aspects of constructivism that Christians condone.

Harro Van Brummelen (2009), a Christian theorist, would agree with constructivists' argument that children are unique and come with various gifts and talents that should be nurtured. A teacher's attention to recognizing and encouraging the gifts in every child is important and should be included in the direction given in the classroom. Disequilibrium arises when the desired "knowledge" or cognitive acquisition that the student will achieve is assumed to flow from individual experiential activity, be it facilitated or directed. This *direction* is not to be confused with teacher knowledge being imposed upon the active learner, but rather with teacher *design* for learning. Since in constructivism, the individual student is the center of learning, it is possible that what the student knows or experiences could, in practice, be valued above what the teacher knows or more significantly, what the student needs to know. Nurturing and developing gifts is a triadic relational activity for the Christian (person, God, and community of faith), not a solo enterprise. The teacher is key here, for from teacher intentionality, instruction flows.

Both Christians and constructivists would be in agreement that students should enjoy, be creative, and be active in learning—these things are wonderful motivation for any learner in the classroom. However, disequilibrium may arise if a focus on process (the means) is viewed as being more important than learning (the end). Just because students appear to be engaged does not mean that learning is occurring. Seasoned educators can attest that happy activity does not ensure learning, no matter how "progressive" the activity may be. In looking at the process and not the person, people become "thing-ified," that is they are seen as "grades" (in the system of national testing) rather than humans who are hopefully learning over time to become better human beings from their learning experiences. If the end is intellectual knowledge and information, students may identify their worth by "the grade" they acquire. The temptation to cut and paste information or purchase papers is evidence of "thing-ifying" knowledge.

Practice and problem solving (also often termed "critical thinking") are valued processes in constructivist and Christian practice. In constructivism, the old saying "practice makes perfect" may come into play, but in my experience, practice does not make perfect. Practice makes permanent. Practice reinforces patterns, attitudes, and dispositional preferences (including grand narratives) for learning, but does not ensure that the learning or knowledge acquired will be meaningful or long lasting. It is possible that the opposite could be true. Problem solving or critical thinking is incorporated within the process of constructive learning, but certain kinds of thinking are valued over others, especially when these concepts relate to science, math, technology, and multiculturalism, or current issues in culture. From a Christian perspective, problem solving only for the purpose of critique is not really good problem solving. Christians are to discern every thought: "We destroy arguments and every lofty opinion raised against the knowledge of God, and take every thought captive to obey Christ" (2 Cor 10:5).

In conclusion, the first theme, *constructivism, knowledge, and wisdom are all linked*, considers the impact of defining language in relation to pedagogy within a liberal arts education and explores "disequilibrium" in the binary opposites of philosophy and faith. In implementing binary opposites as a lens for understanding constructivism's view of knowledge and the biblical concept of wisdom, one can implement the positive aspects of each view constructively. This is needed in order to embrace a fully human educational model for practice where wisdom and humanity, head and heart, become part of learning and teaching.

From Grand Narrative to Metanarrative

All teaching is religious, since God is either excluded or included religiously. A grand narrative for approaching teaching and learning emerges from that decision. Emerging grand narratives, over time, can become adopted as metanarratives for educational practice. In so doing, these metanarratives may drive pedagogical decision making.

Metanarratives are the large, overarching stories that guide us morally, ethically, intellectually, and relationally in life, and they are spiritual in nature. A metanarrative emerges when philosophical perspectives become intentionally verbalized and brought to active engagement as a directive in the act of teaching and learning. This act of teaching and learning is then considered via what poststructural sociologist Pierre Bourdieu termed as epistemic reflexivity.[2]

Christians are urged to move away from childish thinking and to think maturely, in alliance with the mind of Christ (1 Cor 13:11; Rom 12:1, 2). Part of maturity is the ability to consider concepts such as hope, consequences, and resolution to future problem solving, while also considering a past, present, and future reality (Belcher, 2005). Such considerations also apply to understanding the current use of story in the classroom.

CONSTRUCTIVISM: THE EMERGENCE OF CHANGE IN THE ART OF STORY

The second theme, *constructivism creates a new way of interpreting story, and a new way of being or not being a child*, considers the use of modern and postmodern story and the intentionality of teaching from a biblical worldview.

The link between constructivism and postmodern philosophy has greatly influenced the use and interpretation of story in the classroom over the last decade. This movement is not confined to North America.

---

2. This term is further explained in Maton (2003) in light of Pierre Bourdieu's epistemic conditions and in Moss (2005) in understanding epistemic reflexivity as it applies to education. *Epistemic reflexivity* can be understood as similar to what educational texts and research define as *reflective practice* but with the additional consideration of the importance of the structuring effects of educational fields on beliefs. From within action research, narratives are now being critiqued and viewed in terms of how constructivism frames the purpose of story in ethnographic research (Smith, 2006) and in narrative discourse (MacLure, 2003).

The works of those who further constructivism in designing teaching curriculum, educational textbooks, and research often use a story format to expose their findings. This can be seen in the work on multiple readings of a picture book (Johnson, 1999), the development of multiple meanings within narrative (Rosen, 1985), and the work on narrative as social consciousness (Owens & Nowell, 2001). Such research is based on the idea of constructed or revisionist knowledge. Consideration of story and philosophy engages us in the next theme of this chapter.

Of all of the changes that have occurred since the rise of constructivism as a pedagogical methodology, none, in my thinking, is more apparent than that of the approach to and use of story. It is in this area, the area of language arts, that new methods often have profound effects. I suggest that one key tool for opening constructivism to conversation beyond its perspective is the use of the picture book as an instructional device. Much has been written on the use of children's picture books in literature, but I will broadly examine picture books as they relate to story in general.

When I was a child, the modern story was the norm. Modern story could be (and still can be) identified by certain patterns or practices. The modern story has a beginning, middle, and end. It flows logically and has a resolution to any key problem. It focuses on character and consequences. It moves from left to right across the page, and the pictures usually reinforce or add confirmation to the story. The reader knows that there is a message, and that the author intends to tell the story so that the message can be understood. Examples of popular modern story would be *The Tale of Peter Rabbit* by Beatrix Potter (1902) or *The Cat in the Hat* by Dr. Seuss (1957). Modern picture books are traditional in that they tell stories that the "common citizen" can understand. They present a story around which to unite community. The modern story provides hope in difficulty. For the modern story, story matters. It shapes citizens because authors know that stories mean business and that readers are touched and shaped by what they read.

Postmodern story brings another view to young readers.[3] This type of story is not linear and does not necessarily flow from beginning, middle, to end—nor does it need to end at all. Where modern story has a familial and communal context, postmodern story is usually about an individual or ethnic or social group, and it can simultaneously pose a multitude of problems (and it becomes acceptable to do so even

3. For an example of a study of the change in literature from modern to postmodern era across a theme, see Belcher (2008).

if in a rude, aggressive, or degenerate manner) that do not need to be solved at all. No moral or ethical voice is present. Each individual reader interprets the story out of the context of past or current personal experience or interest. Political or social interests are often included to drive the cause of the day home to young readers. Postmodern picture books also feature themes of despair in a broken world; themes that used to be found in adult reading. There is a disappearance of childhood as it was formerly known in premodern and modern story books. Postmodern narratives can be dark and not very comforting as bedtime stories. The reader is presented with more visuals and less print; more fear and less innocence; more chaos and confusion and less joy. Examples of popular postmodern picture books are *Black and White* by David Macaulay (1990) or *The Red Tree* by Shaun Tan (2003).

In my educational experience with postmodern literature, I suggest that most benefit emerges when discussion in community occurs. Regrettably, I have noted that this does not often happen in the reality of the public schoolroom. Postmodern visuals can be complex and disturbing, and children often read independently for periods of time and are thus left to construct their own meaning without any mention of morality, truth, or character formation. Beyond grade four, I have noted in practicum visits to classrooms that less time is given to reading orally to a class and discussing that reading unless it is part of a novel study, which then incorporates student-led literature circles for discourse or activity. A postmodern, constructivist educator may not like to suggest a view or personal opinion on an emerging mind, in a relative world where being politically correct is valued. Cultural issues or themes of the day in postmodern story are often grasped by adults but can be either missed or misconstrued by children. Text and visual often do not tell the same story. Teachers in the classroom may like to teach using these stories, but may not have had time to think about how this could be done. Many are too busy coping with the daily tyranny of the urgent.

Has Pandora's box opened us to a different kind of story, or to the formation of a different kind of child—or the removal of childhood altogether? Some critics believe all of the above, and state in internet chat rooms that the influence of graphic novels and internet blogs will soon triumph over the comfort of the storybook. So what is a teacher to do? Does any of this actually matter? Is there any good in the constructivist view that could be used to unwrap postmodern children's literature, and if so, what is it?

There are many positive aspects to implementing the common ground and strengths of constructivist theory within the use of modern and postmodern picture books. Examining stories for their presentation of culture, worldview, and character development as they relate life issues is enriching for students. The themes of postmodern literature also involve dark areas that are best discussed within a community of care, especially as these relate to areas of social justice. The open-ended endings of postmodern literature also help readers to decide what they value, where they prefer endings to be happy and hopeful, and why. Postmodern books give readers an opportunity to think and develop a voice as they navigate texts written in the context of the cultural experience of the picture book's author. In so doing, a community of learners could be able to consider the consequences of the story to real life over time, which is valuable. Attention could be paid to the language that the story includes or excludes, and the feelings that the story evokes. In community, a teacher and students could engage in discussion about things that may be troubling or feared. This could lead to considering the things that may trouble others. Story can be explored beyond the individual to the communal stage without leaving the individual to construct meaning independently. Discussion in the form of a grand conversation with others, which is advised, can include a teacher perspective to help students consider how and why to respect different points of view, to understand different cultures, and to discern propaganda from reality. Such discussion may even be opened to exploring worldviews. In doing so, it is possible to learn that people are not to be known only for how they differ, but for how they are the same.

There are cautions regarding postmodern literature. Certain texts may induce fear, express chaos, or diminish hope. The writing may also evidence mediocrity in skill and communication, as evidenced in graphic novels, although engaging comparative texts of the same story from different decades is useful in such cases. Students (or the teacher) may fear speaking about anything moral or ethical due to legal or politically correct consequences. However, it has been my experience that students actually expect and prefer teachers to have an opinion on something, or else, what is a teacher for? How does one learn to have an opinion if it is never modeled or discussed?

CONCLUSION

Constructivism is an interdisciplinary and religious view of teaching and learning that uses language and story as a means to promote and deliver critique in a specific way and for a specific end, resulting in an overarching educational metanarrative.

In the final theme of this paper, *constructivism creates a new way of interpreting story, and a new way of being or not being a child*, opportunity is provided to engage the philosophy and perspective of the stories one tells within context and across time. As N. T. Wright reminds the reader: tell the story differently and you change the world. In some postmodern stories, we do have a new type of reader—not the child of innocence, but the child of doubt and critique. But not all stories portray such a child. Engagement about constructivism from a Christian grand narrative in the training of future educators for teaching is both transformative and engaging when educators *intentionally* discuss definitions and presuppositions about constructivism and story in ways that promote discourse and communal understanding. Picture books are worldview tools for opening up binary opposites over decades and creating communal discourse in the act of teaching and learning. Talking about or giving assent to linking theory and practice is wasted unless it is actually implemented in community and the reasons for doing so are expressed. There is a way of de/re-constructing pedagogy and postmodern story to see its grand narratives perspectives and values. There is a way of looking at story over time to consider the consequences of actions, not just to the individual, but to society as a whole. There is a way to consider the philosophic contours and metanarratives that undergird wise and foolish decision making for pedagogical practice. Engaging these ideas with picture books will allow educators to open up communal conversations necessary to discerning life and living in current culture. More research is needed here.

God does not fear or become disillusioned by "isms"—humanism, constructivism, postmodernism—or culture. All "isms" eventually become "wasims" as they are replaced by other educational theories and philosophies. Christians who are called to teach have an opportunity to *constructively* stand in the gap by fostering exciting and engaging discourse. Seize the day.

REFERENCES

Belcher, E. C. (2008). Between the covers: Suffering, trauma and cultural perspectives in children's picture books. *Journal of Christian Education (Australian Christian Forum on Education Incorporated), 51*(2), 41–57.

Belcher, E. C. (2005). The place of worldview in Christian approaches to education. *Journal of Christian Education (Australian Christian Forum on Education Incorporated), 48*(3), 9–24.

Bullough, R. (2008). *Counternarratives: Studies of teacher education and becoming and being a teacher.* New York: State University of New York Press.

Connelly, F. M., & Clandinin, D. J. (1988). *Teachers as curriculum planners: Narratives of experience.* New York: Teachers College Press.

Egan, K. (2002). *Getting it wrong from the beginning.* London: Yale University Press.

Egan, K., & Judson, G. (2008, March). Of whales and wonder. *ASCD Educational Leadership, 65,* 20–24.

Eisner, E. W. (2002). From episteme to phronesis to artistry in the study and improvement of teaching. *Teaching and Teacher Education, 18,* 375–385.

Johnson, G. (1999). Multiple readings of a picture book. *Australian Journal of Language and Literacy, 22*(3), 176–191.

Macaulay, D. (1990). *Black and white.* Boston: Houghton Mifflin Company.

MacLure, M. (2003). *Discourse in educational and social research.* Philadelphia: Open University Press.

Maton, K. (2003). Reflexivity, relationism, and research: Pierre Bourdieu and the epistemic conditions of social scientific knowledge. *Space and Culture, 6*(1), 52–65.

Mills, C., & Gale, T. (2007). Researching social inequalities in education: Towards a Bourdieuian methodology. *International Journal of Qualitative Studies in Education, 20*(4), 433–447.

Moore, R. (2007). Going critical: The problem of problematizing knowledge in education studies. *Critical Studies in Education, 48*(1), 25–41.

Moss, P. (2005). Toward "epistemic reflexivity" in educational research: A response to scientific research in education. *Teachers College Record, 107*(1), 19–29.

Naested, I., Potvin, B., & Waldron, P. (2004). *Understanding the landscape of teaching.* Toronto: Pearson Education Canada.

Naugle, D. (2002). *Worldview: The history of a concept.* Grand Rapids, MI: Eerdmans.

Norsworthy, B. E. (2008). *Being and becoming reflexive in teacher education* (Doctoral thesis, School of Education, University of Waikato, Hamilton, New Zealand).

Owens, W., & Nowell, L. (2001, January/February). More than just pictures: Using picture story books to broaden young learners' social consciousness. *Social Studies, 92*(1), 33–40.

Palmer, P. J. (1993). *To know as we are known: Education as a spiritual journey.* San Francisco: Harper.

Palmer, P. J. (1998). *The courage to teach: Exploring the inner landscape of a teacher's life.* San Francisco: Jossey-Bass.

Postman, N. (1995). *The end of education: Redefining the value of school.* New York: Knopf.

Poplin, M. (2008). *Finding Calcutta: What Mother Teresa taught me about meaningful work and service.* Downers Grove, IL: InterVarsity.

Potter, B. (1902/1992). *The great big treasury of Beatrix Potter*. New York: Derydale Books.

Rosen, H. (1985). *Stories and meanings*. Sheffield, UK: National Association for the Teaching of English.

Seuss. (1957). *The cat in the hat*. New York: Random House.

Smith, D. E. (2006). *Institutional ethnography as practice*. Lanham, MD: Rowman & Littlefield.

Tan, S. (2003). *The red tree*. Vancouver, BC: Simply Read Books.

Van Brummelen, H. (2009). *Walking with God in the classroom: Christian approaches to teaching and learning*. Colorado Springs, CO: Purposeful Design.

Wolterstorff, N. P. (2002). *Educating for life: Reflections on Christian teaching and learning*. Grand Rapids, MI: Baker Books.

Wright, N. T. (1996). *The original Jesus: The life and vision of a revolutionary*. Grand Rapids, MI: Eerdmans.

10

Constructivism in an Era of Accountability: A Case Study of Three Christian Public School Teachers

Jillian N. Lederhouse

INTRODUCTION

The education of a child is always, I would say, either tacitly or explicitly pointed toward a certain way of being in the world for that child. It's true that in assessing an educational situation we must look not only at what the education is pointed toward but at the quality of the situation itself.

—Nicholas Wolterstorff

CONSTRUCTIVISM IS A POSTMODERN theory that contends that humans generate knowledge and meaning from their own experiences. Formalized through the work of Piaget (1970) and Vygotsky (1978), it is a psychological construct that promotes learning through interaction with others and the environment. While constructivism is broader than one particular pedagogy, constructivist educators generally support learning methods that include significant social collaboration and hands-on activities in order to foster the construction of meaning from experience. These approaches are often referred to as educational *best practice* (Zemelman, Daniels, & Hyde, 2005).

However, since constructivists generally see knowledge as determined by time, place, and even culture, Christians who believe in the absolute, eternal, and universal authority of Scripture have long objected to this aspect of the theory (Carson, 1996). Some perceive the practice of teaching critical thinking skills as a means by which children learn to challenge authority and reject all forms of objective truth. This perception is problematic for Christian educators who value the use of constructivist pedagogies to enable their students to understand key concepts and principles.

This study focuses on three such Christian teachers who practice at the early elementary, intermediate, and middle school levels of public education in an educational climate of intense pressure to raise student achievement.

Although social interaction and experiential learning are key components of constructivist pedagogy, they are not the only qualities associated with this approach. Brooks and Brooks (1999) describe five guiding characteristics that highlight the individualistic focus of constructivism. These include (1) posing problems of emerging relevance to students, (2) structuring learning around primary concepts, (3) seeking and valuing students' points of view, (4) adapting curriculum to address students' suppositions, and (5) assessing student learning in the context of teaching. These qualities are important because they are instrumental to independent learning, a necessary framework for continuous learning long after formal education has been completed.

While constructivist pedagogies became influential during the reform efforts in American K–12 education during the 1980s and 1990s as an alternative to direct instruction, Brooks's (2006) hallmarks of instruction are challenging to maintain in an era where curriculum is often externally prescribed and achievement is measured outside the context of teaching and learning through standardized testing. Since the passage of the No Child Left Behind Act (NCLB) in 2001, public school districts who receive federal funding are required to make adequate yearly progress (AYP) as determined by increasing percentages of students who meet or exceed state standards of reading and math achievement. As the law currently stands, all schools by 2014 will need to demonstrate that 100 percent of their enrolled students meet this criterion. This requirement includes all low-income, ethnically and linguistically diverse students, as well as those students who receive special education services. Districts who fail to make AYP are subject to sanctions and state takeover.

In the nine years since the passage of this law, education in many American public school classrooms reflects a greater emphasis on direct instruction and greater reliance on a prescribed curriculum to ensure that all content is covered prior to statewide assessments. Although formal testing does not begin until third grade, even primary grade teachers sense pressure to prepare students for formal assessments in literacy and mathematics.

This research examined how three Christian public school teachers at the elementary and middle grade levels perceived their own practice in light of these changes. Not only do these teachers face a theological challenge to their practice, they also face the constraints of external controls and limited time that often work against collaborative, student-centered, and experiential learning. As accountability measures continue and even increase as 2014 approaches, constructivist pedagogies have become more costly to integrate into one's practice. Despite their focus on active, student-centered learning, these pedagogies are often viewed as too time consuming to employ. This study was designed to explore whether and how Christian educators, who see their work as a calling, continue to use these learning approaches and how they perceive their faith to relate to these professional decisions.

RESEARCH METHOD

All three teachers in this case study taught in different schools within the same suburban school district of thirteen thousand students. They were selected because of their identification as exemplary educators through their long-standing involvement as mentors in our teacher preparation program. This qualitative study primarily involved the use of semistructured interviews with limited classroom observation. Teachers were given the questions two weeks ahead of the individual initial interviews. Due to the need for candid responses, all interviews took place away from the school setting. The interview protocol focused on seven initial questions:

1. Do you see yourself as a teacher who uses constructivist pedagogies? If so, how?

2. Since NCLB have you used these pedagogies at the same level, less, or more frequently? How and why?

3. Have you used direct instruction at the same level, less, or more frequently? How and why?

4. If you have changed your use of constructivist strategies, do you feel it has enhanced learning? If so, how?

5. If you have changed the amount of direct instruction strategies, do you feel it has enhanced learning? If so, how?

6. How do you see your faith as influencing your instructional choices?

7. How do you see your faith as influencing the type of relationships you seek to have with students?

Interview responses were then analyzed for elements of Brooks's (2006) characteristics, and classroom observations were made to find confirmations of the teachers' perceptions. While practice was found to be consistent with all three teachers' views, due to their limited scope, classroom observations did not provide significant additional data for this study. Professional views and practices consistent or contrary to Brooks's (2006) characteristics were noted and are discussed in the conclusion of this study.

MEREDITH STANTON

Meredith Stanton is currently a first-grade teacher in the district where she has worked for twelve years. She has taught kindergarten, first, and fourth grades during this period of time. Meredith graduated from a teacher preparation program housed within a Christian liberal arts college and is currently enrolled in a private nonreligious university pursuing a master's degree in elementary mathematics education. When asked the question, "Do you see yourself as a teacher who uses constructivist pedagogies?" Meredith responded, "I would *hope* to be. I hope that my young students can benefit from my study of Fosnot's (2001) and Hyde's (2006) research. They need to see whole-to-part and part-to-whole concretely in order to understand something as abstract as arithmetic. I also don't see how they can develop strong problem-solving skills apart from constructivist experiences."

An example of this approach is found in her classroom exercise using a basket of green apples and a basket of red apples. Students had to "purchase" only five apples but had to determine how many different combinations of five that could be made from the total. At first they lined up the actual apples and then used five red unifix cubes and five green unifix cubes to represent the different combinations, reproducing their sequential patterns on recording paper.

After graphing the pattern of no green and 5 red, 1 green with 4 red, 2 green with 3 red, 3 green with 2 red, 4 green with 1 red, and 5 green with no red on a wall chart, one student identified a "stair step pattern" more formally know as the concept of compensation. When asked what the "stair step pattern" meant, the class recognized and articulated that as one group of apples increased, the other group had to decrease in order to arrive at the same amount of five.

Meredith reflected that while the entire sequence of activities took short periods of time over several days, the class had mastered the concept through that one brief unit. "It takes a lot longer, but once they get, they *have* it." Identifying the compensatory relationship between two addends laid a critical foundation for mastering all basic facts in arithmetic. Even more significant than constructing answers to specific problems is the value of constructing the properties that govern arithmetic operations such as identity, commutative, associative, or distributive.

When asked if she uses constructivist pedagogies as defined by Brooks and Brooks (1999) more or less frequently over the past eight years, Meredith responded that the decision to utilize this approach is more complex than just proportionality. In her first grade teaching, she stated that she is more committed to it than she has been in the past. However, last year coming back from maternity leave, she taught fourth grade half-time by sharing the job with another teacher. She perceived that covering all the content of upper elementary grades while teaching critical thinking and the "slow and deep learning" it requires is much more challenging.

She remained committed to experiential pedagogy during this year, despite the efficiency of direct instruction. "Initially I tried to follow a faster pace, keeping the mindset that I had to cover this immense amount of material before state testing. But after several lessons, I went back to do what I felt was right. I still had to use more direct instruction, but I integrated as much critical thinking and hands-on learning as I possibly could." When asked how her students performed on the state tests that spring, Meredith reported that she was pleased with the results.

Meredith credited her administration with being supportive of her choices. She was given the freedom to utilize her own instructional approaches as long as she accomplished her district's curricular goals. But Meredith instructs in one of the state's highest performing schools. Performance on the 2009 spring state exams, as indicated on the school's website, demonstrated that 100 percent of all fourth graders at the school met or exceeded state standards in math and 98.5 percent met or exceeded state standards in reading. Although trust is easier to extend in an atmosphere of success, it is accompanied by the pressure to maintain this high level of achievement. Meredith's professional decisions were validated not only by her principal but also by her children's achievement:

> Students did awesome on the state tests, and I think [the approach] had a lot to do with their success. It isn't easy to continue to do what's best for students [in this educational climate], but it's the right thing to do. You have to get past the 'bubble thing' [teaching students how to fill in the multiple choice format on answer sheets] and get back to best practice.

JEROD ANDERSON

Jerod Anderson has taught for nineteen years in the same school, with most of these years spent in fourth grade, his current assignment. Jerod did his undergraduate work in elementary education at a Christian liberal arts college and has earned sixty hours beyond a master's degree from a local university. His long tenure in the same context has earned him the respect of faculty and the four principals with whom he has served the community.

When asked if he would identify himself as a constructivist teacher, Jerod hesitatingly replied, "Yes, but I think I would be more comfortable calling myself a teacher who gets students to think critically about what they are learning. Even before the label [constructivist] became popular, I was prepared professionally to question routine educational practices and to help my students think similarly about their own curriculum. Over the years the label has changed, but that part of my practice has remained."

When one visits Jerod's classroom, one can see the development of critical thinking in action through the number of activities engaging his students. *Engagement* is the most pronounced characteristic of his practice. At the start of the day, groups of four to five students attempt to identify a historical figure or event tied to the day's date, using clues from various curricular areas. In order to do this, they must use geography ("this person was born in a city located at 48°50' N, 02°20' E"), mathematics ("today this person would be 372 years old"), and history. On other days they need to apply their scientific, musical, or artistic knowledge or their awareness of current events.

To solve the puzzle of the day, students walk about the room to check globes, reference books, their own textbooks, and the internet. Although this warm-up fosters a sense of teamwork, Jerod's primary purpose in setting up these initial collaborative competitions is to help his students see that learning is first and foremost multidisciplinary. But this is not an isolated event. Throughout the day, Jerod has incorporated individual, partner, and small group learning activities that offer early finishers a choice of mathematical, scientific, or reading challenges. His goal is to help students make the most of every learning minute through meaningful activity.

When asked to comment on the relationship between his faith and his instructional method, Jerod replied, "God has entrusted these students to me for the year. I need to help them develop to the best of my ability, using whatever approach I can." But holistic development does not come from merely addressing academic and social needs. In fact, it was through these small group and whole class hands-on competitions that Jerod perceived the need to address the moral development of his children.

"I used to award small prizes for winning competitions or for accomplishing these challenges," he said. "But I came to realize that even though I called my class 'people of character,' I was reinforcing a sense of materialism in their motivation." He explained that he often used game formats, such as Jeopardy, to review curricular content, with the winning team receiving small toys or candy for a prize. When they played the game once without Jerod distributing prizes, a student asked why they didn't "get paid." After reflecting on this comment, Jerod sought to address the problem by asking his students to think critically about doing things for the right reasons and then compare it to doing things because they were rewarded. He asked them if they could really call themselves "people of character" if they were only motivated by prizes. Based on this discussion, Jerod and his students revised the reward system to become a recognition system where winners were merely given a gold star on a name tag.

Occasionally, the class does compete for a prize, however the system has been significantly modified. Just as Jeopardy at times features celebrities competing for donations to various causes, Jerod's class similarly plays for charity. Sponsored by an anonymous donor, last year's class earned a two-thousand-dollar contribution to a local food pantry from their winning scores. This activity was also experiential learning, helping fourth grade students tangibly understand what it meant to be a person of character.

When asked if he utilizes constructivist approaches more or less frequently over the past nine years, Jerod reflected that he probably used them less frequently. Because of NCLB, he sees himself as using more direct instructional approaches than when he began his career, but he sees himself as being a better teacher for it.

"I am more organized and more certain that we have covered content. I still use critical thinking, but I believe I reach some of my struggling students better through direct instruction," he stated.

Jerod qualified his response, stating that his improved sense organization may be more directly related to his years of experience, but he characterized himself as being better able to monitor his students' growth through what he identified as a "balanced approach."

In considering how his faith affected his choices in the classroom, Jerod stated that his specific decisions are not necessarily unique to his Christian beliefs but that they reflect who he is in Christ:

> Another teacher with very different values and beliefs might choose to do some of the same things I have chosen to do, but I do them because I believe they honor God and His creation. These classroom approaches may not look very different between us, but mine are based on what I believe God has called me to do. Some of my choices are limited by being in a public school classroom, but I believe strongly in public education and its goals.

ANN COLLINS

Ann Collins has served in her district for thirteen years, teaching sixth grade science all this time at one middle school. Prior to this time, she graduated from a Christian liberal arts college and taught briefly in another district before serving with her husband as missionaries to

Pakistan. Ann has done limited amounts of teaching overseas during this period.

When asked if she would identify herself as a constructivist teacher, Ann stated that she was uncomfortable with the title because she believed in absolute truth. Ann stated that while her curriculum did not include highly controversial topics, she believed it was her responsibility to help her sixth grade students understand the difference between scientific fact and scientific theory. However, she aspired to utilize methods that reflected an active, student-directed focus in order to achieve this goal.

Since the implementation of NCLB, she used constructivist pedagogy less often, but believed that constructivist pedagogies are essential for truly understanding science. She clarified this statement by stating that learning in this discipline must be experiential, as hands-on as possible, and project oriented. But she qualified her use of constructivism in that her projects are not student selected; rather, they are clearly articulated by rubrics and must demonstrate mastery of the goals and standards associated with the unit. She felt there was no opportunity for students to explore their own questions on a topic because of the time constraints imposed by the district's unit-heavy curriculum.

In contrast to her early years, science education in the district was now much more externally controlled. Rather than using six major units and assessments collaboratively designed by science faculty at her school, teachers throughout the district were now required to use textbooks with their corresponding chapter and unit tests. Prior to this formalized textbook adoption, assessments were brief and focused on ten key concepts instructed in each unit. Consequently, she felt there was less time now to study any unit in depth since there were many more units to be covered throughout the year. This she regretted because she believed it is in taking the time to develop the deep questions within a unit that true science is practiced.

While Ann insisted that middle school students "do" science, she assessed that fewer elementary students enter middle school today with much prior hands-on experience. She was astounded to find a number of very capable young adolescents who struggled with lighting a match for one of her activities. Science, she regretted, had been marginalized in the elementary grades in the hopes of raising math and reading scores. She believed this move was shortsighted since many children, who would otherwise struggle in school, connected to learning through the wonder and active nature of science.

Because her middle school students' prior scientific knowledge had decreased over time, Ann now referred to her in-class assignments as "activities" rather than "experiments" since her students needed basic examples employing the scientific method. These activities included weighing balloons to measure air mass and burning candles inside variously sized beakers and recording how long they burned in order to see the effect of oxygen on combustion. Her goal in each of these activities was to enable her students to "see" the concept in practice and then discuss their findings in class. She devoted little of her class time to textbook reading, preferring to have kids active throughout the period.

If students needed assistance with reading the text, she preferred to have them come for help during lunchtime. This was the vehicle where Ann saw her Christian faith most affecting her curricular choices and her teacher-student relationships. She called this time "lunch bunch," offering an open invitation to students who needed help with science readings and makeup labs.

This program began when all science academic support classes were cancelled by the district in order to provide more math and reading instruction. Although she regretted this district move since struggling math and reading students engage in science learning because of its life connections and active format, she saw her lunchtime tutoring sessions as transforming her teaching. "Even though I never get to eat lunch with other teachers now, I really get to know my kids." Getting to know her kids involved academic instruction, counseling, conversation, and often just providing a safe place to do homework. Some of her students asked to complete work for other classes in her room. She welcomed them all, stating that this was a way she could be Jesus to her kids. Two students with special needs requested to eat lunch in her room everyday because it provided a calmer atmosphere than the cafeteria.

Three years ago, Ann took a leave of absence in order to assist her husband with relief efforts in Pakistan after a major earthquake there. Due to the devastation, large numbers of school-aged children had been relocated to Ann's assigned area in Pakistan. Part of her role was to provide professional development for teachers who had been recently hired to accommodate the increased school enrollment. Her task was to model effective science instruction, which she did using a constructivist approach.

According to Ann, this was a significant departure from the methods by which these teachers had been trained. Most learning in Pakistan, she stated, is equated with memorization. The learner there is never taught to question knowledge, merely repeat it. Setting up an environment to hypothesize and test one's hypothesis was antithetical to all other types of elementary or secondary level learning there. Ann found the teachers themselves initially hesitant to engage in her basic experiments. But once they did, they saw the value of conceptually understanding scientific principles over merely memorizing them. Although she doubted that this method transferred to other disciplines, she hoped that her influence in science instruction remained evident in science classrooms there.

CONCLUSIONS

Although these teachers instructed at different developmental levels, they shared several teaching philosophies that were evident in their classrooms. All three teachers reflected a concept of stewardship that guided their practice. They saw themselves as guardians of their students' time and trust. Across primary, upper elementary, and middle school levels, the educators sought to design and implement instruction that enhanced mastery of critical content while increasing students' ability to think and apply that knowledge. Each of the three perceived students to be created in God's image, and therefore instructing them carried a heavy responsibility. As educators they were accountable for far more than adequate yearly progress; they saw their work as holistic, having a sacred charge to do what was best for each individual academically, socially, and morally. They saw the importance of using constructivist pedagogy in order to develop the critical and cross-disciplinary thinking skills needed for a wise, full, and responsible life. They rejected utilizing an instructional methodology that was designed primarily to enhance test scores because it was inadequate for life preparation. They also favored constructivist learning because it brought out children's unique capacities, in contrast to many direct instructional approaches that tend to focus on uniformity and ensuring that every student meets minimal competencies.

Instructionally, all three were committed to collaborative and experiential learning. Across all levels, they valued students' questions in order to promote critical and creative thinking. All three worked to create a learning environment that was safe and inviting for student inquiry.

Each of the three saw the lasting value of their work in developing relationships and was opposed to policies that each perceived to not be in the best interests of all students. Ann saw the elimination of science support classes and the marginalization of science in the elementary curriculum is detrimental to the welfare of her students. She attempted to compensate for this by opening her classroom during the lunch period to provide this support on her own time. She also adjusted her curricular demands in order to meet students at their present experiential level.

Meredith cited the pressure to cover content at a fast pace as counter to the "deep learning" needed by young children and rejected this notion at both the primary and intermediate levels. She also regretted that in many classrooms gifted children's needs were seen as secondary to those who were not meeting state standards. She believed that in many districts, the system was failing these talented students through reduced programs and personnel and feared that these students would be "left behind" in developing their individual potential.

Although Jerod believed the influence of NCLB brought some benefits to his own instruction, he spoke against a system that indirectly teaches children to measure their value by standardized test performance. He also regretted that the current conversation around teaching is too often reduced to academics, neglecting the social, emotional, and ethical components of education.

As Christians, two of the three teachers were uncomfortable identifying themselves as constructivist teachers, preferring to be called teachers who promoted thinking or teachers who used this type of pedagogy. Their reluctance to identify with this title was due largely to their view that most adherents of constructivism reject the concept of absolute truth. Both educators regarded this philosophical foundation of constructivism as incompatible with their belief in the authority of Scripture, which contains God's ultimate truth.

While all three viewed students similarly, they each had their own perspective on the current educational climate. Meredith was strongly committed to constructivist pedagogies and felt administrative support to continue their use. Jerod believed that increased accountability caused him to use constructivist pedagogies somewhat less frequently but that he was a better teacher for it. Ann believed that she faced significant pressure to limit constructivist approaches to learning and felt her students learned less effectively because of it.

Perhaps there is a compensatory principle operating here as in Meredith's mathematics lesson. The amount of freedom to use time-consuming, experiential, and collaborative learning strategies is proportional to the grade level of instruction. As the curricular components expand in upper grades, the time to teach them well appears to compress proportionally.

When these teachers began their careers, they were at times required to justify their instructional choices within their faith communities. Ironically, today they find themselves defending them to members of their own professional communities. Another irony found in this study is Ann's attempts to help Pakistani teachers increase their constructivist pedagogies at the same time she finds their practice decreasing in her own American educational system. What stands out from these teachers' examples is not their allegiance to a set pedagogy but rather a concern for the child and the child's welfare. This concern, grounded in their faith, demand instructional goals that extend far beyond standardized test results.

REFERENCES

Brooks, J. G. (2006). Learning among the mandates. *Constructivist, 17*(1), 1–6.

Brooks, J. G., & Brooks, M. G. (1999). *In search of understanding: The case for constructivist classrooms*. Alexandria, VA: Association for Supervision and Curriculum Development.

Carson, D. W. (1996). *The gagging of God: Christianity confronts pluralism*. Grand Rapids, MI: Zondervan.

Fosnot, C. T. & Dolk, M. (2001). *Young mathematicians at work: Constructing number sense, addition and subtraction*. Portsmouth, NH: Heinemann.

Hyde, A. (2006). *Comprehending math: Adapting reading comprehension strategies to teach mathematics, K–6*. Portsmouth, NH: Heinemann.

Lederhouse. (2009). [A case study of three Christian public school teachers]. Unpublished raw data.

Piaget, J. (1970). *The science of education and the psychology of the child*. New York: Orion.

Vygotsky, L. (1978). *Mind in society: The development of higher psychological processes*. Cambridge, MA: Harvard University Press.

Wolterstorff, N. (2002). Teaching for tomorrow today. In G. G. Stronks and C. W. Joldersma (Eds.), *Educating for life: Reflections on Christian teaching and learning*. Grand Rapids, MI: Baker.

Zemelman, S., Daniels, H., & Hyde, A. (2005). *Best Practice: Today's standards for teaching and learning in America's schools*. Portsmouth, NH: Heinemann. (3rd ed.)

11

Guided Discovery Learning

Cindy Harvel

INTRODUCTION

Picture a classroom filled with flexible tubes lacing tables from floor to ceiling. Students are using metal spheres to roll down the clear plastic hoses, trying to find out how to design the tube to make their "roller coaster" the fastest or slowest depending on the lesson. Add a teacher that intermittently adds instruction as needed, sandwiching each step of trial and error with enough information to inform and pique curiosity, but not enough to give away the expected result. The resulting scenario pictures one example of an emerging pedagogy termed *guided discovery*.

DEFINITION OF GUIDED DISCOVERY LEARNING

Guided discovery learning is a constructivist instructional design model that marries the concept of discovery learning with principles from cognitive instructional design theory. Developed by Charles E. Wales (1978) at the Center for Guided Design, guided discovery was intended to be an improvement to the scaffolding process used in discovery learning. Providing the learner plenty of opportunities for deliberate practice and reflection, guided discovery at the same time provides the supporting information to search that content to satisfy the hungry mind and gratify curiosity.

Kozulin, Gindis, Ageyev, and Miller (2003), call guided discovery a middle ground, a happy medium, between linear didactic teaching and open-ended discovery learning. Using the foundational teachings of Dewey and Piaget, guided discovery calls for a collaborative partnership between instructor and learner. The teacher, like an excellent director to a tantalizing mystery, builds curiosity, provides background information and materials for learning, and then allows for the pregnant pause to allow students to discover and create meaning. If tension is too great and the facilitator senses frustration, increased scaffolding support is provided to build confidence and renew enthusiasm. This dance between the teacher and learner breathes life into learning.

Guided discovery, or guided design, as Wales and Stager (1978) label the pedagogy, combines traditional direct instruction with constructivist applications. In guided design, direct instruction is utilized by insisting that students are given an assignment with predetermined, specific content. These problems, activities, and the meaty lesson of direct instruction then couple with real-world problems and applications driven by social constructivism. The combination proves effective. The framework of a planned lesson "guides" instruction, but action learning fills the gaps between planned segments.

In the math classroom, Norman Labush (2008) describes the steps to utilizing guided discovery. Labush states on his mathematics website that "the teacher must provide all the necessary background knowledge to lead the student to the discovery. The student must recognize the method(s) to be used to make the discovery. To assure this, the teacher may become a model of discovery by demonstrating what the students are expected to do. In this way, guided discovery becomes the goal of the lesson."

There must be a constructive balance between the guidance provided and student discovery for optimal learning to take place. Leutner (1993) explored the idea of guided discovery in the context of e-learning utilizing computer generated simulations. In research involving eighty seventh- and eighth-grade students, advice from the facilitator helped verbal knowledge but actually decreased student performance. If the advice predominantly included background information, students benefited with long-term effects. The "guided" part of the discovery therefore, needs just the right balance between direct instruction and room for discovery. Too much guidance stifles the passion to learn. Too little guidance may leave the learner bewildered and unwilling to proceed with exploring the content.

THE DIFFERENCE BETWEEN DISCOVERY AND GUIDED DISCOVERY

Guided discovery was developed by Charles E. Wales at the Center for Guided Design at West Virginia University (Leutner, 1993). Discovery learning, proposed by Jerome Bruner (1967), paralleling work by Jean Piaget's models of education, is much older and calls for more independent exploration for content on the part of the student.

Discovery Learning

Based on inquiry, discovery learning expects the learner to construct his or her own learning agenda based on questions posed by the student. Because the student uses the foundation of her or his own past experience, new learning takes shape as the inquirer probes, tests, researches, and confirms the facts. By experimenting and wrestling with divergent results, the learner constructs new learning on that underlay of past experience. Bruner (1967) believed students would remember and own the content even though the process of obtaining that content might be more time consuming and tedious.

The advantages of discovery (Allen, 2002) learning can include the learning of time management as students fit discovery learning into the classroom setting, active engagement with content as learners manipulate material in research, a sense of independence as students construct their own learning, and, problem solving and research skills honed throughout the process of discovery. Other possible advantages of discovery learning, cited by Mosston (1972), include cognitive abilities such as hypothesizing, inquiring, inventing, analyzing and recognizing, synthesizing, and discovering, which are exercised as the learner wrestles with and tests material.

Disadvantages also accompany discovery learning. Kirschner, Sweller, and Clark (2006) criticize that discovery learning defies the tenets of cognitive load theory, and that learners cannot retain the amount of information needed to process the content. Critics have cited other disadvantages including the possibility of undetected misconceptions, student frustration, and lack of "worked examples" (Tuovinen & Sweller, 1999).

Guided Discovery

Guided discovery, in contrast, as shown in table 11.1, combines the action learning of discovery learning with the aid of scaffolding from the instructor to produce a rich, blended learning experience that recognizes the boundaries of cognitive load while encouraging the passion of student exploration.

The instructor develops a plan for instruction that includes prompts to guide the learner up the ladder of instruction. In between these "rungs," enticing the student to reach a bit higher, the learner is encouraged to engage in active learning fueled by inquiry. The instructor always keeps the goal in mind, and missteps by the student are caught and redirected to ensure correct information is placed on the foundation of existing student knowledge.

Table 11.1 Guided discovery versus discovery learning

Guided Discovery	Discovery Learning
Goal of instruction Further questions and discussion for future Scaffolding	Discovery
Analysis and synthesis of findings Guided action learning and discovery Scaffolding	Action learning
Student hypothesis Instructor-driven prompt	Student-driven question

FAITH-BASED GUIDED DISCOVERY LEARNING

As a faith-based educator, I must consider how constructivist theory meshes with guided discovery. Hiller (1998) maintains, in light of what he calls the "anastatic option," that constructivism is epistemologically sound pedagogy for the Christian educator. The anastatic option maintains that Christianity provides the scaffolding, the springboard, the trajectory for constructivist pedagogy. The Christian life, experienced as the power and presence of the Holy Spirit, is a launching pad for learning at its best. Hiller encourages Christians to not abandon the sound pedagogy of student-centered constructivist theory with the excesses of constructivism that defy that a body of truth exists apart from the learner. Hiller believes the two can coexist and even nurture one another.

Hiller contrasts instructors (those who teach through directed learning) with constructors (those who teach through individualized constructivist theory). "Instructors" tend to teach a class in a "one size fits all" mentality. "Constructors" vary their teaching to fit their students, helping individual learners to build upon a foundation of their own background knowledge, to further enhance learning. In guided discovery, the Christian teacher depends upon the power and counsel of the Holy Spirit to encourage each student to become the individual each was uniquely designed to be. In constructivism, making meaning takes priority over dispensing nuggets of knowledge. As a result, the Spirit-led teacher can assist each learner to make meaning of her or his accumulating knowledge.

Archer (1998) defines three types of constructivism: social constructivism, individual constructivism, and sociocultural constructivism. Social constructivists propose that knowledge is the result of group-made decisions. Knowledge to a social constructivist does not preexist the knowers. The individuals in the group construct knowledge during the course of their lives. Individual constructivists hold to Piaget's idea that through incremental development, the learner constructs individual knowledge through assimilation and accommodation with the real world. While Piaget believed there existed an independent reality uncovered by the learner, many individual constructivists would assume no such truth exists apart from the learner (Bhattacharya and Han, 2001). Sociocultural constructivists believe knowledge is constructed as Piaget's individual learner interacts with the group, collectively constructing knowledge. Stemming from the writings of Lev Vygotsky (1978), the sociocultural constructivist believes the individual is guided by cultural surroundings and is aided in learning by social interactions. It is this third type of constructivism that is reflected most with guided discovery. As the learner works, processes information, discusses, and interacts with the group, learning is constructed upon a foundation that is not just individual, but is itself composed of all the previous personal interactions that have taken place in the learner's lifetime. The Christian educator works with the empowerment of the Holy Spirit, within the body of Christ to encourage the student in the learning process.

E-LEARNING AND GUIDED DISCOVERY

Allen (2002) encourages those who support blending guided discovery methods with e-learning. Many online applications may initially appeal with glitzy design but actually offer poor pedagogy. These surface-sparklers only provide tired, linear, traditional cycles of poured-out information, with a process of "regurgitate, and cycle again."

Mott, McQuiggan, Lee, Lee, and Lester (2009) investigated the research of guided discovery through the use of an online coach, either a cartoon or real-life picture of an assistant in learning microbiology. This computer-generated assistant guided each task in the lesson. Like the paperclip helper in Microsoft, the coach in this curriculum helped learners as they were taught the scientific method. After becoming adept at the steps to scientific discovery, the caricaturized coach guided students as they delved into specific research tasks. Clark (2008) noted that students perform 24–48 percent more correct solutions in transfer tests when using a cartoon or realistically depicted coach, and 30 percent more correct solutions than groups that performed the task with no coach or cartoon guide. These computer-designed coaches helped to guide instruction by providing the needed scaffolding to encourage students as they went about the work of problem solving.

Aleven, Stahl, Schworm, Fischer, and Wallace (2003) warn that the "on-demand help" of many online interactive environments actually impedes rather than helps learning. Learners need guidance in asking for guidance online: they need scaffolding for developing the metacognitive and cognitive skills needed for effective help-seeking in an online environment.

A MODEL IN CHRIST

Christ modeled guided instruction in the discipleship and training of his followers. The Gospels repeatedly relate stories where Christ told, then modeled, then exhorted his students to go and do likewise. He started by using background experience his learners were familiar with. His tales of lost pearls, wandering sheep, fruitful vines, and flavorful salt equipped his audience with familiar foundations upon which he skillfully provided a framework for spiritual building.

In the parable of the sower (Matt 13:3–23; Mark 4:2–20; Luke 8:4–15; Luke 8:4–15), Christ tells the story of a farmer spreading seed for planting. He told the story to a large crowd by the lakeshore. But after the telling was completed, he offered a bit of guided instruction to those twelve he was intentionally discipling. As he said these things, he called out, "He who has ears, let him hear." The disciples came to him and asked, "Why do you speak to the people in parables?" (Matt 13:9–10). Jesus proceeded to spell out the parable seed by seed, elaborating the metaphor and helping the twelve to apply the gospel to their foundational situation in a community where survival depended on proper planting techniques.

Christ's guided instruction did not end with the narrative, but proceeded with active learning and discovery. "Then Jesus went around teaching from village to village. Calling the Twelve to him, he sent them out two by two and gave them authority over evil spirits" (Mark 6:7). This specific instruction of teaching to be teachers was not limited to the twelve, but extended to his hillside classroom. "After this the Lord appointed seventy-two others and sent them two by two ahead of him to every town and place where he was about to go" (Luke 10:1).

Discovery followed their action as the disciples came back with the delight of a learned lesson. The seventy-two returned with joy and said, "Lord, even the demons submit to us in your name" (Luke 10:17). Jesus did not let the lesson end there, however; he seized the teachable moment and provided additional scaffolding when he replied, "I saw Satan fall like lightning from heaven. I have given you authority to trample on snakes and scorpions and to overcome all the power of the enemy; nothing will harm you. However, do not rejoice that the spirits submit to you, but rejoice that your names are written in heaven" (Luke 10:18–20). With the end of this beautiful guided discovery lesson, he refocuses their excitement toward the true goal of the lesson rather than the temptation to glory in the ministry these followers were about to engage in.

OUR BRAIN AND GUIDED DISCOVERY LEARNING

Instructors need to design curriculum with cognitive load theory in mind. Tuovinen and Sweller (1999) state that effective instruction needs to take into consideration the "architecture of the student mind" (p. 334). Norman states that "human short-term memory can comfortably retain only five to seven" bits of information (1990, p. 65). In order for short-term memory to contain all that is needed in a learning segment, instruction needs to be designed so as to ensure the content being presented is able to be managed in the working memory. If too much content is presented simultaneously, short-term memory cannot adequately manage what is necessary to eventually process it into long-term memory.

In designing teaching, the instructor needs to keep in mind certain principles (Clark & Mayer, 2003) to best get the information across to those who will be learning: the multimedia principle, the contiguity principle, the modality principle, the redundancy principle, the coherence principle, and the personalization principle.

The Multimedia Principle

When teaching content, the instructor should use graphics that enhance the text. Research (Clark & Mayer, 2003) shows that relevant graphics aid in learning in a technical environment. Pictures should not be used to merely decorate the page or screen, but contribute to the learning that takes place. Clark and Mayer cite that in research using ten different studies, "people who learned from both words and graphics produced between 55 percent to 121 percent more correct solutions to transfer problems than people who learned from words alone" (p. 61).

The Contiguity Principle

When presenting graphics, the contiguity principle reminds the instructor to place those graphics in close proximity to the words they illustrate. Research shows that teachers need to avoid four pitfalls in design: (1) never separate visuals from text so far that the learner needs to scroll, (2) never separate visuals needed for practice from the question, (3) never separate secondary linked information that covers what needs to be found on the first screen, and (4) never separate directions from the application (Clark & Mayer, 2003). Presenting information separated from key text or graphics causes the cognitive overload previously mentioned.

The Modality Principle

Because of that same cognitive overload (Clark & Mayer, 2003), an instructor should use audio in place of visual text in addition to the visual graphics. Words will be coming in through the auditory channel of the brain, while visuals will be coming in through the visual channel, instead of words and pictures coming in through the visual channel. The more modes or paths by which learning may enter the brain, the better.

The Redundancy Principle

The instructor should avoid saying words while printed words appear at the same time. Don't add written text to audio text. In research, when comparing groups that tested the redundancy principle, Clark and Mayer (2003) point out that the "animation and narration group generated between 41 to 114 percent more solutions than the animation and onscreen text group, even though both groups received identical animation and words" (p. 93). So for example, if you are adding audio to lecture, use graphics, rather than replicating the verbal words verbatim with identical text.

The Coherence Principle

The coherence principle teaches the instructor to avoid all distractions in the presentation. No extra unrelated stories, graphics, music, or other sounds should take focus away from the instruction taking place. Extraneous information adds, once again, to the cognitive load, taking up too much space in working memory. Clark and Mayer (2003) point out that even in 1913, Dewey "argued that adding interesting adjuncts to an otherwise boring lesson will not promote deep learning" (p. 117).

The Personalization Principle

Research indicates that a conversational teaching style, coupled with an animated or pictorial learning agent increases retention of information. Students will work harder to understand information presented in a conversational rather than formal style (Clark & Mayer, p. 142). In two isolated experiments, learning agents improved performance in student groups. (There was no significance whether the character was in cartoon or lifelike image.) Again, the instructor needs to remember that the learning agent needs to be used to complement learning, not to distract from the learning.

DEVELOPING GUIDED DISCOVERY INSTRUCTION

Research shows that review allows students to better retain the material for an extended period. Mayer found that when instructors provide rehearsal opportunities for working memory to become encoded in long-term memory, learning is impacted in positive ways (Mayer, pp. 149–171). Studies by Ericsson, Krampe, and Tesch-Romer (1993) confirm that "deliberate practice" helps retain information and distinguishes amateurs from experts.

Using Evaluation Instruments
to Determine Instructional Problems

Feedback needs to be addressed from the learner and the instructor's perspective. From the learner's perspective, instruction should be designed in such a way that some sort of positive feedback is given as encouragement. This feedback can be verbal from the instructor or automatic from a computer tutorial. The student learning the content should, from the design of instruction, be able to receive feedback that will help to confirm and validate that learning is taking place. Constructs, in grades, discussion, peer review, and so on can be embedded in instruction to give helpful feedback.

Feedback drives instruction. If error occurs, feedback enables the instructor to determine if it was because of a misunderstanding of content, or a misunderstanding of procedure. Axelson, McGraw, and McEntee suggest a triangulation of observation (observe what the student does), interpretation (determine understanding or misunderstanding), and cognition (understanding what the student knows) to grasp how much instruction has occurred.

Bright and Joyner (2004) conclude that principles of feedback should include (1) focusing on the important idea, (2) being specific to the task, (3) starting from where students understand, and (4) supporting conceptual development. Inferences from the data of individual students need to be made through assessment, interviews, and observation. Questioning should be intentional and contrived to be engaging, refocusing, and clarifying. Assessment and feedback should be data driven to move the student forward in the sophistication of their thinking of the content taught.

Good pedagogy and curriculum design is the meat of the teaching. Guided discovery is simply the container in which to serve the meal. Questions, according to research in classroom assessment (Bright and Joyner, 2004), allow us to observe, classify, and intermediate the next step of efficient instruction. Assessment can be utilized to help students learn both concepts and procedures. In keeping with Bright and Joyner (2004), *concepts* include reasoning and understanding of the major ideas. *Procedures* utilize the manipulation of that understanding. Errors could occur in both *concepts* and *procedures* in two different ways. The student could make mistakes indicating they misunderstood *substance,* the internal understanding of the concepts, or they could err in their *presentation.* In other words, they may have understood the concept but were unable to communicate that understanding. When observing student problem solving during guided discovery, effort needs to be made to distinguish between these types of errors, to give proper feedback, and then to reteach according to the specific need.

INTRODUCTION TO A RESEARCH EXAMPLE

Living examples of the benefits of guided discovery abound in every subject area. Although the roots of guided discovery grow rich in the subjects of mathematics and science, applications have broadened to include language, natural and social sciences, music, and art. The following example involving university students and faculty illustrates how learners chose guided discovery over other methods of instruction while being trained in creating electronic portfolios.

A Practical Application

During the fall semester of 2007, I performed research at a small midwestern university to determine which means of training for an internet-based portfolio development system, Chalk and Wire, was most satisfying to faculty, students, and cooperating teachers (Harvel, 2008). Those building portfolios, both faculty and students, were free to use the discovery method in building their portfolios. Previous background knowledge with computer programs could have enabled portfolio builders to construct their online portfolios systematically on their own through discovery learning. In addition, other implementation was at student and faculty disposal to build their portfolios. Scaffolding strategies included: training workshops advertised at set times and locations, online instruction, hard-copy instruction, one-on-one help from the administrator, and one-on-one help from members of a trained assistance team composed of students.

A fifteen-question survey was given to 171 assessors. Fourteen questions gathered quantitative data, one qualitative. Four cross tabulations completed with a chi square test for independence showed that faculty and cooperating teachers ratings of their success using Chalk and Wire. Qualitative data from the faculty survey question, from the student assistant team survey, and from six interviews revealed several emerging themes:

1. E-portfolio implementation is a formative process in which constituents seemed to prefer continued guidance in training as opposed to the discovery process.

2. All constituents desire clear, easily accessible instructions, conveyed in a simple, user-friendly design, with mapped directions in syllabi for artifact location, available in hardcopy as well as online in a variety of multimedia formats.

3. Time is a valuable commodity.

4. Users appreciate the benefits of e-portfolios such as portability, ease of use, formative and summative reflection, and experience with cutting-edge technology.

5. Advice for improvement included the desire for verification when work has been completed, continuation of educational credit when applicable, and the desire for intermittent use in every class.

6. Problems that surfaced included an unawareness of available help and a consensus that the software changeover was stressful.

7. Trainees desired trainers to be confident, knowledgeable, relaxed, willing to give one-on-one help, available when needed, kind, patient, encouraging, persistent, and flexible.

Recommendations for future research include investigations in best practices regarding length of training times, increasing awareness of available help, and training cooperating teachers.

Embedded in each emerging theme is a recurring reminder that in a variety of ways, students and faculty desired scaffolding and guided instructions to carry out their training. Even though instructions were available after the initial training in both online and hard copy form to view as the trainees needed, participants expressed a desire to not just be allowed to discover information on their own but had a definite preference for guided discovery learning.

Qualitative interviews revealed several traits that trainees desired in guides. Learners wanted administrative and student trainers to not only be confident, persistent, and knowledgeable, but also to be willing to give one-on-one help. They expressed the need for trainers with compassion, who gave words of encouragement and kindness in a relaxed manner. Respondents voiced a desire for a trainer who was able to discern when trainees wanted quick answers from a sage on the stage and when they wanted to have a guide on the side model instruction.

CONCLUSION

Guided discovery learning walks the tightrope, balancing challenge with assistance, independence with support, and encouraging trust of the learner's discovering ability with constructive advice meted out in a systematic, timely manner. The guide needs to be sensitive to the learner, helping only when needed, stimulating the learner to an interdependent quest for knowledge and understanding as the learner intermittently relies on peers, instructor, supporting materials, and background knowledge to be used as stepping stones to reach understanding in the learning process.

REFERENCES

Allen, Michael. (2002). Discovery learning: Repurposing an old paradigm. *LTI Newsline, 17*(17).

Aleven, V., Stahl, E., Schworm, S., Fischer, F., & Wallace, R. (2003). Help seeking and help design in interactive learning environments. *Review of Educational Research, 73*(7), 277–320.

Archer, A. (1998). *Constructivism and Christian teaching.* Presented at the 23rd International Faith and Learning Seminar, University of Eastern Africa, Baraton, Kenya.

Bhattacharya, K., & Han, S. (2001). Piaget and cognitive development. In M. Orey (Ed.), *Emerging Perspectives on Learning, Teaching, and Technology.* Retrieved from http://projects.coe.uga.edu/epltt/

Bright, G. W., & Joyner, J. M. (2004–2005). Classroom assessment in middle grades and high school. *NCSM Journal of Mathematics Education Leadership, 7*(2), 11–17. Retrieved from http://www.fi.uu.nl/catch/documents/AssessmentPaper1999.doc

Bruner, J. S. (1967). *On knowing: Essays for the left hand.* Cambridge, MA: Harvard University Press.

Clark, R., & Mayer, R. E. (2008). *E-learning and the science of instruction.* San Francisco: Jossey-Bass. (2nd ed.)

Clark, R. E. (1995). Media and method. *Educational Technology Research and Development,* 42(3), 7–10. Retrieved from http://www.springerlink.com /content/847312x345gp0374/

de Jong, T., & van Joolingen, W. (1998). Scientific discovery learning with computer simulations of conceptual domains. *Review of Educational Research, 68*(2), 179–201.

Ericsson, K. A., Krampe, R. T., & Tesch-Romer, C. (1993). The role of deliberate practice in the acquisition of expert performance. *American Psychological Association, 100,* 363–406.

Harvel, C. (2008). *Faculty training in developing an e-Portfolio system for formative and summative assessment* (Doctoral dissertation, University of Nebraska at Lincoln). Retrieved from http://digitalcommons.unl.edu/ir information/1

Hiller, H. F. (1998). *The anastatic option: Christian theological scaffolding for constructivist pedagogy* (Doctoral dissertation, University of Calgary). Retrieved from http: //dspace.ucalgary.ca/handle/1880/25997?mode=full

Kirschner, P. A., Sweller, J., & Clark, R. E. (2006). Why minimal guidance during instruction does not work: An analysis of the failure of constructivist, discovery, problem-based, experiential, and inquiry-based teaching. *Educational Psychologist, 41*(2), 75–86.

Kozulin, A., Gindis, B., Ageyev, V., & Miller, S. (2003). *Vygotsky's educational theory in cultural context.* New York: Cambridge University Press.

Labush, N. (2008). *Math for everyone.* Retrieved from http://www.netrox.net/~labush /math.htm

Leutner, D. (1993). Guided discovery learning with computer-based simulation games: Effects of adaptive and non-adaptive instructional support. *Learning and Instruction, 3*(2), 113–132.

Mosston, M. (1972). *Teaching: From command to discovery.* Belmont, CA: Wadsworth.

Mott, B. W., McQuiggan, S. W., Lee, S., Lee, S. Y., & Lester, J. C. (2009). Narrative-centered environments for guided exploratory learning. *Proceedings of the Fourteenth International Conference on Artificial Intelligence and Education.* Retrieved from http://www4.ncsu.edu/~bwmott/papers/crystal-island-abshl-06.pdf

Norman, D. A. (1990). *The design of everyday things.* New York: Doubleday.

Tuovinen, J. E., & Sweller, J. (1999). A comparison of cognitive load associated with discovery learning and worked examples, *Journal of Educational Psychology, 91*(2), 334–341. Retrieved from http://cat.inist.fr/?aModele=afficheN&cpsidt=1862572

Vygotsky, L. (1978). *Mind in society: The development of higher psychological processes.* London: Harvard University Press.

Wales, C. E., & Stager, R. A. (1978). *The guided design approach.* Englewood Cliffs, NJ: Educational Technology Publications.

12

A Constructive, Interactive Approach to Learning

Martha E. MacCullough

INTRODUCTION

THE QUESTION, HOW SHOULD teachers teach? presupposes an answer to the age-old question, how do humans learn? Various answers to this age-old question are offered by learning theorists. Teachers, however, have not always examined the question or the possible answers and are therefore, at times, swept away by every new "wind of doctrine," or else they become close-minded to new research and new ideas. This chapter is designed to help educators think through the question, how do humans learn? in order to promote effective teaching that mirrors, as much as possible, human nature. Assume that you visit the teachers' lounge. You may hear the following conversations among the school teachers.

Marge: Well, what do you think about the article our principal asked us to read on constructivist teaching? I don't think I can buy into this approach. Did you know that constructivism champions the process of knowing and ignores the content?

Jason: Really? I thought that the focus in the article was on something being "constructed" and materials or content are needed for construction. Aren't they?

Marge: Yes, I guess, but the theory is all about what students do in constructing their own personal knowledge and not about the material to be learned. There are no standards other than the personal constructions of the learner. Our subject matter curriculum committee will be out of work.

Tamara: That may not be so bad. I'm on that committee! Look, anyone can use constructivist methods. You don't have to buy into the theory behind it.

Jason: You might be right, Tamara. But, what are constructivist methods anyway? I thought that constructivism was a theory of learning rather than teaching. I am a teacher; I just use what works! Let's have some coffee. This fad will blow over just like the last ten!

Apparently there are conversations similar to the one above in schools around the country today as well as in international settings. My students and educators from Brazil and France voice some of the same understandings or misunderstandings related to constructivism that I hear from private and public educators in the United States. The issue under review in the teachers' lounge, as you might have recognized, reflects a lack of understanding the nature of constructivism and its applications.

Constructivism is a learning theory that tries to answer the question, how do humans learn? It stands in stark contrast to a reactionist theory such as behaviorism. From a philosophical point of view, constructivism is an instructional choice that holds to a set of beliefs that address the nature of the human learner/knower and the nature and source of knowledge. As such, constructivist theories present worldview issues that must be examined by each worldview, including biblical Christianity. Instructional choices come from somewhere. One's underlying beliefs should inform decisions about overall approaches to teaching. Teachers who are serious about building their work upon a solid foundation will not be satisfied with choices and practices that contradict their beliefs. Constructivism, as the reader may have discerned from other chapters in this book, presents both potentials and problems to be examined.

The focus in this chapter is on the constructivist understanding of the learner as "interactive" as opposed to autonomously active or simply passive. Educators who believe one of the latter two descriptors, that the human being relates to the environment in the learning process as, either an active or a passive agent, have been at war for more than 100 years. Even today, most educational articles address the problems in education as being related to passive versus active learning approaches.

This includes many articles on constructivism. If the resolution fails, the war will be continued.

Educational theory tends to swing back and forth between each of these polar views. As my students read educational journal articles, they identify the underlying beliefs of the authors and critique the research or conclusions in light of their own worldview. At times they agree with authors who hold that there is information, eternal truths, objective knowledge, and reality that exist outside the knowing mind and prior to experience. However, the same educator or student will also agree with authors who espouse the active participation and internal construction of the learner while acknowledging the inherent limits in knowing. There are elements and emphases in each viewpoint that are appropriate for "biblically-rooted" educators. Selection, however, is not arbitrary. Christian educators bring to the study of instructional theory and practice their Christian philosophy. Within the boundaries of these beliefs one is free to choose from among the practical options that fit with a Christian worldview.

CONFUSION ABOUT POTENTIALS AND PROBLEMS RELATED TO CONSTRUCTIVISM

Here is an example of a well-written paragraph taken from a Phi Delta Kappa Fastback, *Constructivist Teaching*, (Zahorik, 1995) that helps the reader understand some aspects of decision making but may also lead to some confusion in the selection of pedagogical applications.

> Deciding about constructivist teaching, or deciding about any instructional procedure, is a matter of examining possible instructional methods to determine which are consistent with one's beliefs. Research and theory are helpful in identifying ways to teach. But teachers need to decide for themselves which techniques they will and will not use. When reduced to their essential character, these decisions deal with beliefs about students, their human qualities and learning processes, and with beliefs about knowledge, its form and function. If the beliefs about students and knowledge embedded in the technique or practice match the beliefs the teacher has about the students and knowledge, the technique will be one that fits the teacher. In order to make decisions about constructivist teaching, *two views of students and two views of knowledge are especially important.* (italics added, p. 33)

While the above quote indicates that there are two key views of the student and two views of knowledge, there are at least three of each. Morris Bigge and Samuel Shermis (2004) identify a third view of human nature and learning that may help to solve the one-hundred-year war between active and passive learning. Bigge and Shermis (2004) identify the reasons for various interpretations of experimental research in the field of psychology: "These differences appear to stem from disagreements over the fundamental nature of human beings and their relationship to their environments and the nature of motivation and perception" (p. 45). They go on to warn the educator, "A psychologist's philosophical leaning may not only determine the kinds of experiments one conducts but also may influence the conclusions one draws from the evidence that is secured through experimentation" (p. 45). It is wise, therefore, to discern the underlying assumptions of the researcher before adopting applications related to conclusions.

THREE VIEWS OF HUMAN LEARNING

Constructivism assumes that something inside the learner and something outside work together in the learning event. However, the focus in constructivism seems to be on the construal or construction inside the learner. In that theory, there is either no attempt to affirm an external world that exists as separate from the knower, as Ernst von Glasersfeld's (1995) view suggests, or there is a noncommittal attitude that one need not affirm or deny a world that exists independent of the experiencing learner when developing a purely psychological system, as Bigge and Shermis (2004) suggest. Constructivist positions that deny an independent reality outside the knowing mind or simply ignore the issue altogether, have been responsible, in part, for discouraging some Christian educators from considering the positive concepts of constructivism. This is because they focus on what the learner psychologically makes of the environment or incoming information rather than focusing on both the learner's inside capacity to construct understandings and meanings and the outside factors affecting that construction. This is the point at which a strong position on the interactive nature of the human and learning may help those who are tempted to ignore the insights of constructivists because of their views on the source of knowledge and reality, to look again. A Christian educator may bring his or her worldview to the research and select and use the elements that make sense.

James White (2006) addresses the issue of a great divide when it comes to approaches to thinking that have shaped discourse throughout the ages. In *A Mind for God*, he writes, "the chasm is simple: there is either something outside of ourselves that we must take into account or there is not. The Christian mind is a mind that operates under the belief that there is something outside of ourselves that we must take into account. There is a God" (p. 21). One conclusion, then, for the "Christian mind" might be that, while there is much to appreciate from constructivist approaches, we do not have the luxury of ignoring something that exists outside the knowing mind in its own right even when we are studying how humans learn.

Cognitive interactive learning is a "constructive" theory, as opposed to a "reactive" theory. As a framework for understanding human learning, it acknowledges the innate capacity of the human being to act upon incoming information using prior knowledge, experiences, and language facility (or lack thereof) to construct understandings, meanings, and knowledge. In this composite description, one thing is clear: both inside and outside factors are operating together in the learning event. Constructivists of all subcamps hold to the interactive actional nature rather than the passive/reactive or autonomously active nature. To constructivists, the human learner is certainly not passive, and while the construction process is an active process, there must be something for the human to reach out to, to select, and to bring in to process and construct meaning. This view of the human as interactive offers a third view to present in the one-hundred-year war in education. The pendulum swing between active and passive must now take into account a third, mutually opposing view—interactive.

Bigge and Shermis (2004) use the term *actional nature* to refer to the nature of the relationship between humans and their environment and to refer to the source of human motivation as inside, outside, or inside triggered by either inside or outside factors. Those who hold that humans are active in their actional nature believe that underlying psychological characteristics are inborn; learning comes from forces inside the person. The environment is simply a location for natural unfoldment. Those who hold that humans are basically passive in their actional nature believe that human characteristics are determined primarily by the environment, by forces outside the person. The human is simply a reactor to the environment. Those who hold that the human is interactive in actional nature do not equate learning with the simple unfoldment of inner urges nor with the conditioning process that works on the human being from without only. They believe that psychological characteristics arise as humans take in information from an outside world and try to make sense out of it by processing the information using their innate capacity to know and to learn (Bigge & Shermis, 2004). The three views of human learning are summarized in the table below.

Table 12.1 Three views of human learning

	Active	Passive	Interactive
Relation to environment	Underlying human characteristics are inborn. Environment is merely a location for unfoldment of what is within. Motivation is solely from within.	Human characteristics are primarily products of the environment. Behaviors are the result of outside forces. Humans are nonpurposive. "Motivation" must come from outside in the form of reinforcement.	Human characteristics result from the person making sense of the physical and social environment. Person-environment reciprocal or simultaneous relationship. Motivation is a reciprocal process. Inside is often triggered by outside factors.
Proponents	Rousseau Pestalozzi Froebel Maslow	Skinner Thorndike Watson	Dewey Tolman Vygotsky Bruner Bandura Bigge and Shermis (2004) developmentalists such as Piaget

Teaching model	Draw knowledge out. Instruction moves from activity to activity to activity, with the focus on the enjoyment of thinking and doing.	Put knowledge in. Instruction moves from telling to explaining to testing to reinforcing (grading) with the focus often on the reinforcer, the grade.	Engage the mind. Provide (make available) new information through exploration and explanation. Instruction moves between student processing and construction activities with ongoing assessment (MacCullough, 2008, p. 21).

UNDERSTANDING THE CONCEPT OF CONSTRUCTIVE INTERACTIVE APPROACH

The term *interactive* is often misconstrued and thought of as simply social interaction, talk, cooperative learning, discussions, and the like. Ask any group of teachers to identify which of the statements below fit with their idea of interactive learning, and most will say that all of them do.

- Cooperative learning groups using project and discussion methods

- A class discussion where all are involved together

- At least some time for questions is planned into the lesson (at the beginning, middle, or at the end)

- Creative activities planned by the teacher

- Technology in the classroom

However, interactive learning is more than encouraging student discussions, social interaction, and cooperative learning; beginning a lesson with a question to be answered by one pupil or questions and answers at the end of a lesson; or using interactive technology.

A teacher who has not understood the concept of the "interactive" nature of the pupil and learning might speak like this: "*Well, sometimes students are passive when I am talking and they are listening and other times they are active when they are doing something or talking to each other. Don't you think they can be both passive and active?*"

The answer is no. This confused teacher is referring to methods that are physically active or passive. The three options for the actional nature, passive, active, and interactive, are mutually opposed and refer to the way the mind works in the learning event even during a lecture or reading to find information. The appearance of cognitive science (the forerunner of constructivism) on the educational scene has provided a robust concept that might help us to better understand human learning and thus teaching. The term *interactive* connotes more than a mix or balance between passive and active. It refers to a different way of looking at the nature of the student. In describing the way the mind works in the learning process, the focus is equally on inside factors and outside factors. Constructivist approaches and the interactive actional nature overlap. Constructivism presupposes that the learner constructs as he or she selects from the environment (outside factors) and begins to process and construct meanings and understandings (inside factors).

Behaviorism, the instructional theory that dominated much of the twentieth century, holds that the human actional nature is passive in relation to the environment and that learning happens primarily because of outside factors (the teacher, the text, the DVD, the reinforcers). The learning model derived from this belief is one of outside stimuli soliciting a response or reaction. Future responses (the learning) are determined by the skilled conditioner-teacher and environmental reinforcement. The teacher is everything. The model for teaching is very teacher-centered.

Humanistic theorists that follow the views of the eighteenth-century romantic naturalists Rousseau and Froebel and the modern romantics and existentialists of the 1960s usually hold to natural unfoldment. They believe that the human actional nature is active and that learning occurs primarily because of inside factors naturally unfolding. The environment is simply a location for learning. Learning is autonomous and developmental. The student is everything. The model for teaching is very child or student centered!

Early twentieth-century cognitive interactionists reacting against the behaviorist view of human nature as passive, reactive, and nonpurposive used the term *active learner* to describe their position. This was the prevailing opposing view at the time. Thus the pendulum continued to swing between passive and active and the war did not subside.

With continued research that focused on mental processes that could be inferred from behavior (a scientific approach), a new term emerged to describe the human as one who learns by reaching out to what is available (teacher, text, other students, physical environment) and by using prior knowledge, innate capacities, and language facility to begin to make sense of new information. Another descriptor was necessary; hence, interactive. While there are many educators today whose underlying beliefs are characterized by the terms passive and active, the more recent descriptor has great potential.

A strong interactive position provides an opportunity for the Christian educator to avoid the position of theories that hold that the human is either an autonomous creator of reality or a mechanical, mindless reactor to the environment. One may hold, rather, that the human comes equipped with the innate capacity to know and learn. The world around the learner provides something to know. Both inside and outside factors are vital. The student, the curriculum, and the teacher are in dynamic interplay in the learning process. The model for teaching that arises out of this underlying belief might be more accurately labeled learning-centered rather than teacher-centered or child-centered. The assumption is that the student learner is learning something!

DEVELOPING A TEACHING MODEL FROM A CONSTRUCTIVE INTERACTIVE APPROACH

It is not really accurate to speak of "interactive teaching" any more than it is accurate to speak of "constructivist teaching." Both terms are about learning. However, if one holds to a view that something inside the learner and something outside work together in the learning process, this belief will guide in the development of an overall approach to teaching and in the selection of methods used to carry out the learning plan. Thus, one may develop an approach that is the logical outcome of underlying beliefs.

Take behaviorism as an example. When interviewed by David Goleman (1987) for the *New York Times* in 1987, B. F. Skinner's response to an inquiry related to cognitive and information processing theories was to declare, "The cognitive revolution is a search inside the mind for something that is not there. You can't see yourself process information. Information processing is an inference from behavior and a bad one at that." Skinner never changed his beliefs about the nature of the learner even after the cognitive revolution had taken hold in America. His stimulus response approach to learning lead to an overall teaching model that became:

- Teacher tells.

- Teacher expects students to take notes exactly as given.

- Teacher tests expecting exact answers as given in the notes.

- Teacher reinforces (after the lesson).

On the other hand, Friedrich Froebel (father of the kindergarten) held this belief:

> "All the child is ever to be and become, lies in the child, and can be attained only through development from within, outward. The purpose of teaching and instruction is to bring ever more out of man rather than to put more and more into man." He also said, "Humans unfold like a flower" (in Weber, 1969, p. 279).

Thus a teaching approach for unfoldment (humanistic) theory might look like this:

- Student interest and needs guide activities as the child unfolds.

- Students learn through their own prompting and need no prompting from outside.

- Student activities involve the student in the student's own learning and development.

- Student enjoyment and fun are the focus! Feelings and emotions are central.

- Students are naturally motivated. There is no need to motivate.

The classroom environment is simply a location for student activity.

No wonder the competing theories of learning at war for over one hundred years have been between teacher- or content-centered versus student-centered. Conversations in the teacher's lounge and on some school boards might proceed like the scenario below as educators take sides:

Teacher one: Well, my goal is to teach children!

Teacher two: What do you teach them?

Teacher one: I teach them to think!

Teacher two: Think about what?

Teacher one: Well, they are learning to learn.

Teacher two: Learn what? Look, if you elementary teachers taught kids concepts, rules, and skills, the basics of geography, the framework for history, the basic generalizations of science and math, we middle school and high school teachers would not have to go all the way back to ground zero in our subjects when you send them to us!

Teacher one: Maybe so, but if our focus was like yours, we would be delivering you a bunch of academic clones and psychologically stressed students! Kids are individuals. Personal development is the primary goal of education.

And the war goes on. Do you hear any of your colleagues in this conversation?

An interactive constructive approach would add a third dimension to the conversation above. Assuming that a Christian educator is interested in examining various views before committing to a teaching approach, how does one decide? How might a Christian determine which of the three views of human nature, for example, fits best with the view of humans as revealed in the Scriptures? Upon close examination of God's Word we find that the human is made in the image of God with the capacity to learn and the capacity to seek and know truth. We find, as well, that the one in whose image we are created has also provided something outside of ourselves to know: all of his creation and himself (reality). Christian philosopher Gordon Clark (1981), put it this way, "God has fashioned both the mind and the world so that they harmonize" (p. 316). A biblical view suggests that truth (true information) exists *outside* the knowing mind and can be known, in spite of human limits. The mind (*inside*) has been created with the capacity to learn and come to know. Reason would inform us that learning requires inside *and* outside factors. Furthermore, humans may construe correctly or incorrectly. Ongoing assessment, new information, and opportunities to reorganize and change, are vital in learning. The interactive constructivist view, with a focus on inside and outside factors, leaves room to preserve the concept that reality/truth exists outside the knowing mind as well as the concept that human inside processing and construction of meaning are essential in learning.

Perhaps an accurate view of the actional nature may be inferred from the teaching incidents of Christ. For example, in his teaching ministry, one may readily see his expectations related to the inside processing of information and the receptivity of his teachings that came from outside the learner. On one occasion a lawyer, wishing to trap Jesus, asked him about eternal life. Jesus questioned the lawyer about his prior knowledge of the law. The student gave the right response: "Love the Lord your God with all your heart and with all your soul and with all your strength and with all your mind; and love your neighbor as yourself" (Luke 10:27). Jesus replied, "Do these and you will live" (Luke 10:28). Not satisfied, the student, wishing to justify himself, continued with the question, "Who is my neighbor?" (Luke 10:29). Jesus told the story of a good Samaritan. After the story, Jesus asked the student which of the three in the story he thought was neighbor of the man in need. The teacher was providing information (the story) but assuming that the student would process it and draw a conclusion! His overall approach was interactive. He challenged the mind (inside) with outside information and expected the student to understand and construct meaning.

On another occasion, Jesus asked the question, "Who do men say that I am?" (Matt 16:13). The disciples responded, using prior knowledge, that some believed he was John the Baptist, Elijah, or some other prophet. Jesus asked, "Who do you say I am?" (Matt 16:15). Peter, speaking perhaps for the group, declared, "You are the Christ! The Son of the Living God." (Matt 16:16). Now Jesus knew that the answer given by stimulus response (Who am I? The Christ) was the right answer; however, he also knew that Peter had not constructed complete understanding. The teacher arranged a field trip several days later. Jesus took Peter, James, and John to a mountain where Moses and Elijah appeared to Jesus and the three disciples. Peter revealed a misconstrual in his thinking when he spoke and asked to put up three shelters, one for Jesus, one for Moses, one for Elijah (Matt 17:4). Peter, the student, revealed his misconception through communication. He did not understand that Jesus was the Christ, the Son of God and in a different category (the God-man) than the others. Moses and Elijah were seen no more but Jesus appeared in his glorified form, and God the Father spoke (direct instruction), "This is my son . . . , listen to Him" (Matt 17:5). Both inner and outer factors were considered as both impressive methods (student listening and seeing) and expressive methods (student talking) were used to promote thinking and learning.

Jesus was concerned with the inside processing of the student as well as with the truth to which he was referring. He often used the prior knowledge and experiences of the student to get the student's mind to actively process what he was saying. Is it too much to infer that Jesus knew best how to teach because he knew how we were created to learn?

In the past, Christian educational philosophers have tried to portray the concept of the interactive nature of human beings by including the concepts of active and passive and inner and outer factors in their educational theories (LeBar, 1958, p. 45). While that approach helped teachers design curriculum, it also left the door open for teachers to favor one, active (inner) or passive (outer), over the other, while paying lip service to the other of the pair. There was no overall approach to teaching that could really be described as "constructive" or "interactive." As a young teacher of teachers, I developed a model I called "Directed Inquiry" to try to depict the concept of outer (directed) and inner (mental processes) factors. The concept of the interactive actional nature with its applications for learning and teaching now opens the door for a framework for teaching that more clearly takes into account a biblical view of human learning and knowledge. We owe a debt of gratitude to cognitive theorists for this more recent paradigm that helps to verify the attempts of some Christian educators in the past to answers the question, how do humans learn?

How might the three views of the actional nature lead to different models for learning and teaching? Let's see how this works in the development of an approach to teaching. In developing an interactive constructive instructional model one might think like this:

- If something inside matters in the learning of new information, I must plan to engage that inside something in order to activate prior knowledge and motivate toward learning the lesson at hand.

- If something outside matters, I must study and organize content and skills to deliver these in light of the students' prior experiences and current knowledge base.

- If learning occurs as information is taken in and processed by the individual, I must create student processing activities, both group and individual, that are designed to help the student fit in, make sense of new information, and construct adequate understandings.

- If learning occurs inside as a construction of understandings and meanings and I am a teacher who must assess learning to see how well the student has constructed, I must create ongoing assessment activities that provide feedback to the teacher that answers the question, are they getting it? and feedback to the students answering their question, am I getting it?

TEACHING MODEL CONSTRUCTED FROM AN INTERACTIVE LEARNING MODEL

A learning model based upon the interactive nature of the human is not just passive telling and testing. Nor is it unguided activity, simply drawing out. Rather it is an orchestration of four basic elements (not necessarily steps):

- Engaging the mind (inside) using an activity planned by the teacher (outside)

- Providing new information by *giving it* (outside the student) or creating a student activity that requires the *student to get* the new information from some outside source

- Creating student processing activities to help the student make sense out of new material or skill, to form closure (fit it in), make connections, generalize, draw conclusions, or practice and use a skill.

- Assessing learning by using student expressions of inside constructed understandings in their own words as feedback to see if students are getting it

Interactive learning is the process whereby the learner selects and takes in new information from his or her surroundings and uses prior knowledge to begin to process, construct, and store new knowledge for retrieval and use. (A safe and nurturing environment is helpful in that this process uses both success and failures as intrinsic motivation to learn.) Look at the lesson elements above and determine how each one fits that description.

Finally, check the following issues. Are these true or false?

- Subject matter (content) is vital.

- Prior knowledge of the learner and a knowledge base is important.

- Student processing and constructing activities are not an option; they are a requirement.

- Memory (storage) is essential.

- Understanding is a key to learning and transfer.

- Assessment is vital.

All are true of a robust interactive constructive model of teaching and learning! Please see the appendix for a sample lesson using the interactive constructivist approach to demonstrate the elements of an interactive teaching model.

CONCLUSION

Cognitive interactive theory leads to an approach or model of teaching that will work together with the way humans are created to learn and thus promote learning that is more natural. Teachers who are serious about promoting learning in their students will invite conversation about the potentials of constructionist approaches that are built upon the interactive nature of humans. An interactive constructivist approach, when viewed in its basic form, does not focus on the student or the processes alone and ignore new information and content. Advocates see learning as a unified process involving content and experience, knowing and doing, and information for change. Learning is transformational.

REFERENCES

Bigge, M., & Shermis, S. (2004). *Learning theories for teachers.* Boston: Allyn and Bacon Pearson Education.

Clark, G. (1981). *A Christian view of men and thing.* Grand Rapids: Baker Book House.

Goleman, D. (1987, August 25). Embattled giant of psychology speaks his mind. *New York Times.*

LeBar, Lois E. (1958). *Education that is Christian.* Old Tappan, NJ: Fleming H. Revell.

MacCullough, M. E. *Developing a worldview approach to biblical integration.* Langhorne, PA: Philadelphia Bible University, 2008. (2nd ed.)

von Glasersfeld, E. (1995). *Radical constructivism: A way of knowing and learning.* Washington, DC: Falmer.

Weber, E. (1969). *The kindergarten.* New York: Teachers College Press.

White, J. E. (2006). *A mind for God.* Downers Grove, IL: InterVarsity.

Zahorik, John A. (1995). *Constructivist Teaching.* Phi Delta Kappa Fastback (390). Bloomington, IN: Phi Delta Kappa Educational Foundation.

Appendix

Sample Science Lesson Outline Using the Interactive Model

Concept: Refraction of light

Instructional objective: The student will be able to solve a real-life problem using the concept of the refraction of light. (This is what I want to do in order to promote understanding and the construction of meaning related to the science concept of refraction.)

ELEMENT 1: ENGAGING THE MIND

This element is designed to activate and engage the student's mind toward the lesson at hand by activating prior knowledge and experiences, creating disequilibrium: a question to be answered, a problem to solve, or an issue to be examined.

How will I motivate or engage the student's mind? (This is the method I will use to work through the planned approach.) For the lesson at hand on refraction of light, I might simply write, "Headless Doll," on my lesson plan; however, I would probably write "Demonstration" for the eyes of my administrator.

Method: The teacher provides an aquarium two-thirds filled with water, places it at eye level on a table for the students to observe. As she lowers the doll into the water, keeping the head out of the water, students will observe a "headless doll," the appearance of which is caused by the bending of light as it travels through two different media, air and water. Oohs and ahs are followed by the question, "How did you do that? Can you do it again? Why does that happen?" (to which, the teacher replies, "Let's find out.")

The Headless Doll

Aquarium

* Concept: Refraction of Light

Figure 12.1 Headless doll demonstration

ELEMENT 2: PROVIDING NEW INFORMATION FOR CONCEPT AND SKILL DEVELOPMENT

The purpose of this element is to promote new learning by providing opportunities for students to gather information from well-developed labs to help them begin to construct understandings related to the bending of light as it passes through different media and to connect that learning to previous knowledge and experiences. Carefully organize new and relevant information.

Method: Several hands-on activities (labs) to discover what happens when light travels through different media. (Often provided by the science curriculum.)

ELEMENT 3: GUIDING STUDENT PROCESSING ACTIVITIES

The purpose for this element is to guide the student in the process of making sense out of the new knowledge or skills, to use it, to fit it in, to construct understandings and meaning, to store it.

Methods: Write out questions and/or describe activities in which pupils are guided to organize, relate, connect, and use information and instruction from the labs to answer a question, solve a problem, or practice a skill introduced in the motivation or engagement activity (element 1 above). This element requires the *student* to process information and *make sense* out of new learning by:

Drawing conclusions in writing for each experiment

Sharing conclusions with their team and through eflection, reorganize, if needed, their own conclusions.

Using the discovered and constructed new understandings to define refraction of light in their own words

Checking and comparing their definition with the text

Solving a problem

Each team is given a problem to solve. Here is an example problem: You are in a swimming pool with a friend who drops a hair clip into the water. You see it on the bottom. You reach down and it is not there; it moved. Explain what you think happened and why you think as you do.

ELEMENT 4: ASSESSING STUDENT LEARNING

The purpose of this element is to provide an opportunity for the student and the teacher to know whether or not learning is occurring and whether or not the student has constructed meaning and understandings and an adequate representation of the concepts targeted in the lesson using the available materials, activities, and their prior knowledge and experience.

Method: Provide a problem to be solved by each individual student. Assessment of individual understandings is an individual event. Use at least one question or activity to determine learning. Does the individual learner understand what he or she has stated and discussed or what has been stored in memory? Can the student use the new information or skill? This element may be graded, however, it is not necessary to grade all individual assessments, especially in the formative stage.

For example, show a picture of a fisherman practicing fly casting on dry land. Then show a picture of a spear fisherman and ask the following question: "Can a spear fisherman practice his craft on dry land? Why or why not? Use your lesson on refraction of light to answer the question. Your entry must be carefully written for submission to our class-o-pedia on our home page. Additionally: Research one animal or bird that must be able to compensate for the refraction of light."

NOTE ABOUT METHODS

Use hands-on-minds-on materials as much as possible for science and math. Use demonstrations and modeling in all subject areas. Use advanced organizers of relevant information to aid concept development unless the use of these will squelch curiosity or interfere with problem solving. Make sure you have mastered the concept or skill. Study. Practice. Always describe methods to be used in the plan (overall approach). Methods are tools used to encourage students to construct their experiences.

13

Oobleck: A Constructivist Science Lesson Viewed from a Christian Perspective

Bruce Young

INTRODUCTION

CONSTRUCTIVISM IS BECOMING INCREASINGLY influential in science education. Constructivist approaches to learning and instruction are promoted by national science associations and are becoming normative in science curriculum. Christian educators must be able to evaluate constructivist curriculum materials to discern which practices are compatible with a Christian approach to education. This article examines a constructivist science lesson from a Christian perspective by identifying the philosophical, theoretical, and methodological aspects of the lesson. The article concludes that there are common grace insights as well as misleading philosophical issues in a constructivist approach to science education.

A CONSTRUCTIVIST APPROACH TO SCIENCE EDUCATION

The students were filled with anticipation as the teacher distributed plastic tubs of the green gooey solution to teams of four. The teacher called the solution "oobleck," named after the green substance in the Dr. Seuss book, *Bartholomew and the Oobleck* (1949). The students were told that the oobleck had been retrieved from a distant planet and that they were to play the part of scientists assigned to test the green substance in order to determine its properties. The teacher led a discussion of the term "properties" to activate the students' prior knowledge in preparation for their investigation of oobleck.

Along with the tub of oobleck, each team was given various testing instruments. Students discovered some unexpected results. For example, they found that the harder they pressed on the substance the more resistance they encountered. They found that the solution sometimes acted like a solid and other times acted like a liquid. After completing their investigations the students gathered together to share their findings at a "scientific convention." At the convention the teams shared their list of the properties of oobleck. Once all the lists were shared, "laws of oobleck" were proposed and debated until there was a consensus among the students and a law was established. A follow-up activity involved designing a spacecraft that could safely land on oobleck.

The lesson described above was developed by Cary Sneider (1985) at the Lawrence Hall of Science, University of California at Berkeley and followed a constructivist approach to science education. Constructivism is an approach to teaching and learning characterized by activities where students work collaboratively, encounter discrepant events, and problem solve through hands-on experiments to construct knowledge of the world within a relevant context. A constructivist approach to education creates a learning environment that encourages students to find personal meaning. Cunningham (1992), a proponent of constructivism, explains education from a constructivist's perspective as follows:

> The role of education in a constructivist view is to show students how to construct knowledge, to promote collaboration with others to show multiple perspectives that can be brought to bear on a particular problem, and to arrive at self-chosen positions to which they can commit themselves, while realizing the basis of other views with which they may disagree. (p. 36)

In recent years, science education has been heavily influenced by constructivism (Boudourides, 2003). Perhaps this is because the discipline of science is well suited for the kind of hands-on exploration and personal interpretation that characterizes the constructivist approach. With the current curriculum orientation leaning toward constructivism and national science organizations like the American Association for the Advancement of Science (AAAS) promoting constructivist activities, the Christian educator must ask, does constructivism fit into a Christian educational approach?

THREE MEANINGS OF CONSTRUCTIVISM

Alan Colburn (2000) has made a helpful distinction between three meanings of "constructivism" that can serve as a guide for determining how constructivism may or may not provide useful educational insights for the Christian educator. Colburn identifies three categories of meaning for the term constructivism: philosophical, theoretical, and methodological. The philosophical meaning of constructivism focuses on answering the questions, what is the nature of reality? and what is knowledge? The primary tenet of constructivism as a philosophy is that knowledge is not discovered in the outside world, but constructed in the human mind. There is no objective reality. Personal experience gives subjective meaning to what is known. Everyone perceives the world through their own senses and experiences. There is no way to know what is absolutely "true" because people can only share their personal experiences to find common ground with the experiences of others.

At the philosophical level, constructivism has conflicts with a Christian worldview. The constructivist rejects a belief in transcendent reality and denies the possibility of universal experience and objective truth. A Christian educational philosophy is dependent on the Holy Scriptures and the inspiration of the Holy Spirit to illuminate the truth. At the philosophical level of constructivism, the Christian encounters a paradox. On the one hand, there is what Schaeffer calls "true truth." While our knowledge is not exhaustive, it can be true and unified (Schaeffer, 1968). God has created a universe that is knowable and is governed by laws ordained by the Creator. In this sense the Christian has an objective perspective. On the other hand, it is also true that people view the world through their own eyes. No two people bring the same prior knowledge and experience into their understanding of the world. In this sense the Christian has a subjective perspective. The paradox has been expressed by Fennema (1997):

> There is objective truth. . . . The world is knowable. . . . There is a subjective side to knowing. . . . Revealed truth is known, not constructed. . . . A student's understanding is never the same as that of the teacher, or of any other student, for that matter. (p. 6)

If, through the activities of the oobleck lessons, students are led to believe that there is no objective truth because all that matters is their own subjective, collective experiences, then the lessons would not reflect a Christian philosophical approach to science education as described above.

The theoretical meaning of constructivism concerns learning theory and answers the question, how do children learn? The constructivist views learning as developmental, collaborative, active, and cultural. Here we encounter Piaget's and Vygotsky's influence on constructivist learning theory. Piaget (1969) believed that children construct personal meaning as they interact with the environment. When children encounter new events, they must either assimilate the experience into an existing schematic or make accommodation for the new events. In either case, the acquisition of knowledge is a subjective experience that adds to a child's unique, personal meaning. Vygotsky (1978) emphasized the social and cultural influence on learning. His concepts of scaffolding and the zone of proximal development focused on the collaborative aspect of learning.

At the theoretical level there are some aspects of constructivism that reflect common grace insights[1] fitting into a Christian understanding of how children learn. For example, the Scriptures emphasize the social and cultural role of the community in the teaching of children (Deut 6). The Scriptures also teach the uniqueness of the individual (Prov 22:6; 1 Cor 12). In the oobleck lessons, students investigate the substance in personally meaningful ways while at the same time benefiting from their interaction with other students.

The methodological meaning of constructivism answers the question, what are effective instructional practices? The constructivist describes teaching strategies in terms of cooperative learning, project- and problem-based experiences, situated learning, inquiry, personal meaning, exploration, and discrepant events.

At the methodological level there are many constructivist practices that are compatible with a Christian educational approach. For example, in Deut 6:7–9 the Lord commands that the Lord's words be taught diligently to the children. The passage indicates that children are

1. The term *common grace* comes from a reformed Christian tradition and has been defined by Berkhof (1979) as that which "curbs the destructive power of sin, maintains in a measure the moral order of the universe, thus making an orderly life possible, distributes in varying degrees gifts and talents among men, promotes the development of science and art, and showers untold blessings upon the children of men" (p. 434). A common grace "insight" is an understanding that is beneficial to people or to creation in general and is usually attributed to a non-Christian.

unique individuals who will understand what is taught in different ways. In other words, there is a subjective aspect to learning. According to the Deuteronomy passage some children will get the teaching through auditory means ("talk of [these commandments] when you sit in your house," v. 7, NASB). Some will get the teaching kinesthetically ("when you walk by the way and when you lie down and when you rise up," v. 7). Some will get the teaching through tactile means ("you shall bind them on your hands and they shall be as frontals on your forehead," v. 8). Some will get the teaching through visual means ("you shall write them on the doorposts of your house," v. 9). Rather than using the one-size-fits-all approach to teaching, a Christian approach acknowledges that students are unique individuals with varying gifts and abilities requiring varying instructional approaches.

Proverbs 22:6 provides the same understanding of a subjective aspect to learning. The verse literally states, "Train up a child *according to his way*, even when he is old he will not depart from it" (italics added). If parents and teachers understand the unique way the child learns, then lessons can be taught according to that child's way of learning. The results will be effective and long lasting.

Another constructivist methodology that is compatible with a Christian approach to learning is collaboration. In 1 Cor 12, the Apostle Paul emphasizes the importance of the diversity and unity of the Christian community. God has created people to live within community and work collaboratively. In a school setting everyone benefits from one another's gifts and abilities.

A constructivist teaching practice that would not be compatible with a Christian approach to learning is evident in the obleck lesson when the students came together to decide on the laws of oobleck based on their subjective experiences. While it is true that natural laws are agreed upon by the scientific community, it is important that students understand that the "laws" they create by consensus are actually approximations of the laws God has ordained to govern the workings of God's universe.

CONCLUSION: THE LESSON FROM THE OOBLECK

In the oobleck lesson we find the following constructivist features: First, the teacher activates prior knowledge by asking the students about the meaning of the term "properties." Second, the students investigate the green gooey substance via hands-on experience. Third, the activity is collaborative, and students share their discoveries with one another. Fourth, students construct their own meaning regarding the properties and laws of oobleck. Fifth, students apply what was learned for the practical purpose of constructing a spacecraft that could land on oobleck.

Some features of constructivism are consistent with biblical principles and reflect common grace insights, while other features do not. Christian educators must carefully analyze constructivist methodology to discern practices that can help enrich the students' education.

REFERENCES

Berkhof, L. (1979). *Systematic theology*. Grand Rapids, MI: Eerdmans. (4th ed.)

Boudourides, M. A. (2003). Constructivism, education, science, and technology. *Canadian Journal of Learning and Technology, 29*(3), 5–20.

Colburn, A. (2000). Constructivism: Science's grand unifying theory. *Clearing House, 79*(1), 9–12.

Cunningham, D. J. (1992). Assessing constructions and constructing assessments: A dialogue. In T. M. Duffy & D. H. Jonassen (Eds.), *Constructivism and the technology of instruction* (pp. 35–44). Hillsdale, NJ: Erlbaum.

Fennema, J. (1997, May 29–31). *Knowing in a postmodern age: The Christian's answer begins with a word—the logos*. A paper presented at the With Heart and Mind Conference, Toronto, Canada.

Piaget, J., & Inhelder, B. (1969). *The psychology of the child*. New York: Basic Books.

Schaeffer, F. A. (1968). *Escape from reason*. Chicago: InterVarsity.

Sneider, C. I. (1985). *Oobleck: What do scientists do?* Berkeley, CA: Lawrence Hall of Science, University of California Berkeley.

Seuss. (1949). *Bartholomew and the oobleck*. New York: Random House.

Vygotsky, L. S. (1978). *Mind in society: The development of higher psychological processes*. Cambridge, MA: Harvard University Press.

14

Fostering Online Communities of Faith

Damon Osborne

INTRODUCTION

In considering the teaching and learning process, particularly in the traditional classroom setting, it is easy to envision the creation of a sense of community among the course participants. The learners and instructor are in the same room, sharing communication that extends beyond the verbal into other forms of communication (e.g., body language) that provide context for the course content being discussed. Additionally, the opportunity for spontaneous teachable moments, or the judicious use of humor is also readily present in a traditional setting. This face-to-face context of community also provides strong support for the development of a social constructivist learning environment, in that learners are optimally proximal for such connections to take place.

Yet, when examining the concept of community and constructivism in relation to the online learning environment, questions quickly emerge: (1) How can we create community when we do not see each other face-to-face (i.e., how is this different than in a traditional classroom)? (2) What tools could be used to establish community among online learners? and (3) Is there even a need for community for online learners?

While the practical considerations for the creation and fostering of a community of faith among online learners will be discussed in detail later in this chapter, it is important to answer the final question first, for the simple reason that if there is no need for the establishment of community among online learners, there is no need to expend time, effort, and resources in pursuit of this goal. Rovai (2002b) presents research that suggests a strong correlation between perceived sense of community and both perceived cognitive learning and persistence in asynchronous online learning environments. Additionally, Milam, Voorhees, and Bedard-Voorhees (2004) state:

> Helping students feel that they are a part of a learning community is critical to persistence, learning, and satisfaction. In many cases, human contact is necessary for more than just learning content. Encouragement, praise, and assurance that they are on the right learning path are also critical feedback components that help students get through rough times and keep on working. Knowing that someone is there to help when they get stuck and to get them moving again gives students the confidence that they can succeed. (p. 80)

Having validation from the literature that there is indeed a need for a sense of community among online learners, it is then necessary to understand how community is actually constructed in the online learning environment.

LITERATURE REVIEW

Although the body of literature is limited on the specific topic of establishing a community of faith among online learners, there is substantive literature regarding community in general among online learners. This literature paves the way for the exploratory research discussed later in the chapter. There are a number of challenges that become apparent when studying the issue of establishing community among online learners. One study presents findings that the learners who do not live on campus tend to have a lower sense of community than do their on-campus peers, due to the reliance upon their local communities for social support as opposed to the campus community (Bohus, Woods, & Chan, 2005). Just as commuter learners exist in the traditional college campus setting, learners can become "commuters" within the online learning context, not actually seeking to build community with their peers (Blair & Hoy, 2006), instead opting to "lurk" in the discussion forums without interacting with their fellow learners (Denning & Davis, 2000). Another challenge occurs when learners fail to perceive the other course participants as "real" and do not interact effectively, failing to take advantage of the resources that their peers provide (Russo & Campbell, 2004). Finally, a serious concern raised by a number of researchers (Russo & Campbell, 2004; Song, Singleton, Hill, & Koh, 2004; Tu & McIsaac, 2002) relates to response time between the participants in an online course. This can occur when exploring the interaction between learners in discussion boards (Song et al., 2004), or between the instructor and the learner, when communicating via email (Russo & Campbell, 2004).

The importance of establishing community among online learners is important for a number of reasons, notably: it is a key to successful knowledge generation, and it becomes more difficult for online learners to simply "disappear" from the group (Engvig, 2006). Learners who do not feel as if they are part of the community will either extend more effort in developing the community of the online learning environment, or will instead become frustrated and seek out an alternate educational opportunity (Rovai, 2005). Given the challenges listed above, it is important to consider whether it is even possible to establish community among online course participants. However, even as far back as 1985, Howard Rheingold found that the concept of establishing an online community was not only possible, it was also very rewarding:

> Since the summer of 1985, for an average of two hours a day, seven days a week, I've been plugging my personal computer into my telephone and making contact with the WELL (Whole Earth 'Lectronic Link)—a computer conferencing system that enables people around the world to carry on public conversations and exchange private electronic mail (e-mail). The idea of a community accessible only via my computer screen sounded cold to me at first, but I learned quickly that people can feel passionately about e-mail and computer conferences. I've become one of them. I care about these people I met through my computer, and I care deeply about the future of the medium that enables us to assemble. (Rheingold, 2000, p. xv)

With the understanding that building online communities outside of the context of the educational institution is firmly established, based on the number of social networking websites, discussion forums, and email lists, it then becomes important to consider the elements necessary to include when seeking to create the same, or comparable, sense of community among learners in an online learning environment as that experienced by learners that attend traditional face-to-face colleges and universities. As instructional designers seek to create learning environments that foster a true sense of community among online course participants, there are a number of factors that need to be considered: courses need to be designed with community in mind (Fisher & Baird, 2005; Moallem, 2002; Rovai, 2000; Song et al., 2004; Woods & Ebersole, 2003), course time needs to be dedicated the establishment of community among the participants (Fisher, Coleman, Sparks, & Plett, 2007; Gyllenpalm, 2002; Palloff & Pratt, 2003; Shapiro & Hughes, 2002), and instructors need to continually work to maintain the sense of community in the course through their social presence (Palloff & Pratt, 2003; Tu & McIsaac, 2002; Weiss, 2000).

Designing online courses with community building in mind during the development stage extends beyond adding discussion boards that require weekly postings from the learners (Blair & Hoy, 2006). As previously mentioned, it is important to embed the social interaction aspects of the online learning environment into the course design from the outset (Song et al., 2004). One design component that may be employed is the creation of nontask, or nonsubject-matter-specific discussion forums in the courseroom (Northrup, 2001; Woods & Ebersole, 2003). These discussion forums do not address the course content; instead, these forums allow the learners the opportunity to engage their peers in conversation (Northrup, 2001) and build a sense of connectedness (Woods & Ebersole, 2003).

In fact, a number of researchers contend that the dialogue that occurs in the online learning environment is a primary indicator as to the effectiveness of the establishment of community among the participants. The use of written language, coupled with the concept of public conversation creates a unique opportunity for learners and instructors to engage in an online dialogue that is a combination of conversation and writing (Polin, 2004) that allows participants the ability to metacognitively approach the conversation, altering it when warranted by their educational experience. This online conversation extends into group and individual dynamics as well, demanding that the course instructor become cognizant of the fact that course participants may need private space, in addition to the public space of a discussion forum (Blair & Hoy, 2006). Blair and Hoy also suggest that "a full concept of virtual community includes a range of both group and individual dialogue, in which both are valued equally by instructors, students, and supervisors" (Blair & Hoy, 2006, p. 45).

Course content design plays an important role as well; in fact, there are some advocates that suggest that course design is indeed the most critical factor when seeking to create interactive learning opportunities for online learners (Moallem, 2002). Some online learning advocates state that "when an online course is built with community in mind, it can then be sustained throughout the duration of the course" (Fisher & Baird, 2005, p. 91). Some specific recommendations pertaining to course design include supplementing individual learning opportunities with small group projects to promote community and connections (Rovai, 2002a) and creating worlds within the course that allow learners to interact in virtual cafés (Gyllenpalm, 2002). Gyllenpalm's model hinges on four foundational principles: (1) create a hospitable space by creating an assignment expressly for this purpose where learners introduce themselves to others; (2) explore questions that matter to the members of the community; (3) connect diverse and varied groups of individuals in a small group setting, namely six to nine participants; and (4) listen as a group for patterns and deeper insights by looking beyond personal opinions in order to see the themes that emerge from the group. Gyllenpalm (2002) was surprised to note that participants in his virtual knowledge cafés learned as much, if not more, than face-to-face participants. He cites three possible reasons for this phenomenon: there is more time for reflection, all the contributions are in writing, and there is more time to research appropriate responses.

A number of institutional considerations may also drive the discussion on community building in online learning environments, namely: class size, orientation, and the use of cohorts or cadres throughout the academic career of the learner. Class size is an issue that online learning experts and advocates view as very important to the concept of building community, in addition to the feasibility of facilitating the course from the perspective of the instructor.

For the most effective course interactions, a general guideline of somewhere between eight and thirty learners is recommended (Rovai, 2002a). While this number may not necessarily mean the highest possible profit per section for the institution, the relationships that are possible between instructors and students in smaller groups settings such as those suggested are far more meaningful and effective (Blair & Hoy, 2006).

Orienting students to the online learning environment is a challenging proposition, especially for those learners who are not comfortable with technology prior to embarking on this educational journey. While many institutions offer an online orientation or lab course, designed to familiarize the learner with the functional elements of the online learning environment, some online programs require the learners to attend a face-to-face class or orientation to help build community (Ruhleder, 2004) and begin the online educational experience.

Building on this theme is the concept of utilizing cohorts or cadres of students in order to provide some stability to the learners as they change courses throughout their degree program. While some institutions may provide an online orientation for their cohorts as they begin their online learning experience, others require the cohorts to attend face-to-face sessions at the beginning, middle, and end of their academic career (Riel, 2005). Each of the aforementioned approaches offers opportunities for learners and instructors to begin to build community; however, individual learners may find that their particular needs are best met with a specific solution, such as a periodic face-to-face event.

Once the course has been designed and populated with learners, it is important to dedicate course time to establishing community among the online participants so that they can begin to construct a social identity (Fisher et al., 2007). The time allotted to socialization and establishing community in an online learning environment not only helps facilitate the development of social presence by the course participants, it also builds trust among the learners, which is a key factor for success in collaborative group projects (Palloff & Pratt, 2005). Additionally, studies have shown that persistence is connected to the social content and connection created between course participants in an online learning environment:

> Each small group's message content analysis revealed more than 50% of messages sent online were social in nature, intended to maintain the cohesion of the group and support and encourage the groups' individual members. The social messages gave the students the friendship and sense of belonging that helped to motivate them to apply themselves to their study when they were finding it hard to manage, particularly because of the conditions of studying at a distance. Their accountability and responsibility to the other members of the group for their participation in online collaborative tasks were strong motivators for their per-

sistence and such a sense of a strong group network depended on their establishment of social presence online. (Stacey, 2002, p. 289)

Not only do online instructors need to dedicate time expressly for the purpose of establishing community among the online course participants, they also need to guide the discussion in the courseroom so that there are some casual or light topics (Tu & McIsaac, 2002) in addition to the deep and meaningful conversations that result from peer review or feedback (Fisher et al., 2007). The instructor of an online course should consider spending time on developing online communication competence among the learners that extends beyond the traditional "netiquette" instructions given at the onset of many online degree programs (Shapiro & Hughes, 2002).

Palloff and Pratt (2003) provide a succinct, yet comprehensive, list of instructional techniques that can be employed by the online instructor to facilitate the development of community in the online learning environment:

(a) Post introductions and bios; (b) create a social space in the course; (c) encourage judicious use of chat for socializing; (d) model openness and humor; (e) be willing to give up control and allow learners to take charge of the learning process; (f) involve learners in co-creating learning opportunities; (g) orient students to the role of the instructor and responsibilities of the learners in online learning; (h) provide opportunities for reflection on the role of the instructor, the student, and the course itself; (i) model open, honest communication; (j) orient students to appropriate communication skills and giving and receiving substantive feedback; (k) orient students to the realities of online learning; (l) provide opportunities for feedback, such as posting papers to the course site with the expectation that feedback will be given and received, and post evaluations of collaborative activities online; (m) rotate or share the facilitation role with students by asking them to take charge of a week or two of the online discussion; (n) rotate leadership of small groups; (o) use a "process monitor," or a student who comments on group process and progress on a weekly basis, rotating this role through the group; (p) establish minimum posting requirements and monitor those for compliance; (q) grade on participation; (r) post grading rubrics that establish guidelines for acceptable participation and posting; (s) use collaborative small group assignments and evaluate them collaboratively. (pp. 27–28)

The social presence of the online course instructor is also a key element in establishing and maintaining community in an online learning environment. While instructors in traditional settings may use their voices, body language, facial expressions, and other gestures to represent their presence in the classroom, the use of the instructor's writing and other image-based communications represent the presence of an online course instructor (Downing, 2000). Social presence has been defined as follows: "social presence has traditionally been conceptualized as a medium's ability to convey perceptual and affective characteristics such as warmth and support for personal and sensitive interaction" (Russo & Campbell, 2004, p. 217). In the context of the online learning environment, social presence can also be thought of as the overall feeling of community experienced by the learner (Tu & McIsaac, 2002). While the frequency of interaction in an online courseroom is certainly important (Russo & Campbell, 2004), increased frequency of interaction or participation in an online course does not necessarily result in increased social presence (Tu & McIsaac, 2002). Instead, online instructors should take advantage of the opportunity for one-to-one communication present in the online learning environment and tailor communication to meet the specific needs of each individual that participates in the online courseroom. Russo and Campbell (2004) assert that more important than the volume of communication between instructor and learner is the individualized nature of the communication, where the learner feels as if the appropriate words and language was used, as well as the timely nature of this communication.

The responsibility of initially establishing community and the feeling of social presence rests almost entirely with the instructor in the online learning environment. Not only should the instructor create a learning environment that is robust (Fisher et al., 2007), the instructor is also responsible for setting the tone of the resulting dialogue in the online courseroom (Fisher et al., 2007; Palloff & Pratt, 2003; Rovai, 2002a; Song et al., 2004). Palloff and Pratt continue, suggesting that the online instructor "begin with a set of participation expectations to which students can respond with latitude for negotiation" (Palloff & Pratt, 2003, p. 19). Additionally, the judicious use of carefully worded humor or emoticons (Palloff & Pratt, 2003) may also assist the instructor in establishing social presence and the foundation of an online community of learners.

However, the responsibility for further developing the community found in an online learning environment surely rests with all of the course participants, but perhaps most importantly the learners. In fact, it has been suggested that when learners are able to set the standards by which their community operates, they are more engaged in the online courseroom (Fisher et al., 2007). Other online learning experts agree, indicating that once the instructor has laid the foundation for the construction of an online community of learners, the learners need to be open to collaboration and willing to step up and take on the responsibility of community building (Palloff & Pratt, 2003). Although Palloff and Pratt indicate that the instructor may need to provide continued guidance, it is important to understand the underlying nature of the community found in online learning environments and let go and trust the "social constructivist process" (Fisher et al., 2007, p. 46). This social construction process is extremely important when considering the social bonds formed by the online learners through the collaborative work undertaken in the online courseroom, notably, as these connections become stronger through trust and a heightened sense of community, each individual truly benefits from the collective knowledge developed by the group (Stacey, 2002).

Reviewing the literature also reveals a number of experts in online learning and building online learning communities offering prescriptive advice for instructional designers and online course instructors who seek to establish and foster a sense of community among the online course participants. Rovai (2000), a leading researcher on online community, lists the following factors as essential to establishing community among online course participants: (1) a favorable student-to-instructor ratio may not be as profitable as the high student-to-teacher ratio possible in an online learning environment, but it helps the participants establish community; (2) increase dialog and reduce structure to reduce transactional distance; (3) instructors need to deliberately combat the feeling of isolation that distant learners feel through interaction; (4) lurkers threaten the sense of community, therefore course participants should be required to participate by assessing their participation; (5) course participants should be required to introduce themselves at the beginning of a course in order to make connections; (6) use small groups to work on group goals, while maintaining individual accountability; (7) the instructor must act as cheerleader, diplomat, gatekeeper, and standard setter; (8) when the instructor matches the teaching style to the appropriate stage of self-directed learning, a better sense of community results.

Weiss (2000) advocates the following for making the online classroom more personal: (1) add tone by using written body language or emoticons to get your meaning across; (2) use language that is expressive, such as metaphors or hyperbole; (3) create biographies by supplying biographical information and a photo, while avoiding the inclusion of home addresses and phone numbers; (4) create a virtual break room, which is an informal space for learners to hang out; (5) model appropriate interaction by not dominating the conversation; (6) create an ethical community of learners by working to put out fires before they become raging blazes; (7) hold students accountable.

While the aforementioned prescriptive information provides extensive foundational information for establishing a sense of community among geographically disparate online learners, Christian colleges and universities, and the instructional designers charged with developing online learning environments at these schools, seek to take the sense of community to another level: the establishment of a community of faith among online learners.

RESEARCH

As presented in the literature section prior, the study of developing a community of faith among online learners is still relatively limited. However, as more and more faith-based institutions seek to add online learning elements to their teaching and learning toolbox, the issue of a community of learners becomes increasingly important. One exploratory study (Osborne, 2008) was designed to explore the tools and techniques needed to establish and foster a community of faith among online learners.

The participants of the study were online learners from a single institution, yet were geographically dispersed throughout the United States as well as abroad. In order to obtain a more balanced perspective, even with a limited sample in a qualitative study, the following groups were represented in the study: learners, faculty, administrators, and the chaplain. The study employed grounded theory as the research methodology; in particular, the constructivist grounded theory as espoused by Kathy Charmaz. This variant of the ground theory methodology differs from the traditional model offered by Glaser and Strauss in that instead of discovering data and theories, the researcher constructs the emerging theory from the data as well as from the experiences and perspectives the researcher brings to the research project (Charmaz, 2006).

Participants were asked an initial round of open-ended questions that sought to determine a baseline for understanding their perspective on the availability (or even the need for) an online community of faith. The learner participants were asked the following questions:

> How does your institution make a concerted effort to establish a community of faith among online learners? Please list the tools used (discussion boards, podcasts, emails, etc.) as well as how the tools are used to establish and maintain the community of faith. If you do not feel that your institution makes a concerted effort to establish a community of faith among online learners, where do you see the institution falling short?

Describe your feelings about online community in general. Do you connect with your peers in the online learning environment? If so, what tools do you use to create this sense of community? What stumbling blocks do you see when you think of creating community among online learners? What is your perceived level of need of a community of faith in your educational process? (Osborne, 2008, pp. 62–63)

Similarly, the faculty and administrative participants were asked questions that established a foundation for understanding their perspective on the availability and need for an online community of faith for the learners at their institution:

1. In what ways do you intentionally seek to establish a community of faith among the online course participants at your institution?

2. What tools (discussion boards, emails, blogs, podcasts, etc.) do you regularly use in the pursuit of community? How effective do you feel that these tools are at establishing a spiritual connection between the course participants?

3. In addition to specific course management tools, what course design considerations play a role in establishing a community of faith among the online learners at your institution? That is, are there specific assignments, required interactions, or other instructional tools that are employed in an effort to establish a community of faith among the course participants? How effective are these mechanisms, in your opinion? Please give examples. (Osborne, 2008, p. 63)

Not surprisingly, as the participating institution was intentionally Christian, the majority of the respondents indicated that they sought community, in particular, a community of faith, even though they were not meeting with their colleagues or professors face-to-face. Themes that emerged from this initial round of data collection and analysis seemed to indicate that the required coursework-based discussion questions were prime areas for the development of a community of faith, while the optional areas, such as the virtual prayer room or online chapel services, were virtually unused (Osborne, 2008). However, it should be noted that there were also participants who indicated that there was not the need for a community of faith, as this need was met through corporate worship elsewhere.

Based on their initial responses, and the subsequent analysis of the data collected, additional questions were crafted to delve deeper into the issue. Although additional questions were asked regarding the virtual prayer room, the online chapel services, and an instant messaging system (all specifically designed to connect the learners and faculty in a faith-based situation), the responses indicated that these tools were secondary in importance as compared to the use of threaded discussions. The following set of questions elicited rich data:

> A number of participants have indicated that the discussion boards at [the Christian college] provide the best opportunity for creating a community of faith. However, there is some discussion on whether this occurs primarily in the discussion boards focused on coursework, or the discussion boards dedicated to the Virtual Prayer Room. Based on your experience, which of these discussion boards is the location best suited for the development of an online community of faith, if either? What is your level of participation in either of these discussion areas, and how do you think that impacts the development of a community of faith? What is your perspective on the involvement of faculty or staff in the development of a community of faith through the use of discussion boards (i.e., should faculty be more or less involved)? Please share any other thoughts you may have regarding the development of a community of faith through the use of discussion boards at [the Christian college]. (Osborne, 2008, p. 76)

From the responses, it was clearly evident that the required discussions used for connecting learners to content were also the location of the establishment of community. As learners and instructors interacted in the discussion boards, they formed bonds of trust that allowed the application of faith to the course content in a natural and seamless manner. This is not to say that the optional areas, such as the virtual prayer room, online chapel services, or instant messaging solutions, are not useful for many learners; instead, they form a well-rounded supplementary package that complements the construction work taking place in the course content discussion boards.

Based on the data collected and analyzed in the study described above, a grounded theory emerged:

1. Coursework must be designed with the intention of introducing, establishing, and maintaining a community of faith. The development of a community of faith among online course participants primarily occurs in the discussion boards devoted to the dissemination of course content. The requirement of participation spurs interaction, which in turn increases development of community. When discussion questions are crafted appropriately (i.e., open-ended and inviting a discussion that furthers the understanding of a Christian worldview), the learners and course facilitators are able to interact in a manner that is conducive to the establishment and fostering of a community of faith.

2. As an accompaniment to the use of threaded discussions, institutions may also choose to employ additional means of communicating or disseminating content designed to stimulate discussion that will build the community of faith. Instant messaging tools, such as text-based chat programs, voice-over-IP programs, or even video-conferencing programs can be effective at building the community of faith, provided that they are implemented in a fashion that meets the needs of the learners and that they are not out of the reach of the learners. Scheduling chat sessions at various times that cover topics of faith, using tools that all learners can easily access and use is an effective supplement to the community building effort. Similarly, distributing media, such as an electronic version of a chapel service, can be effective at building the community of faith provided that it is integrated into the curriculum in some fashion, as both learners and faculty alike often ignore optional materials.

3. The online faculty member must make time available throughout the course for the development of community, beginning with an

autobiographical discussion thread, and continuing as appropriate in the formal and informal communications of the group. For the instructor to be truly effective in this venture, coordinated professional development is necessary on the part of the institution. (Osborne, 2008, pp. 118–119)

IN PRACTICE

Combining the literature on establishing faith-based community with the research presented above leads to interesting practical applications for an online course facilitator or institution. Although it may seem counterintuitive at first to consider that strong online communities, particularly communities of faith among online learners, can be established in the context of coursework-oriented threaded discussions, in fact this has been borne out over several sections of a faculty training course. This course is primarily designed to provide training for potential online course facilitators at Mount Vernon Nazarene University and is five weeks in length.

While the course content is similar to other training courses found at faith-based institutions of higher learning (with coverage on issues such as academic integrity, best practices in online course facilitation, and a comparison/contrast between an existing face-to-face teaching practice and an emerging online teaching practice), a substantive portion of the course's appeal to the participants is the behind-the-scenes explanation provided by the facilitator. Although the discussion that follows mentions a number of specific tools, keep in mind that the same tasks can be accomplished in a number of ways.

At the outset of the course, the learners are greeted in two different ways: a text introduction and a video introduction. Using a standard threaded discussion, the instructor posts a forum for all course participants to use in order to introduce themselves to the group. Leading by example, the instructor posts a thread before the course is opened to the learner participants so that they then have an example to follow. Here is an example of an instructor introduction from a recent faculty training session:

> I remember the first day of Kindergarten. Although it was many years ago, there was a slightly embarrassing moment that makes it memorable to this day.

As the teacher was calling roll, I waited anxiously to hear my name. Eventually, she made her way to the middle of the alphabet and called out "Carl Osborne?"

At first I thought, "Weird, there is another kid here named Osborne, but I don't know them. Is this a cousin?" I looked around the room, but I didn't see any of the other children raising their hand.

When she reached the end of the list, she asked if there was anyone who she missed.

I raised my hand.

When she asked me what my name was, I said, "Damon."

She responded, "Damon what?"

"Damon Osborne."

"Could that be CARL Damon Osborne?"

"Maybe?"

Cue laughter from the rest of the class.

You see, I grew up across the road from my grandfather who was Carl Osborne, so my parents just called me Damon.

You can too.

:)

(Osborne, 2009)

In addition to the text-based introduction presented in the familiar context of threaded discussions, the instructor also creates and posts video introductions at the beginning of each course. In order to provide the most seamless viewing experience, as well as reduce the load shouldered by Blackboard (the course management system utilized by Mount Vernon Nazarene University), the instructor creates the video in iMovie '09 (Apple, 2009b) and then exports the final product directly to YouTube (YouTube, 2009), a free video sharing service. The elegance in this solution is that YouTube allows users to copy and paste embedding HTML code into other webpages. Therefore, after the video has finished uploading into YouTube, the instructor simply copies the embed code and then returns to paste it into the appropriate area in Blackboard. This allows learners the ability to access the video content without leaving the course management system, making it appear that the YouTube-hosted content is contained within. Other institutions are using varied means of pushing media-rich content, such as audio or video podcasts through iTunes U (Apple, 2009a) in order to provide a richer experience for their online learners.

Both introductions on the part of the course instructor serve to lay the foundation for social presence, a key element in establishing community among online learners. Instead of merely remaining text on a page to the learners, the instructor becomes a voice and a face. Of course, the extensive use of technology is not without challenges. Learners who are accessing the internet via dialup modem connections may not have sufficient bandwidth to view the videos from YouTube, even though those videos are compressed and flash-based in order to easily stream to the end user. Similarly, downloading podcasts that can become very large, particularly when video is involved, is an extremely time-consuming process for the learner with a limited bandwidth connection.

Once the course is underway and the learners have participated in the introduction in the threaded discussion, the instructor then continues efforts at building community within the group by interacting appropriately in the course content discussion questions. Appropriate interaction, in this context, implies a balanced approach that has the instructor drawing out deep reflection on the part of the learners, while not stifling interaction between the course participants. By modeling the appropriate interaction at the outset of a course, the instructor can set the tone and then get step aside so that meaningful dialog can take place between the course participants. The types of responses the instructor chooses to give sets the tone for the rest of the course, so care should be exercised to keep the interactions positive in nature.

Faculty at faith-based institutions have the added benefit of integrating faith, either directly through the use of Scripture or other devotional material, or indirectly by espousing virtuous attributes in the content of their responses. Although an institution is grounded in faith intentionally, not all of the students are necessarily members of that faith. Therefore, it is important to include elements of good moral and ethical behavior, regardless of religious affiliation, in the responses to the learners. Once the instructor has set the tone for interaction in the discussion board, it is possible to draw the learners in to the optional areas such as a community of faith discussion forum, where the instructor can post devotional material that requires interaction. A key element for success in this area is to pose questions that inspire learners to reflect upon their own experiences and share in community with others.

At the end of each week for the previously discussed course, the instructor posts both text and video feedback. As this is a course that focuses on the facilitation of an online course, the text-based feedback aligns with the course content discussed during the week, while the video-based feedback discusses the facilitation technique employed by the course instructor. By providing a look behind the scenes in this manner, the online course instructor is humanized for the online learners. The key takeaway for the developing online instructor is that it is necessary to find ways to connect and interact with the learners in such a manner as to become more than words on a page; it is necessary to become connected in community in order to develop the level of trust necessary for the exploration of faith-based elements in the course.

CONCLUSION

In summary, while building and fostering community among learners in a traditional face-to-face setting may seem completely natural to course participants, in the online learning environment, community building requires conscious and concerted effort by the instructor and the institution. At a faith-based institution of higher education, generic community is extended to include an element of faith, further compounding the development process. However, when course instructors make intentional efforts to foster community among the course participants in an online setting from the outset of a course, a level of trust emerges that allows the deeper community of faith to emerge.

REFERENCE

Apple. (2009a). *Apple – Education – Mobile learning*. Retrieved from http://www.apple.com/education/mobile-learning/

Apple. (2009b). *Apple – iMovie – Make a movie on your Mac*. Retrieved from http://www.apple.com/ilife/imovie/

Blair, K., & Hoy, C. (2006). Paying attention to adult learners online: The pedagogy and politics of community. *Computers and Composition, 23*(1), 32–48.

Bohus, S., Woods, R. H., & Chan, K. C. (2005). Psychological sense of community among students on religious collegiate campuses in the Christian evangelical tradition. *Christian Higher Education, 4*(1), 19–40.

Charmaz, K. (2006). *Constructing grounded theory*. London: SAGE.

Denning, K., & Davis, M. (2000). Computer-mediated communication in adult education. In D. M. Watson & T. Downes (Eds.), *Communications and networking in education: Learning in a networked society* (pp. 91–100). Boston: Kluwer Academic Publishers.

Dowling, C. (2000). Social interactions and the construction of knowledge in CMEs. In D. M. Watson & T. Downes (Eds.), *Communications and networking in education:*

Learning in a networked society (pp. 165–174). Boston: Kluwer Academic Publishers.

Engvig, M. (2006). *Online learning: All you need to know to facilitate and administer online courses.* Cresskill, NJ: Hampton.

Fisher, M., & Baird, D. E. (2005). Online learning design that fosters student support, self-regulation, and retention. *Campus-Wide Information Systems, 22*(2), 88–107.

Fisher, M., Coleman, B., Sparks, P., & Plett, C. (2007). Designing community learning in web-based environments. In B. H. Khan (Ed.), *Flexible learning in an information society.* Hershey, PA: Information Science Publishing.

Gyllenpalm, B. (2002). A virtual knowledge café. In K. E. Rudestam & J. Schoenholtz-Read (Eds.), *Handbook of online learning: Innovations in higher education and corporate training.* Thousand Oaks, CA: SAGE.

Milam, J., Voorhees, R. A., & Bedard-Voorhees, A. (2004). Assessment of online education: Policies, practices, and recommendations. *New Directions for Community Colleges, 2004*(126), 73–85.

Moallem, M. (2002). Designing and implementing an interactive online learning environment. In P. Comeaux (Ed.), *Communication and collaboration in the online classroom.* Bolton, MA: Anker Publishing.

Northrup, P. T. (2001). A framework for designing interactivity into web-based instruction. *Educational Technology, 41*(2), 31–39.

Osborne, C. D. (2008). *Establishing and fostering a community of faith among online learners: Instructional design considerations* (Unpublished doctoral dissertation). Capella University, Minneapolis, MN.

Osborne, C. D. (2009). You can call me Carl? [Online forum comment]. Retrieved from Facilitating Online Instruction course website, Mount Vernon University.

Palloff, R. M., & Pratt, K. (2003). *The virtual student: A profile and guide to working with online learners.* San Francisco: Jossey-Bass.

Palloff, R. M., & Pratt, K. (2005). *Collaborating online: Learning together in community.* San Francisco: John Wiley & Sons.

Polin, L. (2004). Learning in dialogue with a practicing community. In T. M. Duffy & J. R. Kirkley (Eds.), *Learner-centered theory and practice in distance education.* Mahwah, NJ: Erlbaum.

Rheingold, H. L. (2000). *The virtual community: Homesteading on the electronic frontier.* Cambridge, MA: MIT Press.

Riel, M. (2005). Building communities of learning online. In G. Kearsley (Ed.), *Online learning: Personal reflections on the transformation of education* (pp. 309–320). Englewood Cliffs, NJ: Educational Technology Publications.

Rovai, A. P. (2000). Building and sustaining community in asynchronous learning networks. *Internet and Higher Education, 3*(4), 285–297.

Rovai, A. P. (2002a). Building sense of community at a distance. *International Review of Research in Open and Distance Learning, 3*(1), 1–16.

Rovai, A. P. (2002b). Sense of community, perceived cognitive learning, and persistence in asynchronous learning networks. *Internet and Higher Education, 5*(4), 319–332.

Rovai, A. P. (2005). Feelings of alienation and community among higher education students in a virtual classroom. *Internet and Higher Education, 8*(2), 97–110.

Ruhleder, K. (2004). Interaction and engagement in LEEP: Undistancing "distance" education at the graduate level. In T. M. Duffy & J. R. Kirkley (Eds.), *Learner-centered theory and practice in distance education* (pp.71–90). Mahwah, NJ: Erlbaum.

Russo, T. C., & Campbell, S. W. (2004). Perceptions of mediated presence in an asynchronous online course: Interplay of communication behaviors and medium. *Distance Education, 25*(2), 215–232.

Shapiro, J. J., & Hughes, S. K. (2002). The case of the inflammatory e-mail: Building culture and community in online academic environments. In K. E. Rudestam & J. Schoenholtz-Read (Eds.), *Handbook of online learning: Innovations in higher education and corporate training* (pp. 91–124). Thousand Oaks, CA: SAGE.

Song, L., Singleton, E. S., Hill, J. R., & Koh, M. H. (2004). Improving online learning: Student perceptions of useful and challenging characteristics. *Internet and Higher Education, 7*(1), 59–70.

Stacey, E. (2002). Social presence online: Networking learners at a distance. *Education and Information Technologies, 7*(4), 287–294.

Tu, C.-H., & McIsaac, M. (2002). The relationship of social presence and interaction in online classes. *American Journal of Distance Education, 16*(3), 131–150.

Weiss, R. E. (2000). Humanizing the online classroom. *New Directions for Teaching and Learning, 2000*(84), 47–51.

Woods, R., & Ebersole, S. (2003). Using non-subject-matter-specific discussion boards to build connectedness in online learning. *American Journal of Distance Education, 17*(2), 99–118.

YouTube. (2009). *YouTube Help.* Retrieved from http://www.google.com/support /youtube/bin/topic.py?hl=en&topic=16560

15

Project-Based Learning
in Faith-Based Multicultural Education

Pamela M. Owen

INTRODUCTION

CONSTRUCTIVIST LEARNING THEORY IS viable in the university classroom. I implemented this theory following semesters of observation, reflection, and wrestling with the traditions often found in higher education. The dilemma facing me was the tension between traditional teacher-directed instruction versus the more student-directed focus of the constructivist theory. I promoted constructivist learning for young children in a university classroom of early childhood education students, but teaching the theory from a textbook radically clashed with the methods of the very theory I was teaching. If constructivism is relevant, shouldn't it stand that I model what I believed was best practice? Given the controversy of the constructivist theory, I wondered if I could use it while supporting the goals of our faith-based education. I carefully designed half the semester to resolve the contradiction while simultaneously being compatible with our faith-based goals of a Christian university. This was accomplished through the implementation of the Project Approach (Chard, 2005; Katz & Chard, 1989).

CHARACTERISTICS OF CONSTRUCTIVISM REFLECTED IN THE PROJECT APPROACH MODELING

I chose the Project Approach because it is a constructivist teaching and learning structure. I used it to open the topic of multicultural education to my students. At the end of the semester, students had learned a new teaching method for use with their students, and they had acquired personal knowledge about multicultural education (Owen, 2010; Owen, 2007). The principles of constructivism—basing the curriculum on personally relevant material, building concepts from a common knowledge base, encouraging social interaction, taking the time to fully work through concepts, exploring how to learn, in meaningful contexts, and motivating learners—were evident throughout the work. These principles are fully present in the Project Approach as discussed in this chapter.

Posing Personally Relevant Investigations

Personal experience is foundational to the theory of constructivism. It is vital that the learners have personal experience as it relates to the topic being investigated. It is assumed that learners bring prior experience and opinion to their learning experience. The theory of constructivism challenges beliefs and offers the opportunity to build new knowledge and internalize new beliefs based on personal relevance. Also, it is important that the learner take ownership of the learning. Students are more likely to be invested in learning that they find to be important. Learners need to believe that the topic of study is important to their lives. This component of constructivist theory was evident in the work completed by my students using the Project Approach.

I asked students to construct their own understanding of a particular problem or situation that was relevant to them. Students thought carefully about their learning goals. They had to work within the topic of multicultural education but that was the only limit.

As they discussed multicultural experiences, personal relevancy was revealed. They identified specific interests in the area of multicultural education and developed these interests into investigations. This procedure naturally built on prior knowledge and provided a comfortable segue to further study that was grounded in personal curiosity. Topics ranged from creating an appropriate classroom environment to political and advocacy issues.

Establishing a Shared Knowledge Base

Constructivist theory relies heavily on a shared knowledge base, especially when working in a group setting. To prevent the risk of what Abdal-Haqq (1998) considers idiosyncratic knowledge, common experiences were provided through shared readings, video viewings, and lectures. These experiences were not designed to be prescriptive or considered as direct instruction, to do so would be antithetical to the constructivist theory of learning; instead, they were open-ended for the purpose of promoting inquiry, discovery, and self-reflection. They needed to acquire contextual knowledge to construct their own understanding of the Project Approach and multicultural education.

This was accomplished through the shared readings, viewings, and discussions. All students watched a video (Helm, Katz, & Scranton, 2000) to build their knowledge about the Project Approach. They enriched their knowledge by exploring Chard's website (2005) and locating project samples. Common experiences were provided to build knowledge regarding multicultural education. "An Indian Father's Plea," (Lake, 1990), *Anti-bias Curriculum: Tools for Empowering Young Children* (Derman-Sparks, 1991), *Starting Small: Teaching Children Tolerance* (McGovern, 1997), *A Framework for Understanding Poverty* (Payne, 1998), and *Multiple Social and Cultural Contexts* (RISE, n.d.) were a few of the shared resources.

Transforming Learning into a Social Activity

Dewey, Piaget, and Vygotsky all recognize the importance of social interaction in the learning process. Educators need to not only espouse this idea, they need to encourage, promote, and model the practice. Using the Project Approach to study multicultural education is an example of such modeling.

Learning took place in a social arena. Students learned from each other. Concepts, problems, and interests were identified as experiences were shared. Students interacted with others through interviews, visits, and field trips. Knowledge was constructed as interactions were experienced. Students supported each other as new information was collected and analyzed. Conversation was an essential facet of learning. As Bodrova and Leong (1996) report, "Learning occurs in shared situations. To share an activity, we must talk about that activity. Unless we talk, we will never be able to know each other's meanings" (p. 13). The students shared activities through discussion and verbal reflection.

Taking the Time to Construct Knowledge

Time plays a role in constructivist learning. Learners need more time than a few hours in a classroom or study group. Many times instructors rush through class in an attempt to "cover" all the content, but in reality, learners do not absorb the information. It takes time to build knowledge. Learners need to question content, test hypothesis, inquire of others, wonder at and consider the information before actually understanding. They need time to think, to investigate, to digest, and to share. Quality thinking does not happen in a vacuum. Piagetian constructivists recognize the value of time and the social transmission of knowledge (Bodrova & Leong, 1996).

By dedicating half the semester to only two concepts, Project Approach and multicultural education, students had time to benefit from this principle of constructivism. They had time to think, to revisit ideas, to contemplate, to inquire, and to absorb information; thus, they could construct knowledge.

Much of class time was devoted to discussions of personal experience and discovery. Individuals reported the progress of investigations, which included interviews, observations, surveys, library research, and artifact collection. Often the initial questions were revised, modified, or changed; the research changed direction as more knowledge was gained. Individual research plans were refined.

Learning to Learn

Cognition, the process of knowing and learning, is of critical importance in the theory of constructivism. Constructivists encourage learners to not only build meaning and knowledge based on personal experience and social interaction but to also develop systems of learning, thus identifying personal ways of learning. Students discover "what works for them" and gain information about how they learn as individuals.

The project in my classroom required students to think independently and rely on themselves instead of the instructor telling them what to study, what to think, and how to make application. They acknowledged their individual learning styles and were appreciative to operate within that style. Beyond focusing on their individual learning needs, students also solved social problems, such as problems within the group dynamic, and sought help when it was needed. By doing these things, the students generally felt accomplished and proud. They learned to learn.

Learning in Context

Constructivist tenets hold that learning takes place in a context, and it is not through a set of isolated facts and ideas. Individual lives and experiences greatly impact the content learners are facing. Knowledge, beliefs, fears, and experiences influence what is learned and how it is learned.

The learning that took place in the Project Approach design flowed naturally from the origin of personal context. Individual studies grounded in personal interest were revealed through brainstorming and planning sessions. No limitations were imposed; the study was to be based on students' prior knowledge. This knowledge was stimulated by discussing experiences with various cultures. Students shared stories, photographs, drawings, and artifacts explaining personal encounters and attitudes, thus promoting self-awareness. "Broadening their awareness and learning more about cultures other than their own was at the core of their investigations" (Owen, 2007, p. 223).

Enhancing Learning through Motivation

Motivation is a key component to many learning theories but critical to the constructivist theory. Learners more eagerly approach an academic task if they have a reason to learn the material. We see this demonstrated in people of all ages. An infant is motivated to crawl, thus practices until the skill has been mastered. An adult is motivated to master a sport, thus practices until the skill has been mastered. Learners of all ages want to satisfy their intellectual curiosity as well as develop their physical skills. The need and desire to learn is motivating.

Having control over what to learn and how to learn it transfers the power from the instructor to the learner, enhancing motivation and the desire to learn. The learners using the Project Approach were motivated to learn as evidenced through self-evaluations and end-of-course surveys. Students reported a desire to create a similar environment in their future classrooms. They were engaged learners who were eager to discover answers to questions that were important and relevant to them. They took responsibility for their own learning. In the end, more was learned than initially expected, and the students actually exceeded the course objectives. They reported increased knowledge about both the Project Approach and multicultural education.

The theory of constructivism can clearly be successfully implemented in the university classroom. It takes time, planning, and a measure of risk as the instructor shares responsibility for the learning. The Project Approach is not the only method that can be used. It does, however, offer a structure that provides comfort to both the teacher and the student.

THE PROJECT APPROACH IN A FAITH-BASED SETTING

The principles of constructivism—basing the curriculum on personally relevant material, building concepts from a common knowledge base, encouraging social interaction, taking the time to fully work through concepts, exploring how to learn, in meaningful contexts, and motivating learners—were evident throughout the project work and are fully compatible with goals of faith-based education.

The university in which this project work took place holds the following as some of the goals for their students (Mount Vernon University, 2009–2010):

- Acquire the process of continual self-evaluation of personal values

- Choose a value system eventuating in meaningful service to God and mankind

- Continue to develop the ability to listen receptively, think critically, reason clearly, evaluate objectively, and communicate cogently and clearly

- Analyze, synthesize, and integrate various types of information and structures of knowledge, including the causal relationships of events and the logical relationship of ideas

- Continue to develop and maintain meaningful, rewarding relationships with individuals including those in the wider social context

- Grow with others in community: with neighbors, with fellow citizens, and with members of the Church, the body of Christ

- Acquire attitudes which stimulate awareness of oneself and one's environment enabling one to respond creatively and positively

- Choose a discriminative set of values and communicate them without being coercive or dogmatic

These particular goals were accomplished through the project work as evidenced through student journals, narratives, reports, and discussions. Sample quotations from students follow (Owen, 2007); embedded in the comments is a demonstration of the accomplishment of the university goals: self-evaluation, values, communication, evaluation, service, and living in community.

> "We need to plan, be intentional, to build our awareness."

> "It is our responsibility to learn about cultures other than our own."

> "Teachers have a responsibility to break stereotypes."

Most of the candidates made statements indicating a sense of efficacy toward promoting equity:

> "I want to be responsible and accountable for what I have learned, and I want to be able to apply it. I feel that a professional understanding, with personal experiences, is the basis for understanding multicultural education and anti-bias curriculum."

> "I was able to put all the information together and *understand* it. I feel like I learned a lot and I could just talk about it easily without any notes or anything. I didn't just memorize information: I actually learned and understood the information."

> "I felt the highest accomplishment when we were interviewing parents of adopted international children. I got a lot of information from the parents, and I felt I understood them very well. I felt excited about what we were learning."

> "Project Approach helped me take learning into my own hands. I wasn't given specific guidelines of what to do, so I had to think for myself."

In addition to the faith-based goals, students made comments clearly indicting that the constructivist approach prompted motivation.

> "I was very excited about learning about this topic. It is work I wanted to know more about and is close to my heart. I felt very accomplished."

> "My partner and I dove in head first into the research and the project itself."

CONCLUSION

The constructivist design used in this classroom setting, which has since been replicated annually for nearly a decade, has been highly successful. Thus, it indicates the viability of the constructivist learning theory in the university classroom. The tension between traditional teacher-directed instruction versus the more student-directed focus of the constructivist theory has been, in part, resolved in my practice. I am confident that the principles of constructivism touch the spirit of the learner and can enhance the understanding of Jesus' teaching of love, service, and compassionate understanding.

Who is to say if Jesus used a constructivist approach when teaching? But we do know that when Jesus taught he often told stories. These stories directly connected to the lives of his listeners much like the students' stories connected to their lives. We know that Jesus gave the responsibility to learn to the individual. He never forced a person to follow. We know when individuals did follow they were internally motivated and enthusiastic; they asked questions and sought answers. They were, at times, wrong or misguided, but Jesus responded with patience and gave them time to resolve their issues and concerns. His teaching appeared to often be "student-directed" as well as "teacher-directed." Considering the model of Jesus as teacher and the success of using a constructivist approach, I am encouraged to continue to practice the Project Approach and search for other methods of implementing constructivist theory.

REFERENCES

Abdal-Haqq, I. (1998). *Constructivism in teacher education: Considerations for those who would link practice to theory.* ERIC document ED426986

Bodrova, E., & Leong, D. J. (1996). *Tools of the mind: The Vygotskian approach to early childhood education.* Upper Saddle River, NJ: Merrill.

Chard, S. C. (2005). *Project Approach.* Retrieved from http://www.project~approach.com

Derman-Sparks, L. (1991). *Anti-bias curriculum: Tools for empowering young children.* Washington, DC: National Association for the Education of Young Children.

Helm, J. H., Katz, L., & Scranton, P. (2000). *A children's journey investigating the fire truck* [Video]. New York: Teachers College.

Katz, L. G., & Chard, S. C. (1989). *Engaging children's minds: The project approach.* Norwood, NJ: Ablex.

Lake, R. (1990). An Indian father's plea. *Teacher Magazine, 2*(1), 48–53.

McGovern, M. (Producer). (1997). *Staring small: Teaching children tolerance* [Video]. Montgomery, AL: Teaching Tolerance.

Mount Vernon Nazarene University. (2009–2010). *Catalog.* Mount Vernon, OH: Mount Vernon Nazarene University.

Owen, P. M. (2007). Integrating Katz and Chard's Project Approach with multicultural education in the university classroom. *Journal of Early Childhood Teacher Education, 28,* 219–232.

Owen, P. M. (2010). Increasing pre-service teachers' support of multicultural education. *Multicultural Perspectives, 12*(1), 1–8.

Payne, R. K. (1998). *A framework for understanding poverty.* Baytown, TX: RFT Publishing. (rev. ed.)

RISE (Producer). (n.d.). *Multiple social and cultural contexts* [Video 2 of Tools for Teaching Developmentally Appropriate Practice: The Leading Edge in Early Childhood Education]. Washington, DC: National Association for the Education of Young Children.

16

Until My Change Comes: Assessment in the Faith-Based Classroom with Constructivist Components[1]

Michael D. Dixon

ASSESSMENT AS AN AGENT OF TRANSFORMATION

Assessment is a term that carries broad potential for connotation. Ideological perspective, philosophical orientation, and formal training provide us with cues for interpreting all that assessment may entail. Constructivist thinking holds a perspective of assessment for both teacher and pupil. Since meaning-making is a fundamental aspect of constructivist thought, assessment and its functions from that perspective involve not just a determination of sorts, but a transformation through the process as well.

> Beloved, now we are children of God, and it has not appeared as yet what we will be. We know that when He appears, we will be like Him, because we will see Him just as He is. (1 John 3:2, NASB)

From this Scripture we perceive what assessment is and what is does. It is a comparison against some accepted standard. In this scriptural example, assessment is a comparison with that which is perfect. This process of comparison has a transcendent component that also transforms. We shall become like him because we shall see him as he is.

This view of assessment is crucial as we confront what it means to be a transformed individual. It also provides a context for teachers and

1. I extend my appreciation to Steve Metcalfe for his valuable comments on the early draft of this chapter.

administrators in faith-based schools to be what we want our students to become. Since we will never be perfect in this life, what we strive to be is in process toward excellence.

Assessment does not originate in the field of education. It comes out of judicial and financial arenas, as one discovers from the etymology of the root *assess*. The Online Etymology Dictionary (Harper, 2009) defines *assess* as: " 'to fix the amount (of a tax, fine, etc.),' from Anglo-Fr. *assesser*, from M.L. *assessare* 'fix a tax upon,' originally frequentative of L. . . . *assidere* 'to sit beside' (and thus to assist in the office of a judge)." *Assessment* is a relatively new term in educational reform. It replaced *testing*, which is now interpreted as an examination of learning from a perspective that is: (1) summative (covering a specified amount of material), (2) traditional (matching, multiple choice, and problem solving on paper; reflection writing; etc.), and (3) teacher centered.

In *Redeeming Science*, Poythress (2006) states, "Science is discovering the mind of God" (p. 160). In many ways, education is doing likewise, using assessment as the comparison of what we "presently already know" to our socially discovered and constructed view of God's mind. In this context, this construction is a form of "truth," as measured by predetermined standards. This view aligns well with the scriptural example above and speaks to the constructivist quality of meaning-making that define our *imago Dei* (image of God).

In the context of improving academic quality, assessment is a comparison between what is actually being constructed by students, what is done, and how it is done by students and teachers, to a standard, typically a state standard for a given content area.

Total Quality Management (TQM) has been used to justify the state standards assessment, but at its core TQM is focused on comparisons with an ideal. In TQM, assessment is related to quality and is intended to be human centered and data informed. Unfortunately, it is often applied in the reverse, being data centered and data driven. People assessed become secondary to the data assessment delivers.

The human-centered application of TQM goes beyond what a student did on a test, or how well individual questions on a test were answered. It involves other assessment tools such as journaling, homework, labs, presentations, portfolios, exhibits, letter writing, and work on extended projects. These can provide greater context and understanding beyond mean scores and standard deviations.

Recognizing the gap between the perfect and the current status of achievement impacts faith-based schools because it directs schools and teachers to achieve the shared goal toward transformative perfection. This transformation covers academic and personal arenas including faith and identity formation. Faith-based schools work within those flaws and focus on their ultimate goal of improving the systems they operate within.

Being humbly open about flaws is important. It sets a tone of improvement throughout the school that creates a culture dedicated to improvement. Dedication to improving should be central when faith-based schools determine improvement strategies. These approaches include selecting assessment tools, areas, and subjects to assess and which not to assess; selecting implementation protocols; deciding how assessment data will be used; and deciding how to integrate assessment data to address differentiation and methods of learning.

Assessment in a faith-based school can be a means for creating positive transformation, a means of critiquing and correcting teaching and learning techniques, and a means to positively impact self-identity of students and teachers. From practitioner experience, I view assessment as an interconnected component of healthy student, and classroom, transformation. It involves such things as school vision and resources. In this context, assessment's role in learning is central for both teacher and learner.

ASSESSMENT SYSTEM FOR TRANSFORMATION: BUILDING BLOCKS OF ASSESSMENT

The goal of education is to transform students, not to assess them. Assessment is just one tool to assist human-centered change. Transformation is a radical type of change that creates a new nature in the object that is changed. Transformation is one result of assessment because assessment gauges expected accomplishment and challenges students to strive toward an ideal. Romans 12:1–2 makes this point clear: "Do not be conformed to this world but be transformed by the renewing of your mind, that you may prove what is the good and acceptable will of God." This perspective of "renewing of your mind" should be a faith-based school's standard of quality.

Assessment clarifies how performance has attained to what is expected, consequences for not reaching an expectation, and rewards for achieving expectations. Jesus' disciples were transformed through three years of experiential and constructed learning. During that time they were exposed to his standard of quality, but they were also assessed, encouraged, trained, and rebuked by him.

Jesus used both formative and summative assessment to develop his disciples. One formative assessment is in Luke 10:17–20, where Jesus sent his disciples to practice what they were taught, correcting them when they returned to prioritize the right things, to focus not on what they could do, but on understanding what was truly important, their walk with God, which would ultimately be assessed when disciples met God and their names were found in the book of life.

Jesus' summative assessments mirror components of taxonomies like Bloom's, (updated by Anderson and Krathwohl in 2001) and actually connect evaluation and assessment with knowledge construction as part of higher order thinking. These higher order cognitive skills develop and progress from remembering to understanding to applying to analyzing to evaluating (assessing) to creating (synthesis).

THE TRIAGE OF HEALTHY CHANGE

Healthy academic and personal transformation of an individual is a systems-based process where assessment is one of several components. Just as one has to be examined when going to an emergency room, schools should do triage assessment to identify potential hindrances of constructive, systemic, and healthy change. A framework for triage that I have developed from research and ongoing practice identifies components of health. When components are missing, corresponding symptoms are assessable. Seven components of a healthy classroom and healthy school change include: classroom vision, skill development, student/teacher incentive, resources, a plan, sending forth, assessment.

From my personal experience as a practitioner and administrator, I have seen how assessment can take on a life of its own. Another thing I have seen with school improvement is that there are often other systemic symptoms that arise with plans that can get overlooked, that are unexamined, or that are simply not seen as connected. These symptoms often stem from unfulfilled components of healthy change.

As indicated in table 16.1, when one aspect of healthy transformation is missing, consequences ensue and can be assessed. For example, if the vision of the school or classroom is not clear, confusion arises from those asked to implement or participate in that vision. Or, if a teacher is asked to do something they are not adequately skilled to do, like teach a special education or AP class, that teacher may have anxiety about teaching that class. If a school has a great process, lesson plan, and vision, but the students or teachers don't buy into the process or lack some sense of need or incentive to work hard, the change that is expected will be slower to occur.

Table 16.1 Managing for healthy classroom change

Vision	Skills	Need (Incentive)	Resources	Plan, do, study, act (PDSA)	Sending forth	Assessment (Measure)	Healthy Change
	Skills	Need	Resources	Plan	Sending forth	Assessment	Confusion
Vision		Need	Resources	Plan	Sending forth	Assessment	Anxiety
Vision	Skills		Resources	Plan	Sending forth	Assessment	Gradual change
Vision	Skills	Need		Plan	Sending forth	Assessment	Frustration
Vision	Skills	Need	Resources		Sending forth	Assessment	False starts
Vision	Skills	Need	Resources	Plan		Assessment	Over- dependence
Vision	Skills	Need	Resources	Plan	Sending forth		Disappointing change

Faith-based schools often have challenges with resources. When resources are low, and a teacher tries to prepare students without adequate resources, both the teacher and the students become frustrated. Without a clear plan for improvement, and implementation of that plan, a common result is "false start." This is similar to diet or exercise goals people set that get forgotten or laid aside. This is also similar to many textbook or curriculum adoptions that are soon forsaken.

Teachers and students need opportunities to demonstrate their competence to feel empowered and to mature in their ability and independence. Jesus sent out seventy-two disciples (Luke 10:1) to provide them practice doing what they saw him doing. Sending forth is often not adopted as part of the education process, but students too should make assignments, make their own practice games, do peer editing, etc. Teachers need a professional license in order to make a vision their own. This sort of empowering multiplies the strengths of the teacher and engenders a sense of worth and identity to students that is as important as a lesson, especially in a faith-based classroom. Without a sending forth, students can easily become over dependant on the teacher, and teachers over dependent on administrators for making change happen.

Change requires assessment. Without assessment of the students' present performance, or of where the academic and cultural structure of an organization is, and so forth, there is no mirror available from which comparison to a standard can be made. In order to create effective and healthy change, a comparative evaluation of the assessment results must take place.

The parts of any system are interconnected by definition. Assessment is not an independent activity but a vital member for other components within a system of healthy change. Assessment that corresponds to other factors involved in change, including shared vision, requisite skills development, and appropriate incentive for learners, is critical. Meaningful assessment utilizes available resources, is complementary to the plan that enacts the vision, is regularly applied to encourage improvement (a sending forth, as Jesus did with his disciples). All of these conditions allow for knowledge construction.

THE ISSUES OF ASSESSMENT

Change comes through comparison of reality to a desired outcome. The process of comparison is what I view as assessment. Much of modern school reform is based on assessment principles that come straight from the business world. These include the use of benchmarks, Whole School Improvement plans, and data-driven improvement.

Like Christ's words and the Bible, Deming's (1986) principles can be interpreted and misinterpreted by "Assessment Pharisees," people who use faith and data for personal gain, rather than for sincere transformation. Data-driven instruction has become the norm in schools rather than an intended student-centered instruction that is data informed.

Assessment's Irony: The More One Assesses, the Poorer the Result, When Minimum Standards Are Set

According to the TQM model, regular quality checks should be done away with. Reasons for this perspective include: (1) defects are assumed; (2) defects will be detected at the end of the manufacturing process; and (3) those checks happen too late in the process to improve the system. Implications of this perspective have huge ramifications for students. Instead of using assessment as a mechanism for identifying "bad" students, the assessment process should be pervasive throughout the system, constructed by all stakeholders, and supportive for the system to create fewer "defects."

Tests are important, but it provides a suggestion that personal excellence should be the standard we strive to attain, rather than some minimum standard, or basal test score (Aguayo, 1991). Base expectations can actually have the opposite effect than what educators strive for. In the case of the two car transmissions, one can assume the Japanese manufacturers were proud of their work and not just concerned with getting paid.

From an academic perspective one can see that grading alone can actually make some students lazy. If a student can get 92 points and earn an A, she or he may not have much incentive for striving for 100. The American manufacturer built their transmissions within specifications, which is similar to getting an A, but they stopped there. The Japanese company applied the single standard of perfection. Because that standard can never be reached, striving for it is never fully satisfied. Instead, by following a continuously motivating standard that seeks improved systems, high-quality results becomes the norm.

What Faith-Based Schools Can Learn from Constructivist Limitations and Strengths in Urban Settings

As we determine methods of comparison for educational models, we should examine constructivism and its theoretical and practical bases. Brooks and Brooks (1993) state, "Constructivist teaching practices . . . help learners to internalize and reshape, or transform new information" (p. 15). Consequently, learning is the process of adjusting our schemas to accommodate novel learning experiences.

A concern many faith-based schools have is that if this philosophi-cal perspective is taken too far it can give individuals a license to cre-ate knowledge without academic, religious, or moral boundaries. From my experience with urban education, creating boundaries and utilizing teacher leadership is very important, yet it does not take away from the use of constructivist theory in teaching and learning. Jesus never gave up authority in his classroom, but he used that authority in a human-centered way. This authority-shared model with boundaries is very simi-lar to TQM's human-centered approach, and to complex instruction's structured cooperative instruction methodology called "management of roles," developed by Cohen et al. (1993). Jesus' teaching structure supported a meaning-making process, and ensured comparison (assess-ment) was based on that which was perfect, not on individually con-structed models.

A faith-based perspective assumes absolutes that give structure and boundaries on what can be constructed. For example, creating "knowledge" that eliminates faith is outside a faith-based perspective. Understanding limitations of constructivist thought is therefore helpful in this regard.

Many faith-based schools, especially those who take the biblical mandate to serve those most in need, learn to embrace constructivist frameworks with boundaries that create order and allow them to stay true to their mission. Urban education is currently falling behind in terms of academic performance with respect to its suburban counter-parts. Constructivist pedagogical approaches help bridge this gap and accelerate learning, especially around tasks and products like standard-ized tests.

In this era of standards-based school reform, urban faith-based schools sit at a crossroads. Lisa Delpit (1995) describes the importance of quality products (even those established by a social space that does not fully include people of color):

> Teachers do students no service to suggest, even implicitly, that product is not important. In this country, students will be judged on their product regardless of the process they utilized to achieve it. In addition, that product, based on the specific codes of a par-ticular culture, is more readily produced when the directives of how to produce it are made explicit. (p. 31)

Constructivism, by itself, is not always effective in urban areas (Collins, 1999). Structure is often needed in urban schools (Shearon, 1999), because there is such a lack of structure in the environment of such students. Faith-based schools, like other urban schools, are isolated via a lack of power and language to enact change in the general society. Consequently, instructional structures create order, provide safety, and empower its members. Doing so in an honest way, by any method necessary including instructionalism, allows for a more freeing discourse.

In reality, students have the language they bring, and a language they need to learn for commerce and discourse with other communities, specifically, the majority community. "[Teachers] should recognize that the linguistic form a student brings to school is intimately connected with loved ones, community, and personal identity" (Delpit, 1995, p. 53). Students who are taught to become "bilingual" students, to communicate in their home language and the more widely accepted academic language, are able to enact change in both arenas (Steele, 1994).

For immigrants to be taken seriously in America at the turn of the twentieth century, they had to learn English. At that time, language differences were clear and distinct. Today, the educational influence of our constructivist society is rooted in a paradigm of individualistic standards. If students in faith-based schools are to become successful, they have to understand that there are other viewpoints available to them. They must learn how to translate into their own perspective through acquired skills using whatever resources they have available. Then they need to begin to let the world see the standard they use for true assessment regarding principles such as purpose and justice.

Creating Positive Change from Social Assessment

Using the lens of constructivism, it is easy to see that within similar faith-based orientations there is a diversity of beliefs, boundaries, and priorities. To get desired change from such frameworks requires assessments based on an individual school's vision and how each student connects with that vision. There should always be room for individual accomplishment and goal setting within a local academic setting. As Christians, our model is Christ, but Paul said "follow me as I follow Christ" (1 Cor 11:1), meaning we have a faith mandate to be challenged by, and to imitate others.

This framework allows us to take on challenges we might not otherwise take on. The challenge of assessment becomes what I call the "Tom Sawyer heuristic," where assessment itself helps us to problem solve and to create knowledge of what we are capable of through healthy challenge. Tom Sawyer encouraged some younger children through reverse psychology that white washing the fence he was supposed to paint was a task for bigger kids (Twain, 1876/1987). Likewise, we can use assessment tools as "fences to paint" to encourage students to take on challenges and to build ownership of their efforts.

When teaching AP calculus and physics in an urban public school, I expected more work, developed contracts for students, mandated Saturday classes, and expected all students in these classes to take AP exams at the end of the course. Such a challenge had the opposite effect one might expect in an urban environment. Instead of deterring students from taking the class, the challenge actually encouraged students to participate, and it became my largest class. I did not use psychology as Tom Sawyer did, but instead gave students the opportunity, making them feel better about themselves and their school. At that time, AP courses had not been offered at the school for many years previous. The challenge of the assessment helped create change.

Social and Affective Components of Constructivism and Assessment

Constructivism is not just an educational philosophy. It is a worldview that permeates every aspect of society including business, the military, and education. The governing of the modern soul includes the individuality of Vygotsky and Dewey's democratic constructivism. With constructivism, there is the risk of students constructing destructive knowledge that hinders academic performance itself. A hidden curriculum (Schiro, 1980) often lurks underneath the official curricula of a school. This curriculum may include: lack of academic encouragement of a student, lack of direct focus on stereotype threat (Steele, 1999), and issues such as mathematics phobias, and societal baggage, such as a limited number of parents graduating from college (College Board, 1999, p. 9).

According to Schiro (1980), curriculum can be seen in three ways: as object, interaction, and intent. These encompass the overt curriculum, but also the hidden curriculum that often has just as much effect on students. Such curriculum provides a context for students to accept and create knowledge, including positive and negative perceptions of themselves, their self worth, and their ability.

When the hidden curriculum leads to negative academic perspectives of one's self, it can infect the culture of a school. In many urban schools dominated by people of color, students who achieve academically are often labeled as "selling out" and "acting white" (U.S. Department of Education, 1998, p. 4). Such "learning" can also lead to internalization of stereotypes that result in lower performance on tests due to the stereotype threat (Steele, 1997).

Knowledge construction for higher-order problem solving is one area to build needed storehouses of knowledge in our increasingly technological society. "Given the complexity and pace of technological advancement in recent decades, educational goals have expanded from mastery of basic skills to developing higher-level thinking skills" (Henke, Chen, & Goldman, 1999, p. 1). Vygotsky (1978) formalized the social building mechanism of academic concepts. In order to understand his view of socially supported academic learning (scaffolding), we have to clarify his meaning of the zone of proximal development (ZPD) where scaffolding takes place. Vygotsky (1978) defined the ZPD as: "the distance between the child's actual development as determined by independent problem solving and the level of potential development as determined through problem solving under adult guidance or in collaboration with capable peers" (p. 88).

Higher-order cognitive functions begin with social-cultural interaction, according to Vygotsky (1978). He brilliantly extended this concept of mediation in human environment interaction to the use of signs as well as tools. Like tool systems, sign systems (language, writing, number systems) are created by societies and change across time with forms of society and levels of cultural development. Vygotsky also said, "[All] the higher functions originate as actual relations between [people]" (Vygotsky, 1978, p. 57). If that is true, and higher functions relate to Bloom's updated taxonomy (Anderson & Krathwohl, 2001), then higher-order skills such as assessing and creating come from a social context.

Within this context, assessment is also a social activity. It is not merely something administered to individuals, but a challenge for a group to assume together. Intentional group work has multiple purposes, including:

1. Encouraging group work by national councils, just as Jesus sent out the seventy-two disciples in pairs (Luke 10:1)

2. Developing group problem-solving skills, as Jesus did regularly with his disciples. Business and industry also covet quality workers who are able to work with a team to problem solve.

3. Overcoming the gap between levels of students to their counterparts in standardized tests and skills for employment (Tal, Krajcik, Blumenfeld, 2006)

4. Developing higher-order thinking skills (Bassarear & Davidson, 1992)

5. Intentionally teaching cooperation between students (Cohen et. al, 1994)

6. Empowering students for the changing of their society, rather than enabling them to become victims of it (Lipman, 1998)

7. Providing individual reflection while developing group feedback skills for the feedback itself. Activities requiring peer assessment enable "students to learn while judging their own work or the work of others" (Ma & Millman, 2005).

Assessment's Impact on the Affective Component of Learning

Assessment impacts students at every educational exchange. This means how students perceive an assessment impacts what students feel about themselves as a result of the assessment. The stimuli that impact these educational exchanges are therefore important to explore in understanding of the effectiveness of an assessment.

Dunn and DeBello (1999) consider five stimuli with twenty-three corresponding elements that influence how students learn. For the purposes of this chapter, the five stimuli are categorized into three parts: the locus of exchanges, where they take place (the hand- environmental and physiological stimuli), conceptual methods and types of exchanges (the head-intellectual and psychological stimuli), and affective types and methods of exchanges (the heart-emotional and sociological stimuli). Table 16.2 presents Dunn and Dunn's (1978) stimuli model with regard to the framework of educational exchange. It also shows how social educational methods such as complex instruction and TQM relate to the three elements.

Table 16.2 The framework of educational exchange

	Exchange	Stimuli	Social methods	Total quality methods
Interaction with the environment (hand)	Locus and infrastructure of education exchanges: scaffolding	Environmental Physiological	Group work	Teachers and administrative systems support classes that feed students into the current class.
Intellectual types and methods of exchanges (head)	Conceptual methods and types of exchanges	Academic Psychological	Peer scaffolding and group problem solving	Students can redo assessments until they achieve mastery.
Emotive types and methods of exchanges (heart)	Affective methods and types of exchanges	Emotional Sociological	Team building, confidence building through group work	Teachers design assessments to drive out fear.

If our standard of knowledge is seen as more than a collection of facts and ideas implemented in rote procedures, active individual internalization of knowledge can be thought of as a goal of education that leads to achievement. Active individual internalization should allow students to problem solve utilizing higher-order thinking skills and develop metacognitive strategies regarding how they approach higher order problems. Active internalization allows students to create new knowledge and solve increasingly difficult problems. Vygotsky (1978) describes this internalization process as a series of transformations:

> An operation that initially represents an external activity is reconstructed and begins to occur intentionally. . . . An interpersonal process is transformed into an intrapersonal one. Every function of a child's cultural development appears twice . . . first, between people (interpsychological), and then inside the child (intrapsycholigcal). (p. 57)

Social assessment creates a feedback loop that impacts students cognitively as well as emotionally. If students feel like they never measure up to the standard of an assessment, they may internalize failure. If they come to believe that the standard is not reachable but still a challenge to do their personal best, like one's walk of faith (as being imitators of Christ), then they can also internalize the idea of assessment as a constructive challenge, especially if threat is replaced with a drive to succeed with mastery.

One of Deming's principles of TQM is "driving out fear" (1986). This goes beyond minimizing to actually challenging the sources of fear in the classroom. Language used in educational exchanges can create a healthy culture for assessment, which effectively connects with the head (knowledge), the heart (efficacy), and the hands (performance) of students, or it can create a culture that tears students down so they become less effective learners.

HINDRANCES TO ASSESSMENT TOP DOWN USES OF ASSESSMENT WITH CONSTRUCTIVISM

Teachers are the "closest to meaningful change" (Boggs, 1996), and as with any effort to change someone's job, teachers may become resistant and downright defiant if not included in the reform process. It is important to keep in mind that teachers in a constructivist classroom often can include student peers in addition to the traditional adult in the role of instructor.

Current reform movements based on assessment often don't teach a man to fish, they simply tell the man how many fish he should have caught by now. This lack of vision takes the joy out of fishing. Teaching and learning in the classroom is where the "fishing" takes place. External forces have driven reform over the past forty years. People say we have less fish, and less quality fish than other countries, for example. Similarly, as a response to the Russians "defeating" the American space program, the Physical Science Study Committee (PSSC) was developed that was a university-driven response to Sputnik (Schiro, 1980). Similar outcries were heard after the last set of TIMSS (Third International Mathematics and Science Survey) results. Schools were blamed for the sky falling, and schools had to do something.

Results of PSSC and frameworks are similar, which ultimately translate into an attempt to make learning "teacher proof." In some districts, teachers literally have to be on the same page in their teacher's guides. That is a quality principle that has gone too far. The teacher is in some ways the CEO of the classroom. Many administrators can relate to this. They would not feel positively if their board of directors took decision-making away from them because scores slipped without ever being given a chance to personally address what happened.

Management needs to model what it wants others to become. According to some top-down models, school should apparently be reduced to taking tests. In this context, the very nature of education gets dragged down into mechanistic repetitions. Even components that are constructivist in nature become mechanical and prescribed.

Teachers are often left out of the discussion on reform. The process of design and implementation is usually top-down. As Dolan (1994) makes clear from several management examples, top-down reform is very limited and is often infected with the same disease as what created the need for reform in the first place.

> The overriding lesson of all these stories (about Ford) is that the remedies look dangerously like the dysfunctions that they are meant to heal. They are almost always imposed from above, driven in isolated and un-integrated fashion, focused on short-term quantitative results, and seldom if ever involve people who do the work. The net result is often further dysfunction and deeper anger and frustration. (Dolan, 1994, p.50)

I advocate teacher-centered change because that is where the power and heart of learning lie in the classroom. There are many external forces impeding student success in school, but good teachers can at least have a fighting chance to address those factors if allowed to create change. This would allow them true professionalism. Teacher-centered reform also builds up an environment of learning, and students are also exposed to a model of human excellence that is scriptural, not being perfect, but striving for continuous improvement.

Pharisaical Use of Data That Is Not Student Centered

Whole school improvement plans, data-driven improvement plans, and the like often use benchmarks, timetables, and other TQM tools; these uses of data often prioritize the data over real, meaningful learning. If one uses constructivist components in the classroom, the centrality of the student is evident. Deming (1986) understood the importance of having a bottom-up framework, because those on the bottom are closest to where quality can really be impacted. Like those who misplace priorities with data, Pharisees were religious zealots chastised by Jesus because they missed the gospel by prioritizing the wrong things. They prioritized the external factors of the faith, rather than the internal.

Modern academic Pharisees misuse data by using it to deal with student deficiencies rather than for really improving student learning. For example, as the Pharisees focused on the laws more than the God behind the laws, states focus on getting students to pass a test rather than getting them ready for college and other effective outcomes after high school. States that have mandatory exams often use data to determine whether students need more time preparing for the state tests at the expense of all else, without considering the affective components of learning, causing many to drop out, as well as missing other major goals.

Getting students ready for college using an AP course and AP preparatory courses can have a bigger impact than having more state test math prep courses. How one constructs knowledge at ever increasing levels is more important than what score they get on one test. Though a high-stakes test score may be a great tool to get a snapshot of where a student's skills are for taking those kinds of tests, it is not necessarily an accurate evaluation of what they understand, or how they understand, or what motivation they have to continue in school.

Stereotype Threat a Proof of Constructivism and an Impactor and Impactee of Assessment

Claude Steele (1999) defines "stereotype threat" as:

> the threat of being viewed through the lens of a negative stereotype, or the fear of doing something that would inadvertently confirm that stereotype. Everyone experiences stereotype threat. We are all members of some group about which negative stereotypes exist, from white males and Methodists to women and the elderly. And in a situation where one of those stereotypes applies—a man talking to women about pay equity, for example, or an aging faculty member trying to remember a number sequence in the middle of a lecture—we know that we may be judged by it.

Steele's research (1995) has shown that students of varied racial backgrounds but with fairly identical socioeconomic backgrounds perform similarly when nothing is stated before the assessment is given. When something is stated before an assessment such as, "this is an intelligence test," then an internalized piece of constructed knowledge seems to raise its ugly head. White students performed about the same, but black student scores went down in math.

How can a general statement impact a score? Easily, if the cultural meaning of the statement and implications for the students had been previously constructed and internalized. This research on the impact of stereotypes proves that we internalize and construct ideas about ourselves that impact how we perform. This construction impacts assessment outcomes but also, self-perception is impacted by how we perform on tests. If one always does poorly on assessments, one will tend to sense a threat of poor performance on upcoming tests. Overcoming that requires more than just taking more tests. It requires reordering what one has constructed about one's self.

Deming (1986) emphasizes that we must drive out fear to increase quality, a purpose of assessment. When there is a threat to our knowledge construction and self-image, we tend to live up or down to that expectation. Faith-based schools must be sure to not allow stereotypes to persist, but rather continue to use the understanding that there is neither Jew or Greek, male or female (Gal 3:28) to counter this hindrance. A healthy swagger can be developed based on extraordinary skill development that helps students to see themselves as successful, therefore internalizing a deeper work ethic.

CONCLUSION: HEALTHY USE OF ASSESSMENT IN FAITH-BASED SCHOOLS

In a test-centered educational reform environment, where math and science are becoming more vital components, faith-based schools must assess and accelerate constructivist learning in order to remain competitive, not just in the United States but on a global level. The nature of society in the years to come will be impacted by the contested terrain of all classrooms in the United States, but especially by those that have a transcendent standard, located in faith-based schools.

The form of the assessment is as important as the process itself. It may constitute a Tom Sawyer heuristic in the classroom that makes doing academic work at the highest levels pleasurable for all students. One primary aspect relating to developing healthy assessment of internal thinking is the need to develop an internalized confidence, which I call swagger. This allows students to overcome stereotype threat, as well as develop other affective skills that improve student achievement.

There are many positive things that can come from implementing meaningful assessment and grounded constructivism in a faith-based school. Assessment can help challenge us to become more than we presently are or it can make us feel less than we are. In faith-based schools, we have a foundation and a standard. Constructivism is a part of our educational milieu, and we must be sure what boundaries to place on it as we assess its effectiveness in our classrooms for our primary goal of holistic student transformation. I have developed three healthy applications of assessment during my work as an administrator, practitioner, and researcher. They are how I apply the lessons of assessment and constructivism in the faith-based classroom.

Use Assessments to Accelerate Learning

Accelerated learning creates healthy swagger development and inoculation against stereotype threat. This does not mean teaching ahead of the students but rather, presenting content that is appropriate at earlier levels, and introducing rubrics that allow for early introduction and familiarity. Vygotsky's concepts of mediated learning and Piaget's models for cognition in school-aged students provide parameters and modes for appropriately determining content and strategies for young learners.

Determine the Assessments First

Reverse engineer, or as Wiggins and McTighe (2006) call it, "backward design" (p. 338), the curriculum and assessments, so you know where you are going. Just as, "We shall be like Him because we have seen Him face to face" (1 John 3:2), we shall be what we want to become if we first identify what we want to become. If it is a school that teaches AP classes, reverse engineer the classes, reshape and use rubrics down at lower levels, and vertical team the curriculum so things are introduced earlier. This suggestion intersects with the previous one. Systems consist of complex interdependent parts. Trying to work out all of the details is difficult if you can't keep your eyes on where you are going.

Use Assessments to Develop Systems Thinking

Think about how all of the pieces impacting healthy change work together. Utilize a triage framework to identify weaknesses, but understand that all the parts fit together and that all are important. These components include aspects such as vision, resources/skills, needs, planning, sending forth, and assessment. In order to get the change we want, we must have a mirror. Assessment is that mirror, but the learning that takes place is internally constructed. How we use that mirror dictates whether we only assess the superficial or truly look at where transformation can take place.

REFERENCES

Aguayo, R. (1991). *Dr. Deming: The American who taught the Japanese about quality.* New York: Simon & Schuster.

Anderson, L. W., & Krathwohl, D. R. (Eds.). (2001). *A taxonomy for learning, teaching and assessing: A revision of Bloom's taxonomy of educational objectives.* New York: Longman. (Complete ed.)

Bassarear, T., & Davidson, N. (1992). The use of small group learning situations in mathematics instruction as a tool to develop thinking. In N. Davidson & T. Worsham (Eds.), *Enhancing thinking through cooperative learning* (pp. 235–250). New York: Teachers College Press.

Boggs, Heather. (1996, October 2–5). *Launching school change through teacher study groups: An action research project.* From Midwestern Educational Research Association Conference, Session 35: Teachers as Adult Learners, Chicago, IL. ERIC document ED402286.

Brooks, J., & Brooks, M. (1993). *The case for constructivist classrooms.* Alexandria, VA: Association for Supervision and Curriculum Development.

Cohen, E., Lotan, R., Whitcomb, J., Balderrama, M., Cossey, R., & Swanson, P. (1993). Complex instruction: Higher-order thinking in heterogeneous classrooms. In S. Sharan (Ed.), *Handbook of cooperative learning methods* (pp. 82–96). Westport, CT: Greenwood.

College Board (1999). *Reaching the top: A report of the national task force on minority high achievement.* New York: College Board.

Delpit, L. (1995). *Other people's children: Cultural conflict in the classroom.* New York: New York Press.

Deming, W. E., (1986). *Out of the crisis.* Cambridge, MA: MIT Press.

Dolan, P. (1994). *Restructuring our schools.* Kansas City, MO: Systems and Organizations.

Dunn, R., & DeBello, K. (1999). *Improved test scores, attitudes, and behaviors in America's schools.* Westport, CT: Bergin & Garvey.

Dunn, R., & Dunn, K. (1978). *Teaching students through their individual learning styles.* Reston, VA: Reston Publishing.

Harper, D. (2009). Assess. In *Online Etymology Dictionary.* Retrieved from http://www.etymonline.com/

Henke, R., Chen, X., & Goldman, G. (1999). *What happens in classrooms? Instructional practices in elementary and secondary schools, 1994–1995*. National Center for Educational Statistics: US Department of Education. NCES 1999-348.

Lipman, P. (1998). *Race, class and power in school restructuring*. Albany, NY: SUNY.

Ma, X., & Millman, R. (2005). *Using self-assessment and peer assessment*. National Council of Teachers of Mathematics. Retrieved from http://www.nctm.org/news /content.aspx?id=616

Poythress, V. (2006). *Redeeming science, a God-centered approach*. Wheaton, IL: Crossway.

Schiro, M. (1980). *Curriculum for better schools*. Englewood Cliffs, NJ: Educational Technology Publications.

Shearon, D. (1999). *First set of responses to Marva Collins, carpe diem page*. Retrieved from http://www.shearonforschools.com/marva_collins__first_responses.htm

Steele, C. M. (1997). A threat in the air: How stereotypes shape the intellectual identities and performance of women and African Americans. *American Psychologist, 52,* 613–629.

Steele, C. M. (1999, August). Thin ice: "Stereotype threat" and black college students. *Atlantic Monthly, 284*(2), 44–47, 50–54.

Steele, C. M., & Aronson, J. (1994). Stereotype vulnerability and African-American intellectual performance. In E. Aronson (Ed.), *Readings about the social animal*. New York: Freeman.

Steele, C. M., & Aronson, J. (1995). Stereotype threat and the intellectual test performance of African-Americans. *Journal of Personality and Social Psychology, 69,* 797–811.

Tal, T., Krajcik, J. S., & Blumenfeld, P. (2006). Urban schools teachers enacting project-based science. *Journal of Research in Science Teaching, 43*(7), pp. 722–745.

Twain, M. (1876/1987). *The adventures of Tom Sawyer*. New York: Viking Press.

U.S. Department of Education (1998, March 7), *TIMSS 12th Grade Results*. Retrieved from http://www.ed. gov/ inits/TIMSS/overview.html

Vygotsky, L. S. (1978). *Mind in society: The development of higher psychological processes*. Cambridge, MA: Harvard University Press.

Vygotsky, L. S. (1987). *Thought and language* (A. Kozulin, Ed.). Cambridge, MA: MIT Press.

Wiggins, G., & McTighe, J. (2006). *Understanding by design*. Alexandria, VA: Association for Supervision and Curriculum Development. (2nd ed.)

PART 3

Reflections and Future Concerns

Introduction

S O FAR, THE WRITERS have discussed how constructivism offers many useful learning methods in faith-based education in which students actively participate. However, we need to reconsider the usefulness and congruence of constructivism in faith-based education before a final decision can be made. The two chapters in part 3 offer ways to consider and reflect on the resourcefulness of this philosophy as a means for negotiating alternatives.

Do constructivist thinking and Christian faith-based education have points of agreement? If so, what might these be? In chapter 17 the author considers this question and definitely answers yes. Although disagreement can occur between constructivism and faith-based education, the author concludes that constructivist thought and Christian faith-based education are congruent and harmonious in some aspects. He confirms that constructivism actually provides faith-based education an opportunity to apply the "image of God" to revelation-based learning.

The final chapter of this book, chapter 18, explores constructivism as an alternative, or at least a supplement to training and education methodologies of faith-based education in the information age. With such drastic changes in the social environment, the current paradigm of the educational system of schooling needs to change. Constructivism is potentially a powerful philosophical idea in its ability to lead changes in education. Its principles and its relevance when working with faith-based education are therefore major themes of this chapter.

Although we were not able to cover all the issues on constructivism in faith-based education in this book, this is the first systematic research effort in which Christian educators share ideas and perspectives related to faith-based education. The debate is still in progress, and I hope we will continually communicate with each other until we arrive at a common ground regarding Christian constructivism.

17

Constructivism and Faith-Based Education: Children Separated at Birth?

Stephen P. Metcalfe

INTRODUCTION

MANY CURRENT TEACHER EDUCATION programs place increasing emphasis on preparing candidates with a constructivist philosophical and theoretical posture for educational practice (Andrew, 2007; Hausfather, 2001). However, concepts coming under the constructivist label are broad and not easily limited to a single perspective or set of principles (Boudourides, 2003). At the broad base of all views within the constructivist perspective, though, is the general idea that learners create knowledge and understanding through a process of meaning making and experience, as opposed to knowledge being a thing that exists outside of the learner that is eventually accessed, obtained, realized, and/or clarified (Gijbels, Van De Watering, Dochy, & Van Den Bossche, 2006). This core perspective is fundamental to individually and socially framed learning theories that ground many teacher education philosophies and practices. This perspective also provides a platform for dialogue and debate among and between educational perspectives that hold diverging or contrary epistemological perspectives.

In recent years, concerns have been expressed by some groups within Christian higher education regarding the role or interaction that constructivist thinking may have within a Christian faith-based educational framework or environment. Many Christian college and university teacher education programs promote themselves as faith-based institutions and intentionally link their curriculum for preparing future educators to an ultimate truth that exists outside of the learner, specifically a perspective described as a Christ-centered understanding of ultimate truth. The tacit or explicit contention made by Christian faith-based education programs with concerns about constructivist theory therefore is that all learning is ultimately grounded within a context of truth that falls outside of a learner's individual construction of reality. How then might a learner-centered constructivist philosophy accommodate this view, and conversely, how might a Christ-centered perspective integrate a view of constructed understanding and knowledge?

The question at this point is, do constructivist thinking and Christian faith-based education have points of engagement? If so, what might these be? Both of these areas of thought represent a continuum that contains dissenting camps within each respective field. A simplistic response to this question does more to reflect a position of exclusivity than it does to engage in the scope of either area of thought. A Venn diagram of constructivist thought and Christian faith-based education (see figure 17.1) might instead offer a perspective where some views within each body of thinking are not compatible (Kennedy, 1997), while at the same time there is congruence and shared harmony between many other aspects of these perspectives.

Figure 17.1 Areas of exclusivity and compatibility between constructivism and Christian faith-based thought

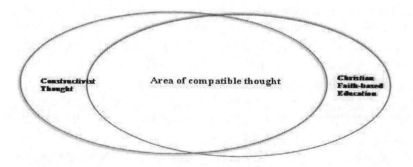

To continue this discussion it would be important to clarify which aspects of constructivist theory and which aspects of Christian faith-based education are complementary and therefore relevant to the implication in the title of this chapter. Similarity of perspectives

regarding learning and understanding between constructivist thought and Christian faith-based education may outnumber differences, if an agreed-upon understanding for both positions is presumed to be centrist-held rather than that of beliefs held by the more peripheral radical elements of either group. The purpose of this chapter is to present descriptions of constructivism and of faith-based learning, and to suggest that in practice as well as in structure, faith-based education can confidently embrace constructivist teaching and learning postulates and incorporate constructivist perspectives in an informed manner to create and become better educators and learners. To begin this effort, a discussion of both constructivism and faith-based education are in order to clarify what is intended when using both terms in this paper.

CONSTRUCTIVISM

Constructivism as a model for learning is based on a premise that individuals understand, know, and learn through a process of meaning making (Driscoll, 2005; Gijbels et al., 2006; Phye, 1997; Posner, 2004; Woolfolk, 2010). Constructive meaning making is informed through the senses and refined and personalized by interaction between cognitive processes and the individual's experiences. As experiences increase, a person integrates and organizes new and additional understanding. Some experiences reinforce or modify what "made sense" previously, while other experiences help alter a person's understanding of a condition or event (Byrnes, 2001; Ginsburg & Opper, 1979). Through this process, understanding is altered, refined and deepened, thus "what a person knows and learns" continues to be constructed and refined throughout her or his lifetime.

Constructivism and assumptions that embody its perspective fall within the philosophical subsets of epistemology and ontology. Epistemology deals with the nature, origin, methods, and limits of human knowledge and knowing (Stein, 1975). Ontology is a study of the nature of existence. Central questions from an epistemological perspective might include, How does a person come to know or understand something? or, Where does what a person knows come from? The simplified central question concerning ontological debate is, What is real?

Constructivist thought is broad in both theory and practice. The spectrum for defining the term *constructivism*, as with almost all branches of philosophy, ranges across conservative-to-radical perspectives and applications of constructivist principles (Pegues, 2007). Most interpretations and applications of constructivist theory in public school and other preK–12 settings fall more toward conservative-centrist perspectives than toward more purely existential views and academic practices. Educational areas where radical perspectives are more often embraced fall within familiar hotbed content areas such as mathematics and natural sciences. Presumably, it is within these fields where the philosophical applications of knowing and reality seem most debatable between secular constructivists and Christian faith-based constructivists.

CHRISTIAN FAITH-BASED EDUCATION

The term "faith-based" can be applied to a broad spectrum of organizations and orientations sharing a common thread of "spirituality" (or faith) linked to the activity undertaken by that organization. The understanding or application of this spirituality is not uniform and can lead to complex issues and misunderstandings in societies (Riley, Marks, & Grace, 2003). The range of spiritual expression reflected by faith-based organizations covers the breadth of religions and spiritual belief systems in our population. As a result, the term itself is not initially defining or clarifying when used as a descriptor for an organization.

Even within the umbrella descriptor of "Christian faith-based education," one will find variation and debate on how one's Christian faith informs or relates to the action of equipping students and nurturing learning. On one end of the spectrum will be institutions whose affiliation with a Christian organization is indirect or historical, and concepts of faith-based education are not formally or corporately structured. On the other end of this spectrum are institutions with personally defined understandings of what *faith-based* entails and prescriptive protocols for ensuring adequate if not uniform application of this understanding. It would be safe to assume that most faith-based institutions fall somewhere along this continuum.

Many Christian faith-based institutions engage in corporate exercises to discuss and clarify "what we believe" and "how this belief is integrated into what we do" to maintain longitudinal consistency in identity and goal setting. The result of this is actively cultivated dialogue on how Christian faith-based educators understand mission, purposes, and practices. This action is constructivist by nature, with an emphasis on constructivist principles such as seeking clarification of concepts, elaboration on thought, and encouragement of dialogue on concepts (Brooks & Brooks, 1993).

Many faith-based Christian institutions of higher learning contend that constructivist perspectives and operational components of constructivist theory in education are not antithetical to perspectives proposed by Christian faith-based educational principles. The questions and debates that perpetuate from the perspective of some faith-based Christian thinkers tend to center on the perceived threat posed by a dogmatic existential pursuit of constructivist reasoning. Questions and debates that are initiated from radical constructivist views tend to center on perceptions of ideologies underlying faith-based views of reality and knowledge. For the former, the issue seemingly boils down to a need to protect the authority of God in a human understanding of knowledge and reality. With the latter, the issues often seem to be related to aspects of reality, morality, and spirituality. At the extreme, both perspectives adopt postures from the other's canon. Radical constructivists uphold a maxim of "no maxims" while faith-based arguers develop understandings and knowledge that reflect sound constructivist principles.

For the purposes of this discussion, the parameters of the term *Christian faith-based education* will be limited to a perspective within the spectrum of Christianity that to some degree shares similar theological views with regard to Jesus, Scripture, and a personal-corporate faith relationship with God. Specifically, a view of Jesus is held that he is God's son and that he represents a sole model and sacrifice for being brought into relationship with God. Scripture is seen as God-inspired, and a means through which God enables Christians to understand life, living, and purpose. Faith is the basis through which Christians engage in relationship with God. It is seen as a gift from God and the basis of the experience of "being Christian."

These parameters are not intended to ignore or discredit other perspectives that may fall under the definition of "faith-based education." As noted above, the term is not singularly helpful in providing direction or definition. Limiting the scope of this term to these few descriptors provides an opportunity for context. Assuredly it also provides the opportunity for welcome debate.

AN INTEGRATIVE DIALOGUE BETWEEN
CONSTRUCTIVISM AND FAITH-BASED EDUCATION

Within the defined parameters of "faith-based" above, it can be proposed that Christian faith-based education actually embraces constructivist theory and practices as it is expressed through the teachings of Jesus. Again, the form of constructivist theory that is embraced is clearly rooted in a sound, established knowledge base that aligns with what we as humans have come to learn about ourselves and with what we have been given to understand through God-based revelation.

With regard to the former supposition, what we have come to learn about ourselves in terms of constructivist theory supports the concept that we are both creative and creators, as we should be in image-of-God likeness. God's purposes to literally place God's active presence in the world (does not "Christian" mean "little Christ"?) through our membership and participation in God's purposes through the Body underscore the reality that we are called to reflect constructivist tendencies. The interactive qualities of constructivist theory also align well with the interactive quality that God has with Christians in faith-based perspectives. God is the ultimate more educated individual (MEI) in Vygotsky's concepts of mediated learning (Kozulin, Gindis, Ageyev, & Miller, 2003). As we secularly continue to learn about and assign meaning to our lives, God continues to provide "kingdom" cultural tools to help us get proper context for our learning. As Vygotsky described cultural tools as a fundamental means for enabling culture-specific mediated knowledge construction, faith-based Christians perceive a dual-citizenship role as members of the human family and members of the kingdom Body. As we adopt these kingdom cultural tool lenses, our understanding of reality and knowledge is informed and transformed. In this context, God actually wants us to be questioners and seekers of better understanding. The more we learn, the more we validate God's role in reality.

The role of revelation in developing a knowledge base is fundamental to faith-based interaction with constructivist theory. The concept of revelation is not exclusively religious, but when used in dialogue closely related to faith-based issues, it is usually interpreted as divine revelation, or knowledge coming from God. Since the breadth and diversity within the body of Christian believers is broad, the exact definition of the term *revelation* is not a singular, uniform understanding. Faith-based Christians believe one source of revelation is Scripture. This belief is expressed across a range of meanings from dogmatic, literal Scripture interpretation (even so far as preferring a particular "translation's" English language wording) to seeing Scripture as God-inspired and dynamic, enabling the believer to hear God's thinking in diverse circumstances through revelation in specific circumstances. While there is sharp argument about *how* Scripture reveals God to believers, it is certainly a commonly held understanding *that* Scripture is a source of God's revelation.

The fact that Christians see core aspects of their faith differently helps suggest that meaning and experience of God have constructivist qualities. This proposal aligns well with the assertion earlier that faith-based education and constructivist educational theory may have more commonly shared characteristics than areas of problematic philosophical conflict. These areas of commonality include our tendency to be in a continuous state of growth and development, the imagery found in Scripture that suggests this tendency is a reflection of image of God, and the fact that the nature of God is never finite and presents us with an eternal process of learning more about God and our relationship to God. The remainder of this section will address each of these shared dynamics.

Continuous Growth and Development

The nature of God is reflected through the first topic introduced in the Bible—creation. Regardless of the particular perspective a faith-based Christian has with regard to the creation story, it is universally agreed by Christians that God created something from nothing. From that point on, one core feature of God's nature and of God's relationship to humanity is commonly understood as transformation. God begins with something (or nothing) and ends up with something completely different. This quality of beginning with one state and synthesizing a new state parallels Piaget's theory of knowledge construction where schemas are formed and modified through adaptation processes of assimilation and accommodation (Ginsburg & Opper, 1979). In this case, in our limited human capacity, we begin with pieces of information, and we organize and develop increasingly complex systems of knowledge and thought. In turn, we then use this constructed understanding to create and construct new and novel things in our personal and social world.

Scripture also reflects a developmental process in how God has chosen to relate to human beings. This is important to note as faith-based Christians see a relationship to God as an open-ended developmental process. God's first interaction with people is close up, personal, and interactive. As "kingdom" cultural tools are disregarded by people, as reflected in the fall (Gen 3), people's constructed understanding of how to relate to God became more distanced. God then initiated a process by which the eventual outcome is a restoration of this close up, personal, and interactive relationship. Faith-based Christians, regardless of where their interpretation of Scripture lies, embrace this perspective. All faith-based Christians feel as though they are "in process" to some extent. Scripture reflects a schism between where humanity is presently and where we expect to be at some point in the future. One example is 1 John 3:2, where we are told we're presently incomplete but working toward a time when we will be more fully developed.

Constructivist learning theory emphasizes the need to help learners move beyond simply stated facts to a place where they are able to do something meaningful with those facts. In addition, constructivist educators help develop better learners by providing opportunities for internalized, personal understanding. This does not imply idiosyncratic, cellular understandings that cannot be shared and mutually agreed upon, but rather understanding of concepts and ideas that are grounded in personally relevant and individually validated engagement. Just as teaching to the test is not an effective strategy for developing broad and deep understanding, an unexplored and unquestioned epistemology is not an effective platform for spiritual maturity.

Constructivism as Image of God

The Bible contains material that was written, collected, selected, and organized over a long period of time. As a piece of literature, it provides careers for scholars who debate the various aspects of its contents. To faith-based Christians, the Bible supersedes literature status and is recognized as a means by which God helps us better understand both who God is and who we are ourselves in relation to God.

It is beyond the scope of this discussion to explore emic versus etic (Franklin, 1996) interpretations of the Bible with regard to humanistic cultural tools or kingdom cultural tools. It is clear enough to safely state that any reading of the Bible is done so through a particular lens at a particular time, in a particular context. This constructivist reality is one explanation for the range of diversity across the scope of Christianity over the centuries.

Emic or etic interpretations aside, the images of God presented in Scripture lead both believers and nonbelievers alike to form perspectives of what God is like. Faith-based believers in particular believe that knowing what God is like helps provide a framework for living since being Christian is a process of being like Christ. Contrasting the simplified secular stereotype of God as a white-robed, white-haired man, Scripture provides a broad view of characteristics and qualities of God that reflect complexity, linear/temporal incongruence, and personality. These characteristics and qualities are descriptions that by default need to be limited to human experience for people to have any frame of reference.

One common historic presumption by some members of the Christian faith has been that these descriptors themselves necessarily remain static. This perspective is grounded in a belief that the cultural and social significance of the imagery has also remained static across the centuries. Other Christians feel as though God's revelations and characteristics are affirmed and supported across time and culture, and as a result, they seek deeper understanding of God's nature through application of accumulating human knowledge. Both groups' interpretation of Scripture is directed toward a faith-based deepening of relationship to/with a God that exists simultaneously both in and out of the bounds of our physical reality. This existence beyond human reality is one implied trait of "image of God" that faith-based Christians eventually aspire toward in eternity with the expectation of being "changed."

"Image of God" as a concept begins for Christians with the creation story in Genesis and progresses throughout Scripture to where New Testament authors provide guidance for reflecting God through our thoughts, deeds, and character (Gal 5; Matt 5, Col 3). In the creation story, "in God's image" does not likely refer to physical traits since God is not physical by nature. New Testament authors reinforce this likelihood with their emphases on relational and character qualities to be developed through interaction and relationship with God and God's nature. Jesus often said, "You have heard it said . . . but I say . . . ," offering perspectives into "image of God" characteristics. Faith-based Christians understand that reflecting "image of God" only takes place through God's active participation and transformation. Constructivist imagery of "something completely new out of former condition" is consistently prevalent in this perspective.

Never Fully Knowing God

To know God is easy; God is looking for you in the first place. To know everything about God is impossible. Eternity isn't adequate for this to be possible. In addition, most often the means through which we attempt to know God are misplaced or misapplied. Media provides an excellent example of this with the plethora of historical programs using geological and anthropological artifacts to dispute or confirm portions of historical biblical accounts.

While there certainly are discreet historical events in the Bible, as well as events and accounts that provide fodder for debate, the central purpose of Scripture is not to prove God to anyone. Scripture exists to act as revelation to believers of the nature and purposes of God. In this context, constructivist thinking is a well-suited perspective. As faith-based Christians continue to interact with Scripture, and as God provides insight, new understanding develops and improved perspectives of "image of God" are generated from parts of previously existing knowledge. This process is well chronicled throughout the history of the church, with both positive and difficult results within the Body. For faith-based Christians, Luther, Calvin, and Wesley are prime examples of interaction between cognitive construction and revelation.

The tendency to misapply evidence-based practices to support or debunk faith-based perspectives, or any other spiritual arena has been common practice since the advent of the Enlightenment. The posture of equating human reason with God wisdom is even older, reaching back into Genesis with the story of Babel. Scripture attempts to steer faith-based Christians toward an understanding that trying to use physical reality and measures as a sole means of reaching an understanding of God (or God's existence) is like trying to measure air pressure with a yardstick. Old Testament Scripture notes that God's ways are not our ways, placing God's self outside the limitations of our understanding. New Testament writers state that our wisdom is God's foolishness and vice versa. Without a faith-based orientation, Scripture is as meaningless as any literature written in an unfamiliar language.

CONCLUSION

There is a place for disagreement and boundary between faith-based educational theories and constructivist philosophies. Since both areas of thought are fairly expansive in terms of interpretative perspective and epistemology, there is adequate opportunity to both presume little interaction as well as to presume little conflict between the two areas, although the former perception is the more prevalent presumption, resulting in this conversation.

There certainly is a great deal of potential for shared thinking, as suggested by the figure in the earlier part of this piece, where faith-based education should employ constructivist theories as they reflect "image of God" in our human character and in our efforts to know more about what God is like through our personal and collective growth and development. Faith-based Christian education should be a forum where learning incorporates all possibilities of understanding with an expectation that God expects us to continually grow, learn, develop, and create as a result. Scripture emphasizes the importance of wisdom, and that wisdom without God-interaction is incomplete. The understanding of how we learn and think as human beings equips us to better engage in the process of making meaning and of making sense of our purposes in this short time as mortal beings.

Many historical episodes of secular-sacred conflict between what human beings have learned about themselves and their world should at some point help us to learn that God is only confirmed by what we can learn. In the past, the church formally sanctioned new thought with regard to understanding and scientific discovery. Since the wane of political power and influence by church-based sources, control over "spiritually correct" perspectives has been maintained on a more parochial level within the various branches of the church universal. In many cases, time has borne out validity or inaccuracy of various assumptions held. Through all of this, God is and still offers a window into God's nature, character, and purposes. Constructivist theory affords another means for us to learn and apply God's will and purposes in our lives as we integrate what we have learned about ourselves into a faith-based practical lens of understanding.

Within this context it might be suggested that constructivism actually provides faith-based education an opportunity to apply "image of God" to revelation-based learning. The concept that something new can come from formerly irrelevant or unrelated subsets comes out of Scripture as much as it comes from secular sources. From the story of creation to the assertion that we are made new creatures in Christ, with old things having been passed away, constructivist thought parallels images provided us of God and God's creative nature. Those faith-based educators who continue to hold cautionary views of radical constructivist assertions of no absolute truths need not disregard all other aspects of constructivist tenets. Much constructivist learning theory supports faith-based perspectives. Like children long separated by distance and time, it may be appropriate to join in a dialogue that considers meaningful application and integration of these two broad and rich areas of thought.

REFERENCES

Andrew, L. (2007). Comparison of teacher educators' instructional methods with the constructivist ideal. *Teacher Educator, 42*(3), 157–184.

Boudourides, M. A. (2003). Constructivism, education, science, and technology. *Canadian Journal of Learning and Technology, 29*(3). Retrieved from http://www.cjlt.ca/index.php/cjlt/article/view/83/77

Brooks, J. G., & Brooks, M. G. (1993). *In search of understanding: The case for constructivist classrooms.* Alexandria, VA: Association for Supervision and Curriculum Development.

Brooks, M. G., & Brooks, G. B. (1996). Constructivism and school reform. In M. W. McLaughlin & I. Oberman (Eds.), *Teacher learning: New policies, new practices* (pp. 30–35). New York, NY: Teachers College Press.

Byrnes, J. P. (2001). Theories of cognitive development and learning. In *Cognitive Development and Learning in Instructional Contexts* (pp. 8–41). Boston, MA: Allyn & Bacon. (2nd ed.)

Driscoll, M. P. (2005). Constructivism. In *Psychology of Learning for Instruction* (pp. 384–410). Boston, MA: Pearson. (3rd ed.)

Franklin, K. J. (1996). K. L. Pike on etic versus etic: A review and interview. *Summer Institute of Linguistics.* Retrieved from http://www.sil.org/klp/karlintv.htm

Gagnon, G. W., & Collay, M. (n.d.) Constructivist learning design. Retrieved from http://www.prainbow.com/cld/cldp.html

Gijbels, D., Van De Watering, G., Dochy, F., & Van Den Bossche, P. (2006). New learning environments and constructivism: The students' perspective. *Instructional Science, 34*, 213–226.

Ginsburg, H., & Opper, S. (1979). *Piaget's theory of intellectual development.* Englewood Cliffs, NJ: Prentice-Hall. (2nd ed.)

Hausfather, S. (2001). Where's the content? The role of content in constructivist teacher education. *Educational Horizons, 80*(1), 15–19.

Kennedy, M. M. (1997). The connection between research and practice. *Educational Researcher, 26*(7), 4–12.

Kozulin, A., Gindis, B., Ageyev, V. S., & Miller, S. M. (2003). *Vygotsky's educational theory in cultural context*. Cambridge, UK: Cambridge University Press.

Matthews, W. J. (2003). Constructivism in the classroom: Epistemology, history, and empirical evidence. *Teacher Education Quarterly, 3,* 51–64.

Matthews, M. R. (Ed.). (1998). *Constructivism in science education*. Dordrecht, Netherlands: Kluwer Academic Publishers.

Papert, S., & Harel, I. (1991). Situating constructivism. Retrieved from http://namodemello.com.br/pdf/tendencias/situatingconstrutivism.pdf

Pegues, H. (2007). Of paradigm wars: Constructivism, objectivism, and postmodern stratagem. *Educational Forum, 71*(4), 316–330.

Phye, G. D. (1997). Learning and remembering: The basis for personal knowledge construction. In G. D. Phye (Ed.), *Handbook of academic learning: Construction of knowledge* (pp. 47–64). San Diego, CA: Academic Press.

Posner, G. J. (2004). Theoretical perspectives on curriculum. In *Analyzing the Curriculum* (pp. 43–66). Boston, MA: McGraw-Hill.

Riley, K., Marks, H., & Grace, G. (2003). Big change question: In a period of global uncertainty, do faith-based schools re-enforce social divisions within societies and between nations? *Journal of Educational Change, 4,* 295–307.

Sikkink, D., & Hill, J. (2006). Education. In H. R. Ebaugh (Ed.), *Handbook of religion and social institutions*. Springer US. Retrieved from http://www.springerlink.com/content/gkp370382r444164/fulltext.pdf

Straits, W., & Wilke, R. (2007). How constructivist are we? Representations of transmission and participatory models of instruction in the Journal of College Science Teaching. *Journal of College Science Teaching, 36*(7), 58–61.

Stein, J. (Ed.). (1975). Epistemology. In *Random House College Dictionary, Revised edition*. New York, NY: Random House.

von Foerster, H. (Ed.). (1984). *Observing systems*. Salinas, CA: Intersystems Publications.

von Glaserfeld, E. (1989). Cognition, construction of knowledge, and teaching. *Synthese, 80*(1), 121–140.

von Glaserfeld, E. (1993). Questions and answers about radical constructivism. In Tobin (Ed.), *The practice of constructivism in science education* (pp. 23–38). Hillsdale, NJ: Erlbaum.

Winchester, I. (2007). Editorial: Construction and education. *Journal of Educational Thought, 41*(1), 1–5.

Windschitl, M. (1999). The challenges of sustaining a constructivist classroom culture. *Phi Delta Kappan*. In L. Abbeduto & F. Symons (Eds.) (2008), *Taking sides: clashing views in educational psychology* (pp. 166–174). Boston, MA: McGraw-Hill.

Windschitl, M. (2002). Framing constructivism in practice as the negotiation of dilemmas: An analysis of the conceptual, pedagogical, cultural, and political challenges facing teachers. *Review of Educational Research, 72*(2), 131–175.

Winters, E. (1996–2006). Shape shifting. Retrieved from http://www.ewinters.com/shapeshift1.html

Woolfolk, A. (2010). *Educational Psychology*. Upper Saddle River, NJ: Pearson Higher Education. (11th ed.)

18

If We Build It, They Will Come! Will Constructivism Matter in the Future of Faith-Based Education?

HeeKap Lee and Gloria Edwards

INTRODUCTION

DOES CONSTRUCTIVISM PROVIDE A viable option to the faith-based education method of the future? Thus far, discussions have centered on the strengths and weaknesses of constructivism when it is used in the faith-based education setting. Throughout this book, most of the chapter contributors have suggested that the principles and ideas of constructivism might provide insightful ways to lead the innovations of faith-based education. This chapter supports previous chapters by reemphasizing the importance of constructivism in leading school change in the information age as well as in strengthening faith-based education. It also addresses and explains three main themes: the reason why constructivism is a powerful means to initiate school change, how constructivism is a useful tool in faith-based education as supported by survey results from the perspective of Christian educators, and where several ideas about constructivist instruction have relevance when working in faith-based education.

PARADIGM CHANGE IN THE INFORMATION AGE

According to Banathy (1991), grand societal changes from the agrarian age to the industrial age are now moving through the information age. The societal shift from the industrial age to the information age means that there are fundamental differences between the two educational paradigms. Education in the industrial age mirrored the old organization of production; most people spent eight to twelve years of their childhood training for cog jobs, while a few were propelled toward top policy and planning positions. However, education in the information age encourages students to collaborate with one another so that their combined skills and insights add up to something more than the sum of their individual contributions (Reich, 1988). Reigeluth (1994; Reigeluth and Nelson, 1997) identified and subsequently updated the major differences between the industrial age and the information age that affect education.

Table 18.1 Major differences between the industrial age and the information age

Industrial age	Information age
Standardization (mass production, etc.)	Customization
Compliance	Initiative
Conformity	Diversity
Bureaucratic organization	Team organization
Autocratic leadership	Shared leadership
Centralized control	Autonomy, accountability
Adversarial relationships	Cooperative relationships
One-way communications	Networking
Compartmentalization (division of labor)	Holism (integration of tasks)

Bluestein (2008a), however, took a different approach to the education dilemma by comparing the industrial age versus the information age classroom differences as they pertained to values, priorities, motivators, authority relationships, student behaviors, and discipline goals, explaining in detail how educational needs have changed based upon the needs of the economy. Whereas employers during the industrial age placed their hiring priority on the singularity of "fitting in" (essentially doing as you were told), employers in the information age place higher priorities on a multitude of performance potential characteristics: networking, people skills, communication skills, creative thinking ("outside the box") and problem solving, initiative, flexibility, adaptability, as well as the ability to multitask, shift gears, and change to shifting demands of the workplace with "vision and attitude" (Bluestein, 2008b, para. 6). As such, schools may have no choice but to seek out teachers that have, at a minimum, a teaching philosophy that balances behaviorism and constructivism, in order to groom the next generation of learners to have somewhat of a constructivist mentality.

Schooling was the by-product of the industrial age paradigm where all students were encouraged to learn the basic skills at the same pace using the same materials by meeting in the same classroom regularly. Schools achieved their most obvious and unambiguous success in the industrial age in the area of acquisition and communication of knowledge. However, researchers and educational practitioners argue that schooling neither functioned well in the information age nor currently meets the needs of individuals in the knowledge age (Livingston, 1999). The sad story is that schooling essentially has not changed since it started in the industrial age. It has become increasingly evident that the educational needs within the current society are not adequately satisfied by the schools as they are now organized (Halbhavi, Prensky, Nixon, Levin, & Francis, 2005; Organisation for Economic Co-operation and Development [OECD], 2009; Partnership for 21st Century Skills, 2009; Singh, O'Donoghue, & Betts, 2002; U.S. Congress, 2002). How can we lead the change in education and schooling, especially in faith-based education?

Price and Nelson (2007) suggested a three-component framework: (1) what to teach, (2) how to teach, and (3) the context for teaching and learning. The "what to teach" component provides a structure for planning curriculum content that is relevant and representative of diverse needs of the world, while "how to teach" concerns instructional methods necessary to address diverse needs of a classroom. The "context for teaching and learning" refers to creating an inclusive classroom environment where all students are supported and accepted. Based upon the framework of Price and Nelson (2007), educational changes need to be made in schools of the information age.

Changing What to Teach (Lesson Content)

Education in the industrial age was much like the mass-production process of the manufacturing system. It focused on basic skills such as reading, writing, and arithmetic capabilities—skills necessary to become routine workers. Students sat individually in rows, completing their individual tasks, memorizing their work, and learning not to question, but rather to obey, authority. Schools were designed to teach individuals adequate vocational skills and tended to be standardized to model a community in which leadership came from the professionals (Tyack, 1974). Uniformity, control, and centralization were core virtues in this paradigm.

However, in the information age the key resource shifted to information, knowledge, and creativity. For example, Reich (1991) argues that abstraction and system thinking should form the focus of study. Students should be trained to gather information, translate the information into abstract symbols, manipulate the symbols towards finding answers, turn the answers into operating instructions, and then communicate the instructions downward. Naisbitt and Arbudene (1985) suggested that three new basic competencies should be taught in the information age: how to think, how to learn, and how to create.

The CEO Forum (2001) identified four twenty-first-century skills that should be taught in a school: digital age literacy, inventive thinking, effective communication, and high productivity. Newby (2005a) went as far as to suggest that by the year 2020, schools would need a curriculum that takes more risks and where learning would be negotiated rather than imposed. Bluestein (2008a), OECD (2009), and the Partnership for 21st Century Skills (2009) have all highlighted and detailed each of these ideals and more, strongly endorsing that in the information age the need exists for a reorganized school curriculum that focuses on strengthening higher-order mental capabilities.

Changing How to Teach (Instructional Method)

Instructional methods in the industrial age are similar to the banking style of education referred to by Freire (1972), in which schools objectify students by teaching memorization of rigid, mystified facts, and thereby remove them from the process of taking an active part in their education lives. In the industrial age, students sat individually in rows, completed their individual tasks, memorized their work, and learned not to question, but rather to obey authority.

However, in the information age, a new set of instructional methods are necessary in order to improve information access and retention, knowledge, and creativity of our students. Rather than teach students to assume that problems and solutions are generated by others, students must be taught to understand that problems and questions are created;

that they as students can have an active role in not only creating them, but also in solving them; and that such critical and creative approaches can guide them through the process (Reich, 1986). Therefore, teachers must help students gain the experiences of working through problems and of thus discovering underlying principles that help define and solve related problems. Teacher-centered lecturing, which was the dominate form of education in the industrial age, has shifted to collaborative learning, service-learning, problem-based learning, learning communities, and a number of other innovative techniques designed to engage the learner in the learning process.

Changing Teaching and Learning Contexts

Lastly, the environmental factors that are surrounded by education have drastically changed in the information age. The teaching and learning environments today are significantly different from those of past days. Rosenberg (2001) summarizes five major areas of transformation in schooling and education: (1) from training to performance; (2) from classroom to anytime, anywhere learning; (3) from paper to online; (4) from physical facilities to network facilities; and (5) from cycle time to real time. Technology has made it possible for students to learn anywhere, anytime, synchronously or asynchronously (Oblinger & Oblinger, 2006). As a result, students may now study whenever and wherever they so choose (MacFarlane, 1998). Online tools (e.g., e-mail, blogs, chat rooms, discussion boards, e-books), and tech "toys" (e.g., Blueberries, iPhones, iPods, PDAs, Notebooks) permit a convergence of information, knowledge, learning, and socialization irrespective of time and place; while online virtual communities (e.g., MySpace, Facebook, Twitter, Flickr) set the stage for meeting friends, establishing relationships, and social networking never imagined within the traditional classroom (Newby, 2005b; Oblinger & Oblinger, 2006; Singh et al., 2002). The new skills sets include facilitative abilities that communicate lifelong learner skills to students and guide computer-savvy learners towards multiple literacies inclusive of the new basics (Kalantzis, Cope, & Harvey, 2003), all of which prepare the information-age students for the numerous rapidly changing careers that await them.

In addition, diversity in our schools has increased in the United States and in the nations of the world (OECD, 2009). In 2000, 62 percent of the students in the public schools were white; however, by the year 2020, over 66 percent of all school-age children in the United States will be African American, Asian, Latino, Native American, and multicultural (Woolfolk, 2004). Also, most of constituents of current colleges and universities are called the "millennial generation," (McAlister, 2009; McGuire & Williams, 2002), "generation next," or "net generation" (Beyers, 2009). McGuire and Williams (2002) identify the characteristics of that generation with three ideas: (1) consumer mentality, (2) ubiquitous computer access, and (3) intolerance of nonengaging pedagogical techniques. They are open to embrace change and are comfortable with cultural, racial, and sexual orientation diversity. However, many of them are formally diagnosed as ADD or ADHD, and they lack basic study skills (McGuire & Williams, 2002).

How can we organize teaching and learning contexts in order to teach these students effectively? First of all, because they are comfortable and confident when it comes to working with computers, using technology in classrooms would gain their attention. Secondly, students appreciate the multisensory engagement that comes from working with a variety of media (McAlister, 2009). Considering multiple ways of information presentations and organizing lessons based on multiple learning styles would be one of the best strategies to teach them.

CAN CONSTRUCTIVISM MAKE A DIFFERENCE IN EDUCATION IN THE INFORMATION AGE?

Can constructivist instruction have relevance when working with the new generations? Could constructivism make a positive impact regarding what to teach, how to teach, and the teaching-learning context in general in the information age? Reich (1986) presented the key issues of education in the information age that are closely related to the principles of constructivism. He said:

> We can no longer train the majority of our young people for cog jobs requiring primarily discipline and responsibility. They must be prepared to take advantage of whatever opportunities present themselves for improvements in product and process. To recognize such opportunities, they must be educated to think critically and to continually learn on the basis of new data and experience. (Reich, 1986, p. 21)

What is the image of effectively functioning education and schooling in the information age? Edwards, Lee, and Tan (2007) envision schools in the information age as potential playgrounds after comparing them with that of the factory image of schooling from the industrial age. Table 17.2 conveys a summary comparison between the schools of the industrial age (school as a factory) versus that of information age (school as a playground). The school of the information age appears more indicative of a playground where students learn how to recognize and solve problems, comprehend new phenomena, construct mental models, and regulate their own learning.

Table 18.2 Comparisons of school paradigms

	School as factory	School as playground
Service to super-system	To produce workers as a cog in a wheel	To facilitate student's self-directed learning
Role of school	Dispensers of information	Creators of new knowledge Organizers of knowledge
Learning activity	Drudgery, compliance	Excitement, creativity
Teacher	Knowledge provider Source of information	Guide to information source
Student	Knowledge receiver	Knowledge producer
Main learning activity	Conveying particular piece of information	Discovering underlined principles
Character of knowledge	Something discovered	Something constructed

Can constructivist principles transform our schools into playgrounds? Theoretically, the image of playground and the principles of constructivism share many features. In a playground, children sing songs, play games, and create opportunities where they learn how to cooperate and how to communicate with others in informal learning situations. They constantly explore their worlds and frequently encounter phenomena that they do not understand. By asking questions and collaborating with one another in authentic settings, they ultimately construct their own modes of their experiences. Constructivism redefines learning as the active and constructive mode of the meaning-making process in which learners articulate what they have accomplished and reflect on their activity and observations (Jonassen, Howland, Moore, & Marra, 2003). In the constructivist classroom, learning becomes fun and exciting. The different learning styles and potential capacities of all students are celebrated in the class. This powerful aspect of constructivist learning can be compared to the situation of Aslan changing the witch's courtyard in C. S. Lewis's book, *The Lion, the Witch, and the Wardrobe*.

> For a second after Aslan had breathed upon him the stone lion looked just the same. Then a tiny streak of gold began to run along his white marble back, then it spread, then the color seemed to lick all over him as the flame licks all over a bit of paper, then, while his hindquarters were still obviously stone, the lion shook his mane and all the heavy, stone folds rippled into living hair. Then he opened a great red mouth, warm and living, and gave a prodigious yawn. And now his hind legs had come to life. Then, having caught sight of Aslan, he went bounding after him and frisking round him whimpering with delight and jumping up to lick his face. . . . Everywhere the statues were coming to life. The courtyard looked no longer like a museum; it looked more like a zoo. Creatures were running after Aslan and dancing round him till he was almost hidden in the crowd. (Lewis, 1950/1978, p. 168)

How can we change the classroom into a living place where the potential of all children is identified, similar to the transformation by which Aslan changed a silent environment into a place full of joyful noises? Can constructivism be a useful source in transforming a classroom from that of a museum where the diverse backgrounds and differences of students has been suppressed into something better? Why not believe that constructivism can be the foundation where teachers build a thriving classroom and where learning, sharing, and engagement take place among peers and teachers? The classroom is a community where activities are designed and integrated into the learning process. Using constructivist principles and ideas, the classroom can be built like a playground to meet the new needs in the information age.

There are many more questions to be asked and hopefully answered. Can constructivism be an alternative approach to education in faith-based environments? Is constructivism a good match with Christian education? Does constructivism fit effectively within faith-based education? To a certain extent, one could say yes to these questions. First and foremost, the theories and practices of constructivism have strengthened faith-based education by emphasizing the roles of self-directed students, teachers as facilitators, and well-organized learning experiences. In fact, Jesus knew that learning was an active knowledge-creating process requiring the full participation of learners. He always encouraged his disciples to think deeply and to delve beyond the surface level. Jesus knew that learning was not simply memorizing facts or reciting the law of Moses. This is in contrast to the passive learning paradigm at the time of exact memorization of content established by the Jewish leaders.

Edwards, Lee, and Tan (2007) argued that the current school movement has failed because it neglects to focus on the role of schools in nourishing the spirit. All previous school change movements tended to highlight the external structure or the means rather than the internal changes sought, which would ultimately have produced students who were better equipped for the current age in terms of knowledge, skill, socialization, and character. However, constructivism could become a powerful tool when integrated with the loving and encouraging spirits of teachers. Educators and parents of diverse backgrounds should come together to find ways in which to bring a renewed awakening towards learning back into the schools.

HOW DO CHRISTIAN EDUCATORS VIEW CONSTRUCTIVISM?

Irrespective of the outcomes of the debate regarding compatibility of constructivism with faith-based education, many Christian educators who contributed to this book have suggested insightful and practical ideas when applied to faith-based education. Additionally, the constructivist principles and perspectives provide useful ideas for setting up a Christian school to become a playground. However, it would be beneficial to understand how other Christian educators view constructivism. Do they perceive constructivism to be a powerful tool in the information age for leading educational innovation in Christian schools?

To explore answers regarding the perception of Christian educators about constructivism, an informal survey of eight questions and three demographical questions (see Appendix 1) was designed and distributed (electronically and by regular mail) in May 2009 to selected Christian educators who currently teach in teacher education departments at Christian colleges and universities. Twenty-nine faculty responded. Analysis of the survey data was as follows.

Diverse Definitions of Constructivism but Compatible with Faith-Based Education

There was no consensus of agreement among the surveyed Christian educators regarding the definition of constructivism; however, most understood constructivism to be either a theory of learning (ten responders, or 36.48 percent) or a learner-centered teaching practice (nine responders, or 31.03 percent). On a Likert scale from 1 to 5 with 1 being not compatible and 5 being very compatible; twenty educators (68.9 percent) responded that they believed constructivism is very compatible with faith-based education. The average rating among the twenty-nine respondents was 4.59, which suggests a very positive agreement regarding the compatibility of constructivism with faith-based education. Written comments included:

- Each person's sense of spirituality makes him/her receptive to constructing meaning of content that contains at least one element of dimension of spiritual faith.

- By active, guided discovery we enable students to conceptualize learning truth in the way that best fits God-given abilities.

- Salvation rests on free will, on personal choices, on making personal meaning of Christ's birth, death, and resurrection. Constructivism is based on making sense of the world too, not just memorizing the world.

- Enabling a child to construct understandings from lesson experience is entirely natural and has been practiced since antiquity. More modern nineteenth- and twentieth-century approaches have often led to more constraints and convergence in approaches to learning.

- It encourages students to think deeply, reflecting students' learning styles and diverse needs.

None of the respondents felt that constructivism was incompatible with faith-based education. However, three respondents provided a rating of 3 when asked their views about the compatibility of constructivism with faith-based education. Two felt they could embrace constructivist theory up to a degree, but that it compromised faith-based educational philosophies, while one felt that we need to point out important dangers inherent in constructivist theory.

Respondents Use a Constructivist Teaching Method

All twenty-nine respondents said that they use constructivist methods in their instruction. Seven said that they used divergent questions to sharpen the critical thinking skills of their students, and six said that they use small group discussion format in their teaching. Problem-based learning (two respondents), inquiry-based learning (two respondents), and differentiated instruction (two respondents) were also identified as frequently used constructivist teaching formats.

Jesus Was a Constructivist

One of the survey questions asked was "Do you think that Jesus used constructivist methods when He taught?" All agreed that Jesus used constructivist methods. The following is a sample of their responses:

- The parables intentionally caused people to think in creative ways.

- There was so much mystery in his teaching. Even the disciples didn't know what was right and had to be open to ambiguity.

- Parables require the listener to construct understanding of what the meaning of the parable might be.

- I think parables were a form of constructivist teaching, where there weren't necessarily right answers but listeners were challenged to think through the new information/perspectives Jesus described and come to new understandings (construct new meanings).

- Jesus taught in authentic settings, challenged his followers to think critically, allowed them to make decisions for themselves, and got them actively involved in the content.

- He used everyday examples that related directly to the culture of the day to which his pupils could understand.

He used everyday items for which people would have strong understanding in his teaching. He then built analogies for spiritual principles and teachings using those everyday items as a starting point and often ended his lessons with questions to force people to internalize his lessons so they would be personally meaningful.

Constructivism Is the Future of Faith-Based Education

Approximately two out of three (nineteen, or 65.51 percent]) respondents agreed that constructivism will be more completely embraced in faith-based education circles in the future. Three respondents (10.34 percent) disagreed with this idea, and seven respondents (24.14 percent) abstained from making a decision. However, one interesting finding was that no one raised the issue of incompatibility of constructivism and faith-based education. Others said the reason of disagreement was that constructivism is only one approach of many educational theories and they preferred to take an eclectic approach.

WILL CONSTRUCTIVISM MATTER IN FUTURE FAITH-BASED EDUCATION?

Can constructivism make a positive impact in faith-based education? As previously suggested and as several Christian educators agreed in this book, constructivism can make an impact in faith-based education. First of all, constructivism can lead to instructional innovation in faith-based education by integrating teaching strategies that emphasize active class participation of students. Similar to how Jesus taught with a higher-level inquiry method and used essential questions to intrigue the learning capacity of his disciples, Christian teachers will use constructivism to inspire students' learning. Lee (2006) pointed out that Jesus taught through the discovery learning process, which resulted in changed lives in his audience.

> Jesus used questions to inspire his audiences to formulate new schema that challenged their existing framework of ideas. Learning is a changing process in which assumptions of old principles and beliefs must be dealt with before accepting new ideas and new learning. In order to accept new knowledge and skills, learners should explore the new relationships and new regularities through the discovery process. Jesus' questions always inspire his audiences to unlearn old schemata and to explore a new way of thinking and encourage his listeners to change their perspectives. (Lee, 2006)

Secondly, constructivism provides several benefits that reflect schooling and school innovation by redefining the goals of the school and education. Constructivism argues that a school is more than a physical meeting place. It is a community where activities are designed for and integrated into the learning process. Collaborative efforts and partnerships between parents, schools, and corporate institution are necessary, in addition to a societal commitment to make schools successful. A school continues to be an establishment for learning; however, inclusive in its mission should be opportunities where learning becomes fun and exciting. It should also be a thriving environment where learning, sharing, and engagement take place among friends and teachers.

Lastly, constructivism can be more effective when integrated with the loving and encouraging spirits of teachers. Many school innovations have failed because they have not been integrated with the concerns and perceptions of teachers, who become the major stakeholders in leading school renovations (Pershing, Lee, 2002). The future of schooling depends on caring enough to invest time and money to help engage our students (Halbhavi et al., 2005).

So where do we, as Christian educators, start when we embrace constructivism in our teaching? Perhaps we can start by planning our instructions well, whereby all students are actively participating, being encouraged to share their ideas and perspectives, presenting information in different forms and modes, and evaluating the performances of students in authentic ways. Appendix 2 summarizes the key ideas to identifying whether you are a constructivist teacher or not. It also provides insights for reviewing your teaching and learning process.

CONCLUSION

The drastic shift from the industrial age to the information age requires a new form of schooling and educational approach. Equipping the next generation with the knowledge, skills, and attitudes to survive and be successful in the twenty-first century presents many challenges that as of yet are still unknown. What is known and agreed upon is that future generations will need new skill sets in which current schooling continues to fall short. The school should also be a place where students are fed spiritual nourishment and intellectual excitement. Kessler (2000) was correct when he said:

The body of the child will not grow if it is not fed; the mind will not flourish unless it is stimulated and guided. And the spirit will suffer if it is not nurtured. A soulful education embraces diverse ways to satisfy the spiritual hunger of today's youth. When guided to find constructive ways to express their spiritual longings, young people can find purpose in life, do better in school, strengthen ties to family and friends, and approach adulthood with vitality and vision. (p. x)

The good news, however, is that constructivist principles and ideas can lead to building schools like a playground. Many Christian educators agree with this, and hopefully other Christian educators will share their successful stories and practices after applying constructivism principles in their teaching settings. Therefore, in constructivist learning, three important factors should be emphasized: self-directed students, the teacher as facilitator, and well-organized learning experiences. The role of students is extremely important in the learning process because learning based on the constructivist approach takes a student-centered perspective that encourages student autonomy, initiation, and leadership. The role of the teacher should be shifted from expert to that of guide for the direction of inquiry and encouraging of innovative thinking patterns. And finally, to encourage active participation and practice, well-organized learning materials and learning experiences are important factors for successful learning. Therefore, tasks demanding high levels of processing are frequently learned with strategies advanced by the constructivist perspective (Ertmer & Newby, 1993).

REFERENCES

Banathy, B. H. (1991). *Educational systems design: A journey to create the future.* Englewood Cliffs, NJ: Educational Technology Publications.

Banks, J. A., & Banks, C. A. M. (2005). *Multicultural education: Issues and perspectives.* John Wiley & Sons. (5th ed.)

Beyers, R. N. (2009). A five dimensional model for educating the net generation. *Journal of Educational Technology and Society, 12*(4), 218–227.

Bluestein, J. (2008a). *The win-win classroom.* Thousand Oaks, CA: Corwin.

Bluestein, J. (2008b). *Industrial age classrooms vs. information age classrooms.* Retrieved from http://www.janebluestein.com/handouts/info_age.html

CEO Forum (2001). *Key building blocks for student achievement in the 21st century: School technology and readiness report.* CEO Forum on Education and Technology.

Drucker, P. F. (1993). *Post capitalist society.* New York: Harper Collins.

Edwards, G., Lee, H., & Tan, R. (2007). Exploring paradigms of school innovation for the 21st century. *Teaching with Compassion, Competence, and Commitment, 1*(1), 55–73.

Ertmer, P. A., & Newby, T. J. (1993). Behaviorism, cognitivism, constructivism: Comparing critical features from an instructional design perspective. *Performance Improvement Quarterly, 6*(4), 50–72.

Freire, P. (1972). *Pedagogy of the oppressed.* Harmondsworth, UK: Penguin.

Halbhavi, S., Prensky, M., Nixon, L. A., Levin, D., & Francis, L. (2005). The leadership imperative. *Technology and Learning, 26*(4), 12–13.

Jonassen, D. H., Howland, J., Moore, J., & Marra, R. M. (2003). *Learning to solve problems with technology: A constructivist perspective.* Columbus, OH: Merrill Prentice Hall. (2nd ed.)

Kalantzis, M., Cope, B., & Harvey, A. (2003). Assessing multiliteracies and the new basics. *Assessment in education: Principles, policy and practice, 10*(1), 15–26.

Kessler, R. (2000). *The soul of education: Helping students find connection, compassion, and character at school.* Alexandria, VA: Association for Supervision and Curriculum Development.

Lee, H. (2006). Jesus teaching through discovery. International Christian Teachers Journal, 1(2). Retrieved from http://icctejournal.org/issues/v1i2/v1i2-lee/

Livingstone, D. W. (1999). Lifelong learning and underemployment in the knowledge society: A North American perspective. *Comparative Education, 35*(2), 63–186.

Lewis, C. S. (1950/1978). *The lion, the witch, and the wardrobe.* London: HarperCollins.

MacFarlane, A. (1998). Information, knowledge, and learning. *Higher Education Quarterly, 52*(1), 77–92.

McAlister, A. (2009, August/September). Teaching the millennial generation. *American Music Teacher, 59*(1), 13–15.

McGuire, S. Y., & Williams, D. A. (2002). The millennial learner: Challenges and opportunities. *To Improve the Academy, 29,* 185–196.

Naisbitt, J., & Aburdene, P. (1985). *Re-inventing the corporation.* New York: Warner Books.

Newby, M. (2005a). A curriculum for 2020. *Journal of Education for Teaching, 31*(4), 297–300.

Newby, M. (2005b). Technology 2020. *Journal of Education for Teaching, 31*(4), 265–267.

Oblinger, D., & Oblinger J. (2006). Is it age or IT: First steps toward understanding the net generation. *CSLA Journal, 29*(2), 8–16.

Organisation for Economic Co-operation and Development (OECD). (2009). *Education at a glance 2009: OECD Indicators.* OECD, Paris. Retrieved from www.oecd.org /dataoecd/32/34/43541373.pdf

Partnership for 21st Century Skills. (2009). *The MILE guide: Milestones for improving learning and education.* Retrieved from http://www.21stcenturyskills.org /documents/MILE_Guide_091101.pdf

Pershing, J., & Lee, H. (2002). Leadership Competencies: A Case Study of Leadership Development, International Society for Performance Improvement (ISPI) Conference, Dallas. April, 2002.

Powell, W. W., & Snellman, K. (2004). The knowledge economy. *Annual Review of Sociology, 30*(1), 199–220.

Price, K. M., & Nelson, K. L. (2007). *Planning effective instruction: Diversity responsive methods and management.* Belmont, CA: Thomson & Wadsworth. (3rd ed.)

Reich, R. B. (1988). *Education and the next economy.* Washington, DC: National Education Association.

Reich, R. B. (1991). *The work of nations: Preparing ourselves for twenty-first-century capitalism.* New York: Alfred A. Knopf.

Reigeluth, C. M. (1994). The imperative for systemic change. In C. M. Reigeluth & R. J. Garfinkle (Eds.), *Systemic restructuring in education* (pp. 3–11). Englewood Cliffs, NJ: Educational Technology Publications.

Reigeluth, C. M., & Nelson, L. M. (1997). New paradigm of ISD. In R. M. Branch & B. B. Minor (Eds.), *Educational media and technology yearbook* (pp. 24–35). Englewood, CO: Libraries Unlimited.

Rosenberg, M. J. (2001). *E-Learning: Strategies for delivering knowledge in the digital age.* New York: McGraw-Hill.

Singh, G., O'Donoghue, J., & Betts, C. (2002). A UK study into the potential effect of virtual education: Does online learning spell an end for on-campus learning? *Behavior and Information Technology, 21*(3), 223–229.

Toffler, A. (1980). *The third wave.* New York: Bantam Books.

Tyack, D. B. (1974). *The one best system: A history of American urban education.* Cambridge, MA: Harvard University Press.

U.S. Congress. (2002). *No Child Left Behind Act of 2001.* Public Law No. 107-110, 115 Stat. 1425. Retrieved from http://www.gpo.gov/fdsys/pkg/PLAW-107publ110/pdf /PLAW-107publ110.pdf

Woolfolk, A. (2004). *Educational psychology.* Boston, MA: Allyn and Bacon. (9th ed.)

Appendix 1

Perception of Christian Educators about Constructivism

1. Which of the following describes constructivism for you? You may choose more than one.

   a. It is a philosophical orientation reflected in postmodern educational applications.

   b. It is a theory of learning that is applicable to one's teaching repertoire.

   c. It is a set of teaching-learning methods that emphasize learner-centered teaching practices.

   d. Other (Supply your own definition.) _____

   _____

   _____

2. Is constructivist theory compatible with faith-based education? Indicate your view on the Likert scale below.

Not compatible		Very compatible		
1	2	3	4	5

3. If you feel constructivism *is* compatible with faith-based education, list reasons why here, and then proceed to item 6.

   _____

   _____

   _____

4. If you feel constructivism is *not* compatible with faith-based education, list your reasons why here, and then proceed to item 5.

_____

_____

_____

5. If constructivism is *not* compatible with faith-based education, how should Christian educators respond to constructivism?

    a. We need to identify constructivism as antithetical to Christian philosophical perspectives.

    b. We need to point out important dangers inherent in constructivist theory.

    c. We can embrace constructivist theory up to the degree that it compromises faith-based educational philosophies.

    d. Other (Supply your own definition.) _____

_____

_____

_____

6. Do you use any constructivist teaching methods in your instruction?

    ____ No

    ____ Yes (If so, describe these.)

_____

_____

_____

7. Do you think that Jesus used constructivist methods when he taught?

    ____ No

    ____ Yes (Explain why or why not.)

_____

_____

_____

8. Do you agree with the statement below?

"Constructivism will be more completely embraced in faith-based education circles in the future."

_____ No

_____ Yes (Explain why or why not.)

_____

_____

_____

Please check the items below that reflect your demographic data:

Gender:

_____ Male

_____ Female

Current teaching role (check all that apply):

_____   K–12 teacher

_____   College professor teaching educational foundation courses

_____   College professor teaching educational psychology

_____   Other courses (Please specify.)

_____

Age group (check one)

_____ Under 30

_____ 30–34

_____ 35–39

_____ 40–44

_____ 45–49

_____ 50–54

_____ 55–59

_____ 60 or older

Thank you!

Appendix 2

Seven Essentials for Constructivist Lessons

	Criteria	Descriptors and examples
Grab attention ("hook")	Lesson begins in a manner likely to encourage students to look forward to what comes next.	Questions and activities tap into the students' personal experiences. Small group activities have students share their experiences. Activities require students to frame their own questions on a topic. Questions and activities that assess create curiosity and challenge prior knowledge.
Authentic tasks	Lesson provides students with learning tasks that are as authentic (real-world) as possible.	Students identify and work on real-life problems using a variety of resources (most authentic), simulations (less authentic), complex problems (more authentic), and real-life data.
Appropriate resources	Lesson's design makes resources necessary to accomplish the task available or provides ways these resources to be accessed.	Resources support every task option. Resources support students' multiple intelligences. Possible resources: data, books, videos, experts, contacts, websites.

Cognitively rich questions	Lesson poses questions that require students to think critically and requires students to pose *their* questions in a manner that requires critical thinking.	Questions help students visualize. Questions refocus the small group on the underlying concepts. Questions introduce contradictory concepts. Tasks are framed to pose questions that require critical thinking.
Quality student engagement	Lesson involves activities, exercises, and dialogues that focus student thinking, excite imagination, and prepares students to meet lesson learning objectives.	Activities create student disequilibrium. Activities elaborate and challenge student thinking. Activities prime students using their own experiences. Lesson requires students to analyze data, draw conclusions, and apply knowledge.
Opportunities for reflection	Lesson provides opportunities for the students to think about their thinking: to assess their progress and their decisions.	End-of-the-lesson activities elicit evidence of what has been learned. Questions and activities move students to externalize their thinking and observations. Lesson encourages students to put concepts together and pull them apart through the lens of learning activities such journaling, discussions, carouseling on the main points learned from a working on a task, and concept mapping. Lesson asks students to frame questions that challenge their classmates' concepts on content.
Multiple assessment measures	Lesson utilizes multiple forms of assessment using rubrics to judge student achievement and improve instruction.	Teacher adopts many modes of assessing students' performance such as: demonstration, design, essay, construction and production of products, accomplishment of tasks, and teacher observation. Individual student assessments of student understanding and knowledge is acquired through group work.

Subject/Name Index

Scripture Index